Acclaim for
Secrets of the Baby Whisperer

"A reassuring guide for new parents . . . one that calms the baby and restores peace to the household."
—*USA Today*

"Tracy Hogg has given parents a great gift—the ability to develop early insight into their child's temperament."
—*Los Angeles Family*

"The perfect gift for a new mom and family . . . Every aspect of care for mom and baby is covered, with interesting charts and clear references. There are many good books on baby care . . . but this book possesses unusual tenderness and heart, and it respects babies as people, albeit little ones."
—*Library Journal*

"The extent of Tracy's knowledge on all things baby-related is truly hard to comprehend. She combines this with extraordinary intuition, and most importantly, makes it accessible to everyone."
—Christa Miller
Actress, *The Drew Carey Show*

Secrets of the Baby Whisperer for Toddlers

Also by Tracy Hogg and Melinda Blau

Secrets of the Baby Whisperer:
How to Calm, Connect, and Communicate with Your Baby

Secrets of the Baby Whisperer for Toddlers

Tracy Hogg
with Melinda Blau

Ballantine Books • New York

A Ballantine Book
Published by The Ballantine Publishing Group

Copyright © 2002 by Tracy Hogg Enterprises, Inc.

All rights reserved under International
and Pan-American Copyright Conventions. Published
in the United States by The Ballantine Publishing Group, a division
of Random House, Inc., New York, and simultaneously in
Canada by Random House of Canada Limited, Toronto.

Ballantine and colophon are registered trademarks of Random House, Inc.

www.ballantinebooks.com

Library of Congress Control Number: 2002096001

ISBN 0-345-44092-7

Jacket photo © Tony Bakhtiar/Mere Images Photography

Manufactured in the United States of America

First Hardcover Edition: February 2002
First Trade Paperback Edition: February 2003

10   9   8   7   6   5   4   3   2   1

To Sara and Sophie

Contents

Acknowledgments

I want to thank Melinda Blau, my coauthor, for all her hard work and the friendship we have developed over the past two years. Her ability to capture my voice in these pages has been remarkable, forever convincing me that she truly is a gifted writer.

I appreciate my husband and family for all their love and support, and especially my two daughters, Sara and Sophie, who are my pride and joy.

Thanks to Gina Centrello for her loyalty and honesty; to Maureen O'Neal, who is a wonderful editor and mum; to Kim Hovey for her excellent hard work and friendship; to Marie Coolman for coordinating my West Coast tour; and a big thanks to Rachel Kind for sharing her experiences as a new mum and for her efforts in licensing foreign rights.

Last but not least, I owe a huge debt of gratitude to my families, who have opened their hearts and homes to me. You all know who you are. I want to especially thank Dana Walden, who not only is a wonderful mother but a woman I'm proud to call my friend; and Noni White and Bob Tzudiker, who have been an integral part of my life for the past three years and whose advice has always been, as we say in Yorkshire, spot on.

—*Tracy Hogg*
Encino, California

I want to thank Tracy Hogg for her time, patience, and her wonderful sense of humor. She is able to spin sagas of toddler life with an exquisite eye for detail and an uncanny sense of what life is like from a two-foot-tall perspective.

During the course of researching and writing these *Secrets of the Baby Whisperer* books, I've encountered many wonderful parents on the phone, in person, and through e-mail. In every instance, their identities and stories have been disguised. Nevertheless, I appreciate their generosity and am grateful that they allowed us to peek into their lives. In particular, I want to acknowledge Noni White and Bob Tzudiker, Susanna Grant and Christopher Henrikson, Barbara Travis and Dan Rase, Libby and Jim Hawkes, Owen and Jack Kugell; and a special tribute to my nieces, Karen Sonn and Heidi Sonn, who, with the help of their spouses, Bruce Koken and Louis Tancredi, conveniently (for me at least) gave birth to Reid and Sander as these books were being written and my nephew Jack Tantleff and his wife, Jennifer, who gave birth to Jacob just in time to be included in these acknowledgments.

Seeing groups of toddlers in action was immensely helpful in portraying the play sessions described in this book, which are fictional but based on snippets of actual children and their interactions. I am grateful to Dana Walden and Christa Miller, who allowed Tracy and me to observe their respective daughters at play; to the mothers (Natalie Matthews, Suzie Zaki, Kaydee Wilkerson, Jamie Garcia, and Dana Childers) and grandmothers (Karen Verosko and Beverly Childers) who invited us to attend their play group; and to Darcy Amiel, Mandi Richardson, Shelly Grubman, Jill Halper, and Sara Siegel, who took part in a "reunion" of toddlers I'd first met as babies.

I am deeply indebted to the creative team at Ballantine who have done so much to nurture and support the *Baby Whisperer* books: Maureen O'Neal, our gifted editor; Allison Dickens, her able and always helpful assistant; Kim Hovey, the tireless director of publicity; Rachel Kind, subsidiary rights manager, who also shared with us her experiences as a new mother; and Gina Centrello, president, who has been behind these projects every step of the way. You exemplify the best in publishing—a rare compliment from a writer. Behind the scenes, Alix Krijgsman and Nancy Delia transformed our manuscript into a book, with the help of an ace freelance copy editor, Helen Garfinkle, who also happens to be one of my oldest and dearest friends.

Finally, thanks to Eileen Cope and Barbara Lowenstein, my agents, who repeatedly reassure me that book writing can be an excellent adventure; to Barbara Biziou, for allowing me to draw from her work on rituals; to my neighbors, Joan Weigele, Henry "Waterboy" Simpkin, Sophie, and Adam, whose abiding kindnesses are overwhelming (and indispensable); to my Northampton crew, especially Ellen Lefcourt and Sylvia Rubin, who save me from becoming a recluse when I write; to Carla Messina and Reggie Weintraub, who provide shelter and love in New York; to Jessie Zoernig, masseuse extraordinaire, who kept me from becoming a pretzel; to Lorena Sol, for urging me to find a better word than *template*; and to my children—my daughter, Jennifer, her loving husband, Peter, and my son, Jeremy—whose pride in my work keeps me going.

—*Melinda Blau*
Northampton, Massachusetts

Toddler Whispering

As parents, we are our children's first
and most important mentors: their
guides to life's lessons and adventures.
—Sandra Burt and Linda Perlis,
Parents as Mentors

The Challenge of Toddlerhood

You know the old saying, luv: "Be careful what you wish for—you just might get it." If you're like most parents, I suspect that you spent a good part of the first eight months of your baby's life wishing things would get easier. Mom prayed he* would get over that colicky period, sleep through the night, and start taking solid food. And if Dad is like most men, he probably wished his little man would soon become less of "a blob" and more like the son he dreamed of playing touch football with. You both looked forward to the day Junior would take his first step and say his first word. You happily envisioned the day he'd pick up a spoon, put on a sock, and someday—please God—go potty by himself.

Now that your baby is a toddler, your wishes have come true— and I'll wager that some days you'd just as soon turn back the clock! Welcome to what is probably the most strenuous and awe-inspiring stage of parenting.

The dictionary defines a toddler as "a small child roughly between the ages of one and three." Other books mark this phase of childhood when a baby first begins to "toddle," or walk with short, unsteady steps. For some, this can be as young as eight or nine months. Either way, trust me, if you have a toddler on your hands, *you* know it, no matter what a book tells you.

Though at first your toddler may be a tad shaky on her feet, your little darlin' is now truly ready to explore people, places, and things—without your help, thank you very much. She is becoming social, too. She loves to imitate. She can clap, sing, dance, and play side by side with other children. In short, she's more like a miniature person now than a baby. She's wide-eyed with curiosity, full of energy, and courts trouble constantly. The developmental leaps at this age are miraculous, but given the rapid changes and the rambunctious moments, it's no wonder you feel like you're under siege. Every container, every object your toddler can grasp, every electrical outlet, every cherished knickknack is fair game. From her

---

*To give a fair representation of gender, the pronouns "he" and "she" are alternated throughout this book.

perspective, it's all new and exciting; from your perspective, it can feel like an assault on you, your house, and everything in sight.

Toddlerhood clearly marks the end of infancy. It's also a sneak preview of adolescence. In fact, many experts think of this period in the same vein as the teenage years, because a similar separation process is under way. Mum and Dad are no longer the beginning and end of a toddler's world. In fact, as she rapidly acquires new physical, cognitive, and social skills, she also learns how to say "no" to you—a skill that also will serve her well in adolescence.

Be assured, ducky, that's the good news. Indeed, it is through your child's exploration and struggles (often, with *you*), that your toddler begins to gain mastery over her environment and, most important, gains a sense of herself as a competent and independent being. Of course, you want your child to grow and to become more self-sufficient, even though at times the process is maddening. I know, because I lived through it with my own children who, after all, were my first guinea pigs (and my best students). I think I did a pretty good job with my girls, who are now nineteen and sixteen. But that's not to say that it has been smooth sailing all the way. Believe me, raising any child is a very difficult job and comes with heaps of frustration and brick walls, not to mention tears and tantrums.

Now Your Baby Is a Toddler . . .

I've been asking mothers what were the most significant changes from infancy to the toddler years, and here's what they said:

"I have even less time for myself."

"She asserts herself more."

"I can't take him to a restaurant."

"She's more demanding."

"It's easier to understand what he wants."

"I'm a slave to her naps."

"I have to chase him around."

"I'm constantly saying 'no' to her."

"I'm amazed at what he can learn."

"She imitates everything I do."

"He's into everything."

"She tests me all the time."

"He's curious about absolutely everything."

"She's so much more like . . . *a person!*"

Baby Whispering:
The Foundation of Good Parenting

Aside from my own experience, I have counseled countless parents of toddlers—often those whose children I first met as babies—and I can help you get through these difficult years, which I define here as roughly the period from eight months (not so coincidentally where my last book ended) to two years plus. If you read my first book, *Secrets of the Baby Whisperer,* you already know my philosophy about children. All the better if you adopted a structured routine from the day your baby came home and if you've been using some of my strategies. I daresay you're probably ahead of the game, because you already *think* in a way that will help you with your toddler.

However, I also recognize that some of you are new to my ideas, which were sparked when I first worked with children who had a range of physical and emotional impairments—children who often had no language skills. In my work with disabled children, I had to observe the nuances of their behavior and their body language and make sense of their seemingly unintelligible sounds in order to understand what they needed and wanted.

Later, spending my time almost exclusively with infants (including my own), I discovered that those skills worked just as well with babies. Having cared for over five thousand babies, I fine-tuned what one of my clients dubbed "baby whispering." It's quite like what a horse whisperer does, but here we're talking about infants. In both cases, we're dealing with sensate creatures, living beings who can't actually talk but express themselves nevertheless. In order to care for and connect with them, we must learn *their* language. Hence, baby whispering means tuning in, observing, listening, and understanding what's happening *from the child's perspective.*

Even though toddlers are beginning to acquire language and express themselves better than newborns do, the same principles of baby whispering that guide my work with infants can be applied to this age group. For those of you who didn't read my first book, below I offer a quick review of its major themes. If you have already read my first book, the following will be familiar. Think of it as a refresher course.

Every child is an individual. From the day a baby is born, she has a unique personality, as well as likes and dislikes of her own. Therefore no one strategy works for all. You have to find out what's right for *your* toddler. In Chapter One, I provide a self-test that will enable you to gauge what kind of temperament your child has, which in turn will help you understand what parenting strategies might work best with her. But even when divided into so-called types, each child is a one-of-a-kind phenomenon.

Every child deserves respect—and must learn to respect others as well. If you were taking care of an adult, you'd never touch, lift, or undress that person without asking permission and explaining what you're about to do. Why should it be any different with a child? As caretakers, we need to draw what I call *a circle of respect* around each child—an invisible boundary beyond which we don't go without asking permission or explaining what we're about to do. And we need to know who that child is before rushing in blindly; we must take into account what he or she feels and desires, rather than just doing what *we* want. Admittedly with toddlers this can be tricky, because we also have to teach them that the circle of respect goes both ways. Children at this age can be rather demanding and obstinate, and they have to learn to respect us as well. In these pages, I'll teach you how to respect your toddler and meet her needs without compromising your own boundaries.

Take the time to observe, listen, and talk with children, not at them. The process of getting to know your child starts the day he or she comes into the world. I always forewarn parents, "Never assume that your child doesn't understand you. Children always know more than you realize." Even a nonverbal toddler can express himself. Therefore, you have to sharpen your senses and pay attention. By observing, we begin to understand a toddler's unique temperament. By listening to him, even before he acquires spoken language, we begin to know what he wants. And by having a dialogue—conversing rather than lecturing—we allow the child to express who he really is.

Every child needs a structured routine, which gives his life predictability and safety. This principle, important in the early months of your baby's life, is even more important now that your child is toddling about. As parents and caretakers, we provide consistency and safety through ritual, routines, and rules. We let a child's nature and her growing abilities guide us and tell us how far she can go, and at the same time, remember that *we* are the grown-ups—we're in charge. It's a paradox of sorts, allowing a child to explore and simultaneously making sure she knows that she has to live within the safe confines we create for her.

The above simple, down-to-earth guidelines provide the foundation upon which a solid family is built. Children thrive when they are listened to, understood, and treated with respect. They thrive when they know what's expected of them and what they can expect of the world around them. At first, their universe is small—limited to their home, their family members, and the occasional outing. If this first environment is safe, relaxed, positive, and predictable, if it's a place where they can explore and experiment, if they can depend upon the people in this tiny world, then they will be better equipped to take on new settings and new people. Remember that no matter how active, curious, difficult, or infuriating your toddler seems at times, for her, it's all a dress rehearsal for the real world. Consider yourself her first acting coach, director, and most adoring audience.

My Intentions: The Road to Harmony

Common sense, you say. Easier said than done, you say, especially when it comes to toddlers. Well, that's true enough, but I have a few toddler techniques up my sleeve that will at least help you understand what your toddler is all about and will, at the same time, give you a greater sense of competency and authority.

Although I've peppered these pages with research from some of the most respected child-development experts of our time, there are plenty of books out there documenting scientific advances. What good is science if you don't know what to *do*? To that end, what you find here will help you see your toddler through fresh eyes and act more responsively toward him. By seeing the world from his perspective, you will gain greater empathy for what goes on in his little mind and body. With hands-on strategies for dealing with the inevitable everyday challenges you both face, you will have an arsenal of tools at your fingertips.

I've outlined below a list of more specific goals. What I'm trying to create here is a solid mooring for your family. It's no accident, by the way, that these goals are equally applicable to older children, even teenagers (although hopefully they don't need potty training!).

This book will encourage, teach, and demonstrate through example, how to:

• *View—and respect—your toddler as an individual.* Rather than categorizing him by age, allow him to be who he is. I believe that children have a right to express their likes and dislikes. I also believe that adults can validate a child's point of view, even when it frustrates us or we don't agree.

• *Cheer your toddler on toward independence—without rushing him.* To that end, I provide tools that will help you gauge her readiness and teach her practical skills, such as eating, dressing, potty training, and basic hygiene. I bristle when parents call to ask, "How can I get my toddler to walk?" or "What can I do to make my child talk earlier?" Development is a natural phenomenon, not course work. Besides, pushing children is not respectful. Even worse, it sets them up for failure and sets you up for disappointment.

• *Learn how to tune in to your child's verbal and nonverbal language.* While toddlers are infinitely easier to comprehend than newborns, they vary greatly in their ability to communicate. You must exercise patience and restraint when your child is trying to tell you something, and at the same time, know when to step in and offer your help.

• *Be realistic—toddlerhood is a time of constant change.* Sometimes a parent whose toddler suddenly stops sleeping through the night might ask, "What's wrong with her?" when in fact, their little girl is just going through another stage of child growth and developing. One of the biggest challenges of parenting a toddler is that just when you get used to a certain kind of behavior or a particular level of competence—bam!—your child changes. And guess what? She'll change again and again and again.

• *Promote your child's development and family harmony.* In my first book I promoted my *whole family* approach in which the infant becomes part of the family rather than dominating it. That principle is even more important now. It's critical to create a happy, safe environment that enables a child to venture forth, and at the same time, keeps him out of harm's way and doesn't allow his antics to disrupt the family. Think of your home as a rehearsal hall, where your child learns to practice new skills, memorize his lines, and learn proper entrances and exits. You're his director, readying him for the stage on which the drama of his life will be played.

• *Help your toddler manage his emotions—particularly his frustrations.* The toddler years mark a time when children take giant emotional steps. In infancy, your child's emotions were based on physical elements, such as hunger, fatigue, hot or cold, and feelings overtook her. As a toddler, though, her emotional repertoire will expand to include fear, joy, pride, shame, guilt, embarrassment— more complex emotions caused by her growing awareness of herself and of social situations. Emotional skills *can* be learned. Studies have shown that children as young as fourteen months can begin to identify and even anticipate mood (theirs and their caretakers'), feel empathy, and as soon as they're verbal, talk about feelings as well. We know, too, that temper tantrums are preventable, or if not caught in time, are at least manageable. But the management of mood is far more important than simply keeping tantrums at bay. Children who learn to moderate high emotions eat and sleep better than children who don't; they have an easier time learning new skills and fewer problems socializing as well. In contrast, children who lack emotional control are often those whom both other children and adults would just as soon avoid.

• *Develop a strong meaningful bond between Dad and your toddler.* I know, I know: it's just not fashionable these days to suggest that Mum has more contact with the children, but in real life that's usually the way it is. In most families, it still takes extra effort for Dad to be more than a Saturday helper. We need to look at ways for fathers to be *truly* involved, connecting emotionally, not just as a play pal.

• *Facilitate your child's becoming a social being.* Toddlerhood is a time when your child starts interacting with others. At first your child's world will be somewhat limited to perhaps only two or three regular "friends," but as he marches toward the preschool years, social skills become increasingly important. Therefore, he will need to develop empathy, consideration of others, and the ability to negotiate and handle conflict. These skills are best taught through example, guidance, and repetition.

• *Manage your emotions.* Because dealing with a toddler is so demanding, you must learn how to be patient, how and when to praise, how to see that "giving in" isn't loving (no matter how adorable your toddler acts), how to put your love into action (not *just* words), and what to do when you're angry or frustrated. Indeed, the most current research on early childhood brings out a fact that is critical to good parenting: your child's temperament doesn't just determine her strengths and vulnerabilities, it influences how you treat her. If you have a "handful" of a child who seems to save up her tantrums for public places, unless you learn how to modify your own responses, get help, or exit from a stressful situation, there's a good chance that you will lose patience quickly, respond sharply, even resort to physical restraint which, sadly, will only make your child's behavior worse.

• *Nourish your own adult relationships.* Toddlerhood deprives mums of downtime. You need to learn how to spend guilt-free time away from your toddler and to make opportunities (because they may not naturally present themselves) that will enable you to re-plenish your own reserves. In short, you need to *get* quality time as much as you need to *give* it to your toddler.

Are the foregoing lofty goals? I think not. I see them met in families every day. Certainly it takes time, patience, and commit-ment. And for working parents, it sometimes involves tough choices—for example, whether or not to come home from the of-fice a bit earlier so that your child doesn't stay up later than he should.

My intention is to arm you with information, help you feel more secure about your parenting decisions, and support you in discovering your own best approaches. In the end, I hope you will be a more sensitive parent, too, a toddler whisperer who is tuned in, confident, and loving.

How This Book Is Designed

I know that parents of toddlers have even less time for reading than parents of babies, so I've tried to design this book to be a quick read, and equally important, to make sense even if you start somewhere in the middle. Lots of charts, sidebars, and boxes will help you zero in on important concepts and can offer you at-a-glance guidance when you're too busy to actually pore through the pages.

I would suggest, though, that in order to acquaint yourself with my philosophy, you read through Chapters One, Two, and Three before skipping to particular topics. (I assume you've actually read the Introduction as well; if you haven't, please do that, too.) In Chapter One, you'll find a discussion of nature and nurture, which work together. The "Who Is Your Toddler?" quiz will help you understand your child's nature—in other words, what he came into the world with. In Chapter Two, I offer "H.E.L.P.," an overall strategy for dealing with the nurture part of the equation. And in Chapter Three, I stress that *toddlers learn through repetition.* I underscore the importance of "R&R"—instituting a structured routine and creating other dependable rituals as well.

Chapters Four through Nine deal with the specific challenges of parenting a toddler. Read them in order or as particular issues present themselves.

Chapter Four, "Nappies No More," looks at how you can foster your child's growing independence—but not push her before she's ready.

Chapter Five, "Toddler Talk," is about communication—talking *and* listening—which can be both exhilarating and frustrating when we're dealing with children in their first two or three years of life.

Chapter Six, "The Real World," focuses on the all-important move from home to play groups and family outings, and helps you plan "rehearsals for change," controlled situations that allow your toddler to practice social skills and test out new behaviors.

Chapter Seven, "Conscious Discipline," is about *teaching* your toddler how to behave. Children don't come into this world knowing how they're supposed to behave or the rules of social interaction. If *you* don't teach your toddler, be assured that the world will!

In Chapter Eight, I talk about "time-busters," chronic, undesirable behavior patterns that can erode the parent/child relationship and drain time and energy from the whole family. Parents are often unaware of the many ways that they "train" their children . . . until the resulting difficulties upset their lives. This *accidental parenting*, a phenomenon I talked about in my first book, is the cause of just about every sleep-related, eating, or discipline issue I see. When parents don't recognize what's happening or know how to stop it, the problem becomes a time-buster.

Finally, Chapter Nine, "When Baby Makes Four," is about growing a family—making the decision about having another child, preparing your toddler and helping her deal with the new arrival, dealing with siblings, and protecting your adult relationships and nurturing yourself in the bargain.

You won't find many age-related guidelines in these pages, be-cause I believe that you should *look at your own child*, rather than read a book to learn what's appropriate for her. And whether the subject is toilet training or tantrums, you won't find me telling you, "This is the right way," because the greatest gift I can give you is the ability to figure out *for yourself* what works best for your child and your family.

As a last word, let me remind you that it's important to main-tain a long-term outlook and keep a cool head. Just as time didn't freeze when your child was a very young baby—even though it *seemed* as if infancy would never end—toddlerhood is not forever either. During this time, just put away all your valuables, lock cup-boards containing poisons, and take a deep breath: For the next eighteen months or so, you've got a toddler on your hands. Right before your very eyes you will watch your little one make that gi-ant leap from a fairly helpless baby to a walking, talking child with a mind of her own. Enjoy the incredible journey. For each amazing new bit of mastery and each thrilling first, there will be electrifying calamities to contend with. In short, nothing you ever experience will be more exhilarating, and at the same time, more exhausting than living with and loving your toddler.

CHAPTER ONE

Loving the Toddler You Have

It is a wise father that knows his own child.

—William Shakespeare,
The Merchant of Venice

Babies Revisited

In the course of writing this second book, my coauthor and I held a class reunion for some of the babies who had attended my groups. Infants between one and four months old when we last saw them, the five alumni were now in the thick of toddlerhood. What a difference a year and a half had made. We recognized their slightly more mature faces, but physically the tiny dynamos who poured into my playroom bore scant resemblance to the babies I had known—sweet helpless things who could do little but stare at the wavy lines on the wallpaper. Where once holding up their heads or "swimming" on their tummies was a feat, these children were into everything. When their mums plopped them down, they crawled, tottered, or walked, sometimes holding on, sometimes on their own, desperate to explore. Eyes aglow, babbling sense and nonsense alike, their hands reached here, there, and everywhere.

Recovering from the shock of seeing this miracle of instant growth—it was like time-lapse photography without the middle stages—I started to remember the babies I once knew.

There was Rachel, sitting in her mum's lap, cautiously eyeing her playmates, a bit fearful to venture out on her own. It was the same Rachel who cried as a baby when presented with a stranger's face and who balked during the class on infant massage, letting us know she wasn't ready for so much stimulation.

Betsy, one of the first of the babies to actually reach out and touch another child, was clearly still the most active and interactive of all the children, curious about every toy, interested in everyone else's business. She was extremely frisky as an infant, so it didn't surprise me when she began clambering up the changing table with the skill of a monkey and a nothing-can-stop-me look on her face. (Not to worry: Her mum, obviously used to Betsy's athletic feats, kept a close eye on her and a ready hand near her tush.)

Tucker, who had reached every baby milestone on cue, was playing near the changing table. Every so often, he'd glance up at Betsy, but the brightly colored forms of the shape box were more intriguing to him. Tucker was still right on track—he knew his colors and was able to figure out which shapes fit into which holes, just like "the books" said a twenty-month-old could.

Allen was in the play garden by himself, set off from the others, which made me think of his serious-looking, three-month-old self. Even as an infant, Allen always seemed to have a lot on his mind, and he had that same concerned expression now as he tried to insert a "letter" into the play mailbox.

Finally, I couldn't take my eyes off Andrea, one of my favorite babies because she was so friendly and adaptable. Nothing fazed Andrea, even in infancy, and I could see that she was her old unshakable self as I watched her interact with Betsy, now down from her perch and tugging mightily on Andrea's truck. In turn, this self-possessed toddler looked at Betsy and calmly sized up the situation. Without missing a beat, Andrea let go and began playing contentedly with a dolly that had caught her eye.

Though these children had grown light-years ahead of where they had been—in effect, they were six or seven times older than when I last saw them—each was a reflection of his or her infant self. Temperament had blossomed into personality. Babies no more, they were five distinct little people.

Nature/Nurture: The Delicate Balance

The constancy of personality from infancy through toddlerhood comes as no surprise to me or others who have seen scores of infants and children. As I stressed earlier, *babies come into this world with unique personalities*. From the day they're born, some are inherently shy, others stubborn, still others prone to high activity and risk taking. Now, thanks to videotapes, brain scanners, and new information about gene coding, this isn't just a hunch; scientists have documented the constancy of personality in the lab as well. Particularly in the last decade, research has proven that in every human being, genes and brain chemicals influence temperament, strengths and weaknesses, likes and dislikes.

One of the most hopeful by-products of this latest research is that it has cut down on parent-blaming—a once-fashionable psychology. But let's be careful not to swing totally in the other

It's Nature *and* Nurture

"The studies [of twins and adopted children] have important practical implications. Since parenting and other environmental influences can moderate the development of inherited tendencies in children, efforts to assist parents and other care givers to sensitively read a child's behavioral tendencies and to create a supportive context for the child are worthwhile. A good fit between environmental condition and the child's characteristics is reflected, for example, in family routines that provide many opportunities for rambunctious play for highly active children, or in child care settings with quiet niches for shy children to take a break from intensive peer activity. Thoughtfully designed care giving routines can incorporate helpful buffers against the development of behavior problems among children with inherited vulnerabilities by providing opportunities for choice, relational warmth, structured routine, and other assists."

—from the National Research Council and Institute of Medicine (2000), *From Neurons to Neighborhoods: The Science of Early Childhood Development*, Committee on Integrating the Science of Early Childhood Development. Jack P. Shonkoff and Deborah A. Phillips, eds. Board on Children, Youth, and Families, Commission of Behavioral and Social Sciences and Education. Washington, D.C.: National Academy Press.

direction. That is, let's not allow ourselves to think that parents don't matter at all. We do. (Otherwise, luv, why would I share *my* ideas for being the best parent you can be?)

Indeed, the most current thinking about the nature/nurture debate describes the phenomenon as a dynamic, ongoing process. It's not nature *versus* nurture. Rather, it's "nature *through* nurture," according to a recent review of the research (see sidebar). Scientists know this from analyzing countless studies of identical twins as well as research on adopted children, whose biology is different from their parents. Both types of cases demonstrate the complexity of the nature/nurture interplay.

Twins, for example, who have the same chromosomal makeup *and* the same parental influences, don't necessarily turn out the same way. And when scientists look at adopted children whose biological parents are alcoholics or have some type of mental illness, they find that in some cases a nurturing environment (created by their adoptive parents) provides immunity from the genetic predisposition. In other cases, though, even the best parenting can't override heredity.

The bottom line is that no one knows exactly how nature and nurture work, but we do know that they work *together*, each influencing the other. Hence, we have to respect the child Nature has given us, and at the same time, give that child whatever support he or she needs. Admittedly, this is a delicate balance, especially for parents of toddlers. But following are some important ideas to keep in mind.

You first need to understand—and accept—the child you have. The starting point of being a good parent is to know your own child. In my first book, I explained that the infants I meet generally fall into one of five broad temperamental types, which I call *Angel*, *Textbook*, *Touchy*, *Spirited*, and *Grumpy*. In the next sections of this chapter, we'll look at how these types translate into toddlerhood, and you'll find a questionnaire (see pages 21–24) that will help you figure out the type of child you have. What are her talents? What gives her trouble? Is she a child who needs a little extra encouragement or a little extra self-control? Does she plunge willingly into new situations? Recklessly? Or not at all? You must observe your child impartially and answer such questions honestly.

If you base your replies on the reality of who your child is, not on whom you'd like her to be, you will be giving her what I think every parent owes their child: respect. The idea is to look at your toddler, love her for who she is, and tailor your own ideas and behavior to do what is best for her.

Think of it: You wouldn't ever dream of asking an adult who hates sports to join you at a rugby game. You probably wouldn't ask a blind person to join you on a bird-watching expedition. In the same way, if you know your child's temperament, her strengths, her weaknesses, you'll be better able to determine not only what's right for her, but what she enjoys. You'll be able to guide her, provide an environment suited to her, and give her the strategies she needs to cope with the ever more challenging demands of childhood.

You can help your child make the most of whoever he is. It is well documented that biology is not a life sentence. All humans—and even other animals (see sidebar)—are a product of *both* their biology *and* the world into which they're born. One child may be "born shy," because she inherits a gene that gives her a low threshold for the unfamiliar, but her parents can help her feel safe and teach her strategies for overcoming her shyness. Another child might be "a natural risk taker" because of his serotonin levels, but his parents can help him learn impulse control. In sum, understanding your child's temperament enables you to plan ahead.

Your child's needs aside, you must take responsibility for what you do, too. On the stage of life, you are your child's first acting coach and director, and what you do to and for her will shape her as much as her DNA does. In my first book, I reminded parents that everything they do teaches their babies what to expect from them and from the world. Take a toddler who whines constantly. When I meet such a child, I don't think he's being willful or spiteful. He's just doing what his parents taught him.

Suomi's Monkeys: Biology Is *Not* Destiny

Stephen Suomi and a team of researchers at the National Institute of Child Health and Human Development purposely bred a group of rhesus monkeys to be "impulsive." In the monkeys, as in humans, a lack of control and high risk taking is associated with low levels of the brain chemical serotonin (which inhibits impulsiveness). It seems that a recently identified serotonin-transporter gene (found in humans as well) prevents serotonin from metabolizing efficiently. Suomi found that when monkeys who lacked this gene were raised by average mothers, they tended to get into trouble and end up at the bottom of the social hierarchy. But when they are assigned to mothers known to be exceptionally nurturing, their futures are far brighter. Not only do the monkeys learn to avoid stressful situations or to get help dealing with them (which, not surprisingly, raises their social status in the colony), the extra nurturing actually brings the baby monkeys' serotonin metabolism into normal range. "Virtually all of the outcomes can be altered substantially by early experiences," says Suomi. "Biology just provides a different set of probabilities."

—adapted from "A Sense of Health," *Newsweek*, Fall/Winter 2000.

How did it happen? Every time their little boy whined, they stopped their adult conversation, picked him up, or started playing with him. Mum and Dad truly believed they were being "responsive," but they didn't realize the lesson their child was learning: *Oh I get it. Whining is a surefire way to get my parents' attention.* This phenomenon, which I call *accidental parenting* (more about it on pages 235–236 and in Chapter 8), can begin in infancy and continue into early childhood, unless parents are aware of the impact of their own behavior. And believe me, the consequences are increasingly serious, because toddlers quickly become proficient at manipulating their parents.

Your perspective about your child's nature can determine how well you deal with it. Of course, some children are more difficult than others, and it's also a well-documented fact that a child's personality can influence a parent's actions and reactions. Most people find it easier to be even-tempered around a child who is malleable and cooperative than around a child who's a bit more impetuous or demanding. Still, perspective means everything. One mother might respond to her headstrong daughter by saying, "She's incorrigible," while another might see the same nature as a good thing— a child who knows her own mind. It will be easier for the second mum to help her daughter channel her aggressive tendencies toward more suitable applications—for example, leadership. Likewise, one father may be very upset to realize his son is "shy," while another sees the same reticence as a positive trait—a child who weighs every situation carefully. The second father is more likely to be patient rather than push his son as the first probably would—a strategy that would only make his boy even more fearful (examples of this can be found on pages 35–37 and 311–313).

Who Is *Your* Toddler?

In a way, temperament is an even greater consideration in toddlerhood, both because your child is now truly growing into his personality and because this is a time when every day presents new challenges to your child. Temperament determines your child's ability to handle unfamiliar tasks and circumstances, her "firsts."

You may have already determined what type of baby your toddler was—an *Angel, Textbook, Touchy, Spirited,* or *Grumpy* child. If so, the following questionnaire will only confirm your perception. That means that you started tuning in to your child *early*—and that you've been telling yourself the truth about her personality.

Get two clean pieces of paper, and working independently, both you *and* your partner should reply to the questionnaire below. If you're a single parent, ask the help of another caretaker, the child's grandparents, or a good friend who knows your toddler well. That way, you at least have another pair of eyes and can compare notes. No two people see the same child exactly the same way, nor does any child act the same way with two different people.

There are no right or wrong answers here, luv—this is a fact-finding exercise, so don't argue if your answers are different. Simply allow for a broader view. The goal is to help you understand your toddler's makeup.

You may question the outcome, as did many parents who read *Secrets of the Baby Whisperer*, by saying, "My child seems to be a cross between two types." That's fine, just use the information for both types. However, I've found that one aspect is usually dominant. Take me, for example. I was a Touchy baby, a rather reticent and fearful toddler, and I've become a Touchy adult as well, although some days I can act like a Grumpy person and other days a Spirited. But my main nature is Touchy.

Keep in mind that this is just an exercise to help you tune in and become more observant about your child's natural inclinations. Believe me, *you* and other elements in her environment will shape your child as well—in fact, this is the time when every encounter is an adventure, and often, a test. This questionnaire is meant to give you an idea of your child's most significant behavioral traits—how active she is, how distractable, intense, and adaptable, how she deals with the unfamiliar, how she reacts to the environment, how outgoing or withdrawn she is. Note that the questions ask you to consider not only what she is doing now, but also what she was like as a baby. Mark the answers that reflect your toddler's most typical behavior—the way she *usually* acts or reacts.

Who Is Your Toddler?

1. As a baby, my child
    A. rarely cried
    B. cried only when she was hungry, tired, or overstimulated
    C. often cried for no apparent reason
    D. cried very loudly, and if I didn't attend to her, it quickly turned into a rage cry
    E. cried angrily, usually when we veered from our usual routine or from what she expected

2. When he wakes up in the morning, my toddler
    A. rarely cries—he plays in his crib until I come in
    B. coos and looks around until he gets bored
    C. needs immediate attention, or he starts crying
    D. screams for me to come in
    E. whimpers to let me know he's up

3. Thinking back to her first bath, I remember that my child
    A. took to the water like a duck
    B. was a little surprised at the sensation but liked it almost immediately
    C. was very sensitive—she shook a little and seemed afraid
    D. was wild—flailing about and splashing
    E. hated it and cried

4. My child's body language has been typically
    A. relaxed almost always, even as a baby
    B. relaxed most of the time, even as a baby
    C. tense and very reactive to external stimuli
    D. jerky—as a baby, his arms and legs often flailed all over the place
    E. rigid—as a baby, his arms and legs were often fairly stiff

5. When I made the transition from liquids to solid food, my toddler
    A. had no problem
    B. adjusted fairly well, as long as I gave her time to adapt to each new taste and texture
    C. scrunched up his face or his lip quivered, as if to say, "What the Dickens is this?"
    D. dove right in, as if she had been eating solid foods her whole life
    E. grabbed the spoon and insisted on holding it herself

6. When interrupted from an activity she's involved in, my toddler
    A. stops easily
    B. sometimes cries but can be cajoled into a new activity
    C. cries for several minutes before she recovers
    D. wails and kicks and throws herself on the floor
    E. cries as if her heart were breaking

7. My toddler displays anger by
    A. whimpering, but he can be quickly consoled or easily distracted
    B. displaying obvious signs (clenched fist, grimace, or crying) and needs reassurance to get through it
    C. having a meltdown like it's the end of the world
    D. being out of control, often tending to throw things
    E. being aggressive, often tending to push or shove

8. In social situations with another child or children, such as a play date, my toddler
    A. is happy and actively involved
    B. gets involved, but every now and then gets upset with other children
    C. whines or cries easily, especially when another child grabs her toy
    D. runs around a lot and gets involved in everything
    E. doesn't want to be involved, stays on the sidelines

9. At nap or bedtimes, the sentence that best describes my toddler is
    A. She could sleep through a nuclear blast.
    B. She is restless before falling asleep but responds well to a gentle pat or reassuring words.
    C. She is easily disturbed by noises in the house or outside the window.
    D. She has to be coaxed into bed—she's afraid of missing something.
    E. She has to have total quiet to go to sleep, or she begins to cry inconsolably.

10. When brought to a new house or unfamiliar setting, my toddler
    A. adapts easily, smiles, and quickly engages
    B. needs a little time to adapt, gives a smile but turns away quickly
    C. is easily distressed, hides behind me, or buries himself in my clothes
    D. jumps straight in, but doesn't quite know what to do with himself
    E. tends to balk and get angry, or may go off by himself

11. If my toddler is engaged with a particular toy and another child wants to join in, she
    A. notices, but stays focused on what she's doing
    B. finds it hard to stay focused once the other child catches her eye
    C. gets upset and cries easily
    D. immediately wants whatever the other child is playing with
    E. prefers playing alone and often cries if other children invade her space

12. When I leave the room, my toddler
    A. shows concern initially, but resumes playing
    B. may show concern but usually doesn't mind unless she's tired or sick
    C. cries immediately and looks forlorn
    D. hotfoots after me
    E. cries loudly and lifts up her hands

13. When we come home from any kind of outing, my toddler
    A. settles in easily and immediately
    B. takes a few minutes to get acclimated
    C. tends to be very fussy
    D. is often overstimulated and hard to calm down
    E. acts angry and miserable

14. The most noticeable thing about my toddler is how
    A. incredibly well-behaved and adaptable he is
    B. how much he has developed precisely on schedule, doing just what the books said he would at each stage
    C. sensitive he is to everything
    D. aggressive he is
    E. grouchy he can be

15. When we go to family gatherings where there are adults and/or children my child knows, my toddler
    A. scopes out the situation, but usually gets right into the swing of things
    B. needs just a few minutes to adapt to the situation, especially if there are a lot of people
    C. is shy, stays close to me, if not on my lap, and might even cry
    D. jumps right into the center of the action, especially with other children
    E. will join in when he's ready, unless I push him, and then he becomes reluctant

16. At a restaurant, my toddler
    A. is good as gold
    B. can stay seated at the table for around thirty minutes
    C. is easily frightened if the place is crowded and loud, or if strangers talk to her
    D. refuses to sit at the table for more than ten minutes, unless she's eating
    E. can sit up to fifteen or twenty minutes, but needs to leave when she's finished eating

17. A comment that best describes my toddler is
    A. you hardly know there's a little one in the house
    B. he's easy to handle, easy to predict
    C. he's a very delicate child
    D. he's into everything—I can't take my eyes off him when he's out of the crib or playpen
    E. he's very serious—he seems to hold back and ponder things a lot

18. The comment that best describes communication between my toddler and me, since she was a baby, is
    A. she has always let me know exactly what she needed
    B. most of the time her cues are easy
    C. she cries often, which is confusing
    D. she asserts her likes and dislikes very clearly, physically, and often loudly
    E. she often gets my attention with loud, angry crying

19. When I diaper or dress my toddler, he
    A. is usually cooperative
    B. sometimes needs a distraction in order to lie still
    C. gets upset and sometimes cries, especially if I try to rush him
    D. balks because he hates to lie or sit still
    E. gets upset if I take too long

20. The type of activity or toy that my toddler likes best is
    A. almost anything that gives her results, like simple building toys
    B. an age-appropriate toy
    C. single-task activities that aren't too loud or stimulating
    D. anything she can bash or use to make a loud noise
    E. almost anything, as long as no one interferes with him

To score the self-test above, write *A, B, C, D,* and *E* on a piece of paper and next to each one, count how many times you've used each letter, which denotes a corresponding type.

A's = Angel Baby
B's = Textbook Baby
C's = Touchy Baby
D's = Spirited Baby
E's = Grumpy Baby

Hello, Toddler!

When you tally up your toddler's "score," you'll probably find that one or two letters appear most frequently. As you read the descriptions below, remember that we're talking about a way of being in the world here, not an occasional bad day or a type of behavior associated with a particular developmental milestone, like teething.

You may find that your toddler is a dead ringer for a particular type, or you may see him in more than one of the following thumbnail sketches. Be sure to read all five descriptions. Even if one doesn't fit your child, reading about all the types might help you understand other children, relatives, or playmates who are part of your toddler's social circle. I've exemplified each profile with the babies you met at the beginning of this chapter who fit almost exactly.

Angel. The baby who was "good as gold" turns into an Angel toddler. Usually very social, this child is immediately comfortable in groups and can fit into most situations. She often develops language earlier than her peers or at least is clearer when making her needs known. When she wants something she can't have, it's fairly easy to distract her before her emotions escalate. And when she's really out of sorts, it's fairly easy to calm her before she gets to the tantrum stage. At play, she has a lot of staying power at a single task. This is a child who's dead easy and highly portable. For example, Andrea, whom you met at the beginning of this chapter, travels a great deal with her parents and goes effortlessly with their flow. Even with time changes, Andrea gets back on schedule straightaway. Once, when her mother wanted to change Andrea's nap time because it was disrupting Mum's day, it took only two days for this little one to shift gears. Andrea also went through a stage of impatience with diaper changes—a common toddler occurrence. But giving Andrea her pendant to hold was enough to distract her.

Textbook. As in infancy, this toddler is right on time with developmental milestones. You could say he does everything by the book. He's generally pleasant in social situations but can be shy at first with strangers. He's most comfortable in his own environment, but if outings are planned well, and you give him sufficient time and preparation, he won't have much trouble adapting to new surroundings. This is a child who loves routine and likes to know what's coming next. Tucker is such a child. All along, he's been fairly easy to care for, predictable, and good-natured. His mum continues to be amazed at how punctual he is, even when it comes to the not-so-welcome phases of toddlerhood. Eight months to the day, he started feeling separation anxiety. At nine months, he cut his first tooth. He walked at a year.

Touchy. True to her baby self, this little one is sensitive and typically slow to adapt to new situations. She likes the world ordered and knowable. She hates to be interrupted when engrossed. For instance, if she's deeply involved with a toy or a puzzle and you ask her to stop, she gets upset and is likely to cry. It's this toddler who is often labeled "shy," rather than people assuming, "Oh, it's her temperament." Granted, a Touchy toddler may not do well in social gatherings, especially if she feels pushed, and she often has difficulty sharing. Rachel fits this profile to a tee. If people try to force things on her, she has a major meltdown. Her mum, Anne, had a terrible time when she wanted to put Rachel in a Mommy-and-Me class that some of Anne's friends were attending. Rachel knew several other children in the group, but it took her three weeks to even get off her mum's knee, which made Anne question her decision. "Shall I try to stick it out with her, hoping she'll get acclimated to the group, or leave her at home, which would be very isolating?" She chose the former, but it was a struggle—one that often began again with any new situation. If she's not pushed, though, the Touchy child can mature into a thoughtful, sensitive thinker, a child who weighs situations carefully and likes to ponder problems.

Grumpy. The same mad-as-hell personality that marked this child's early years carries into toddlerhood. He's obstinate and needs things to be *his* way. If you force yourself on him before he's ready to be picked up, expect major squirming action. His mum might try to show him how to do something, but he'll push her hand away. Because he likes his own company best, he's great at independent play. However, he may lack the staying power needed to learn or complete a task and is therefore easily frustrated. When upset, he's prone to crying as if it's the end of the world. Because this toddler often finds it hard to express himself, he also may become a biter or pusher. I tell *all* parents of toddlers who want to thrust their children at me, "Don't make him come to me. Don't *make* him do anything. Let him get to know me on his timetable, not yours." This is especially important with Grumpy toddlers. The pushier you are, the more stubborn they'll be. And don't you dare ask him to "perform" on cue, as Allen's parents found out. Here was a little boy who was sweet as can be . . . if you left it up to him to pick and choose his activities. However, when anyone suggested that Allen perform ("Show your auntie how you make pattycake"), this little boy would put on his best scowl. (Actually, I don't like to see *any* child put on display; see sidebar, page 93.) At the same time, grumpy children are "old souls"—they tend to be insightful, resourceful, and creative, and sometimes even wise, acting as if they've been here before.

Spirited. Our most active toddler, she's very physical, often willful, and may be prone to temper tantrums. She is very social and curious and will point to objects and reach out for them and for other kids early on. This child is the consummate adventurer; she will have a go at anything and is very determined. She displays a great sense of achievement when she accomplishes something. At the same time, she needs very clear boundaries so that she doesn't act like a steamroller, trampling anyone or anything in her path. Once they start crying, these toddlers have stamina and staying power, so you're in for a long haul if you don't have a good routine going at night. They're also keen observers of their caretakers. Betsy, who scampered up the changing table in my studio, was perpetually testing her mum, Randy. Typically, Betsy would set her sights on something—say a plug she was told not to touch—and then, as she moved toward it, she'd keep looking back at Randy, to gauge her reaction. Betsy, like most Spirited toddlers, has a mind of her own. If she's with Mum, and Dad tries to pick her up, she'll push him off. Given good guidance and an outlet for her energy, however, a

Spirited toddler can become a leader and very accomplished in whatever area interests her.

You probably recognized your toddler in the above descriptions. Maybe he's a cross between two types. In either case, this information is meant to guide and enlighten you, not to alarm you. After all, each type has advantages as well as challenges. Also, it's less important to figure out a label per se, than to know what to expect and how to deal with your baby's particular temperament. In fact, labeling is not a good idea. All humans have many faces, and children, like adults, amount to more than single aspects of their temperament.

For example, a child who's "shy" can also be thoughtful, sensitive, musically inclined. But if you think about that child only as "shy"—worse, if you constantly chalk up all his behavior to shyness, you're seeing a stick figure, not a dynamic, breathing, whole child. You're not allowing that child to be an authentic, three-dimensional person.

Remember, too, that when you tell a person that he is one particular thing, he soon becomes that thing. In my own family, I have a brother who was termed "antisocial" as a child. Looking back, he surely was a Grumpy type. Still, his whole being was much more than that label. He was curious, inventive, creative. As an adult, he still is curious, inventive, and creative—and he still loves to be alone. You could spoil your own day by constantly looking for him, hoping to spend more time with him than he'd like. But if you just accepted that he preferred his own space—did not take it

---

Nature or Toddlerhood?

The one constant of toddlerhood is change. Because they're perpetually growing, exploring, and testing, toddlers are transformed literally every day. Yours may be cooperative one moment, obstinate the next. Sometimes he gets dressed without fuss, sometimes you have to chase him. He may eat with gusto on Friday, pick at his food on Saturday. At such trying times, you may *think* that your toddler's personality has changed, but your little one is simply in the process of yet another huge developmental leap. The best way to ride these waves of change is to not make too much of them. Your child isn't having a setback or changing for the worse. It's all part of his growing up.

personally and remembered that he was like that from the time he was a baby—he'd be fine. In fact, he'd probably seek you out faster than if you tried to push him into spending time with you.

Granted, you may not like everything you see in your child. You might even secretly wish you had another type of child. No matter, you must deal with reality and take those blinders off. Your job as a parent is to structure the environment to minimize the pitfalls and bolster the benefits of your child's nature.

Accepting the Toddler You Love

Knowing your toddler's type is not enough; it's also important to *accept* what you know. Sadly, I meet parents every day who don't grasp who their children are. These mums and dads don't seem to appreciate what they see or what they know, deep down inside, about their own children. They may have the sweetest, most docile child, whom other parents would love to have, and yet they wonder, "Shouldn't he get more involved with other kids?" Or their child might be on the floor, screaming because they wouldn't let her have another cookie, and they're saying, "I don't understand— she's never done this before." Right. Instead of accepting, such parents go into denial. They make excuses for their child or constantly question her nature. They're inadvertently saying to their toddler, "I don't like who you are—and I'm going to change that."

Of course, parents don't mean to negate their children, but in effect, that's what happens. They either see a difficult child through rose-tinted glasses or fail to see what a wonderful child they have. Why? I've isolated several reasons and have used parents I know to explain what seems to happen.

Performance Anxiety: Amelia. I can't believe the numbers of young women today who seem to have performance anxiety about their parenting. It starts in pregnancy, when they read every book they can get their hands on, with the hope of seizing on exactly the "right" child-rearing advice. The problem is that in any book (including this one), the advice is not tailored specifically to *your* child.

You may be using a particular technique as instructed, but your child doesn't respond. You deduce that it's something *you* did wrong. And feeling bad about yourself doesn't translate into good parenting.

What's more, performance anxiety obscures a clear view of the little human being in front of you. Take Amelia, twenty-seven when she had Ethan, the first grandchild on both sides of the family. Amelia had read a great deal of parenting literature, joined mothers' chat rooms, and was particularly determined to track little Ethan's development "by the book." She called me regularly throughout Ethan's infancy, always beginning each question with, "In my *What to Expect* book, it says Ethan should be . . ." Every call heralded a different concern: smiling, rolling over, sitting up. By toddlerhood, the questions changed a bit: "What can I do to help him to climb better?" or "He should be into finger food now. What can I give him so he won't choke?" Or she'd read about a new theory—for instance, teaching babies sign language—and immediately rush to try it. A new class for toddlers? She was eager to join it, insisting that Ethan "needed to

---

Signs of Denial

Parents who have trouble accepting their children for who they are tend to make certain kinds of statements. Pay attention to what you *really* mean if you hear yourself saying . . .

- **"It's a stage—he'll grow out of it."** Is that reality or a wish? You might have to keep waiting.

- **"Oh, you're fine."** Are you trying to cajole your toddler out of feelings?

- **"Once he starts talking he'll be easier to handle."** Development can modify behavior, but it rarely overrides temperament altogether.

- **"Oh, she won't always be a shy violet."** But she might always have trouble in new situations.

- **"I wish he were . . ."** or **"Why can't he be more . . ."** or **"He used to . . ."** or **"When will he . . ."** Whatever words you fill in, it might mean you don't truly accept who he is.

- **"I'm sorry she's so . . ."** When parents apologize for a child, no matter what he's doing, they're giving him the message that it's not okay to be himself. I can imagine the child ending up in a psychologist's office, saying, "I was never allowed to be myself."

---

develop his motor skills" or "develop his creativity." Any new toy on the market? She'd buy it. There never seemed to be an ordinary day in this mum's life. She was always presenting a new gadget or activity that she believed would help Ethan develop, teach him a new skill, or give him an edge on other children.

"Ethan is always in a bad mood," Amelia told me when her son was eighteen months old. "I'm worried that he's becoming a difficult child." Spending a few hours with mother and son, it was clear that she was getting more joy out of the activities and toys she foisted on him than he was. Instead of observing and accepting him for who he was, she had been schlepping him all over town. Instead of allowing him to explore and take the lead, she kept buying him more "stuff." His room looked like a toy store!

"Ethan has been who he is all along," I assured her, remembering the knitted brow I had so often observed on his baby self. "He hasn't changed. He was a Grumpy baby, and now he's a Grumpy toddler, who likes to play on his own time and terms and to pick his own activities." I explained to Amelia that in her eagerness to be the best mum in the world—an enthusiasm that clearly bordered on overinvolvement—she wasn't seeing the little boy in front of her. Maybe subconsciously she was trying to change Ethan's nature. In any case, that wouldn't work; she had to accept who he was.

There's an old Buddhist expression: *When the student is ready, the teacher appears.* This, apparently, is what happened in Amelia's case. Her favorite aunt, she admitted, had been telling her for the last several months, "You're overdoing everything, overthinking, and overscheduling that poor little boy of yours," but Amelia owned, "I didn't even know what she meant. I guess part of the problem was that with everyone telling me what a good mother I was, I felt like I had to prove something." Needless to say, when Amelia eased off a bit, Ethan became more manageable. It's not that he suddenly became a cheerful chap, but he certainly wasn't balking at everything the way he had been. Amelia changed, too. She realized that parenting was a process, not an event, and that each minute didn't have to be "enriched" or filled with meaningful activity. She learned to hold back when Ethan was playing to allow him to show her what *he* liked to do, and she began to appreciate Ethan's independence and drive.

Perfectionism: Magda. Perfectionism is performance anxiety taken to the extreme—and it further darkens the tint on one's rose-colored specs. I often see this in women in their late thirties and forties who opt for motherhood after a successful career in which they've had everything under control. Magda is a classic example. People thought she was bonkers to have a baby at forty-two. Part of her maternal anxiety about doing everything "just right" stemmed from her desire to prove to people that she had indeed made the right decision. In addition, she had envisioned herself giving birth to a child similar to her sister's good-as-gold son, an Angel baby who would easily fit into her own busy schedule.

As it turned out, though, Magda's son, Adam, was a Spirited baby, and she was totally thrown by the fact that she didn't seem able to cope with him. Here was this woman who oversaw a large company and sat on the boards of many others and was a gourmet cook to boot. She was so successful in all other aspects of her life, she expected to experience the same ease as a mum. When her pediatrician diagnosed Adam's crying as "colic," Magda tenaciously held on to her belief that Adam *was* an Angel after all—and that he'd "grow out of it."

But long past the natural course of colic (five months at most), Adam was still going strong, and by the time I met him, at thirteen months, he was a boisterous tyrant. Magda tried to make excuses. "He hasn't had a good nap. . . . He's just out of sorts. Or maybe it's his teeth. . . ." She was not only in denial about Adam's being a Spirited toddler, she was also ashamed that *she* needed help. When she called me for a consultation, at the suggestion of several friends who had been clients of mine, she asked me not to tell anyone that I visited her.

Aside from her perfectionist tendencies, which made her put more energy into trying to control Adam than into listening and observing him, she had no idea about setting clear boundaries for Adam; instead, she cajoled him constantly, hoping to sweet-talk or bribe him out of his raucous behavior. Magda also was very isolated. She had gone back to work quickly. Though she had made time to be with Adam, it was usually just the two of them or maybe with Dad, but rarely with other children and parents. I urged her to get involved in a play group so that she could see how other children interact. Talking to other moms and being exposed to other children enabled Magda to gain a new perspective. Instead of her holding on to the illusion that Adam would change, she accepted his nature and started to make fewer excuses for his behavior. She began having different expectations of her little boy, made clearer boundaries, and became better able to set limits without losing her temper. She also incorporated lots of active play into Adam's daily routine, thereby giving him appropriate outlets for his energy.

Admittedly, it was rough going in the beginning. It's not easy dealing with a Spirited toddler who has never had limits. Also, Magda still wanted people to see her as a perfect mum—a goal no woman can attain. "Mothering is like any set of skills you are taught in other walks of life," I explained. "It's something we *learn*." Of course, there are no schools for parenting, but I pointed out that Magda could utilize the resources around her—parents whom she respected, parenting workshops, consultants. Most important, she needed to see discipline as a way of teaching and nurturing, not something punitive that would flatten her Spirited child's ego (more on that in Chapter Seven).

Voices In—and Out of—Your Head: Polly. Some parents can't see clearly because they are haunted by other people's opinions and expectations—real or imagined. We all succumb to this to some degree. We hear our own parents' opinions; we worry about what neighbors or doctors or friends might say. Some questioning is good, and utilizing wise parenting tips makes sense (if they work for you). But sometimes, the voices drown out our own inner wisdom.

Such was the case with Polly, twenty-six, who was married to thirty-six-year-old Ari, a wealthy man of Middle Eastern descent who had had two children from a previous marriage. A dental hygienist before they met, Polly was an only child who came from more humble beginnings than her new mate. Now she lived in a huge home in Bel Air, a very exclusive Los Angeles neighborhood. Polly called in tears one day, asking for help with Ariel, who was going on fifteen months. "I wanted everything to be right for this little girl, but I feel like nothing I do is right. She's so demanding—I don't know what to do for her."

Polly felt guilty and incompetent. Her own parents called often from the Midwest, and naturally asked about their granddaughter. Polly viewed their concern as criticism, which it may or may not really have been (never having met them, I only heard their comments secondhand). Ari's mother lived nearby, though, and it seemed clear that she not only preferred her son's first wife, Carmen, but she thought little of Polly's parenting skills. Mum-in-law constantly hurled offhanded remarks in Polly's direction, like, "Oh, Carmen was so good with the children," or "My *other* grandchildren never whine." Every now and then the disapproval would be less veiled: "I don't know what you're doing with this child."

Talking further with Polly, I realized that she also had the absurd but sadly common notion in her head that if a baby cried it meant she wasn't a good mother. Consequently, she had spent a good part of the last year or so doing everything in her power to prevent Ariel from crying. As a result, her Textbook baby had become a demanding toddler who had never learned patience or self-soothing. Now, even worse, Ariel had begun picking up on her mother's anxiety and was becoming even better at manipulating her. Because this little one routinely grabbed other children's toys and even resorted to hitting to get what she wanted, Ariel was no longer welcome at play group. The other mothers resented the fact that Polly never disciplined her.

The first step in my helping Polly was to get her to acknowledge how the voices in her head had prevented her from seeing who Ariel really was. She needed to observe for herself that Ariel's behavior wasn't necessarily her *nature*; it was the result of Polly's inability to set limits for her. She wasn't an innately "bad" or "spiteful" or "willful" toddler—far from it, in fact, she was a Textbook toddler who was quite cooperative when given clear limits. It took a few months, but awareness helped Polly really tune in to Ariel, and repeated intervention helped stop the tantrums before they got out of hand (See pages 233–239 and 271–274 for tips on handling tantrums).

In time, Polly was even able to admit to her mother-in-law that she didn't find her remarks helpful. "She commented one day that Ariel seemed 'more cooperative than usual,' and I thanked her for noticing. But I also came clean: I told her that Ariel had always been pretty easy but I just needed practice in responding to her needs. My daughter, I explained, had become more accommodating because I'd gotten better at seeing her. It was really funny, but after that my mother-in-law became much more helpful and less critical."

Plagued by Childhood: Roger. From the moment babies are born, everyone starts to catalog which of his parts belong to whom: "his dad's nose," "his mum's hair," "Granddad's frown." Parents almost can't help identifying with their children; it's a natural process. Here's this lovable little being that comes from your genes, your lineage. Who could resist? Problems arise, though, when such connections override the child's own individuality. Your toddler may look like you, even act somewhat like you. But he is a separate human being who may or may not turn out like you, and he might not respond to the same kind of tactics your parents used. Sometimes, though, too-close identification with a child prevents a parent from understanding this. Such was the case with Roger, the son of a career officer in the air force who believed in "toughening up" his son. As a boy, Roger had been painfully shy, but his father was determined to "make a man out of him," even at age three.

Cut to thirty years later. Roger is now the father of a Touchy toddler, Samuel, a little boy not unlike Roger's childhood self. As a baby, Sam was frightened by sudden noises and thrown by any changes in his routine. Roger constantly asked his wife, Mary, "What's wrong with him?" When Sam was eight months old, Roger decided it was time to "toughen up" his son, just as his dad had done with him. Despite Mary's objections, Roger insisted on throwing Sam in the air. The first time he tried it, Sam was so scared, he wailed for a half hour afterward. Roger couldn't let it go. He tried again the next night, at which point Sam threw up on him. Mary was furious. "I was exposed to all kinds of things," Roger said in his own defense, "and it made *me* a stronger person."

Throughout the following year, Roger and Mary battled over Sam—he thought Mary was making a sissy out of their son; she thought Roger was mean and thoughtless. When Sam was two, Mary enrolled him in a music class. She patiently sat through the first few sessions with Sam on her lap. When Roger heard this, he said, "Let me take him. I'm sure he'll be fine." Frustrated because Sammy wouldn't even pick up one of the instruments, let alone interact with the other children, Roger used his dad's approach and tried to goad his son into participating. "Take this tambourine," he insisted. "Get in there."

Not surprisingly, Sam took a giant step backward from that day on. If Mary so much as drove into the parking lot where the music class was held, he screamed, sure that he was going to be forced to return to that scary place. Mary called for my help. Hearing her plight, I suggested that we include Roger in our meeting. "You have a sensitive little boy here," I said to the two of them, "who has very definite likes and dislikes. To make the most of his nature, you have to be more patient with him. Allow him to dip his toe into activities in ways that are comfortable for *him*." Roger protested, giving me the it-toughened-me-up speech. He explained that whether it was family gatherings or events with other children on the air force base, his dad had always pushed him into the fray. It didn't matter if the situations made the young Roger uncomfortable or whether or not he was ready to handle it. "I lived through it," he insisted.

"Maybe your father's approach did help you, Roger," I offered, "or maybe you've forgotten how scary it was. In any case, we can see that it's not working for your son. All I'm saying here is at least give it a go—try another way. Maybe you could buy Sam a tambourine to play with at home. If you give him a chance to explore in his own way and on his timetable, not yours, he probably will become more adventurous. But meanwhile, Sammy needs your patience and encouragement to build his self-esteem, not your put-downs." Roger, to his credit, was able to back off. Many fathers have to learn this lesson, but when they do, it's really a gift, especially for their sons. Giving young boys gentle support without bullying them or trying to toughen them up makes these lads more willing to explore and enables them to master skills in the bargain.

Bad Fit: Melissa. The idea that some parents and children are a "bad fit" is not a new one. Some twenty years ago, when psychologists started looking at temperament as an inborn phenomenon, it was only natural to observe parents' nature, too. Some combinations can be quite combustible, but of course even when it's a mismatch, we can't give the child back! Rather, one has to become aware of potentially dangerous and damaging clashes. Melissa, for example, is a Spirited woman, a television producer who thinks nothing of putting in sixteen-hour days. Her daughter, Lani, is an Angel who barely has any downtime. I worked with this family when Lani was born. And I remembered all too well that when Lani was only four months old, Melissa had already begun campaigning to get her daughter into the "right" preschool. She had also decided Lani would be a dancer. Goodness me, poor little Lani was in a tutu even before she could stand up! Melissa thought nothing of this, nor did she think that overscheduling two-year-old Lani might be a bit much—but the situation came to my attention at one of my toddler groups.

"We're going from here to music class," Melissa announced to the other mums.

"Really?" questioned Kelly. "Sean is pooped after this group. I have to put him down for a nap . . . unless I want a grouch on my hands for the rest of the day."

"Well, Lani catnaps in the car on the way over," Melissa offered. "Then she's fine. She's a real trouper, this one," she added proudly.

That day, I took Melissa aside after the other mothers had left. "You know you mentioned to me that Lani seems to be in a bad mood more often these days. I think she's just plain knackered, Melissa." Melissa looked a bit miffed, but I went on. "If she's not at one of the many classes you've signed her up for, she's on the set of a TV show with you. She's only two. She can barely catch her breath during the day, no less show sustained interest in anything."

At first Melissa protested that Lani "liked" going with her to work and "enjoyed" all the activities she'd planned for her, but I suggested another possibility. "It's not that she's happy. She goes along because she's so good. But on some days she's clearly exhausted. That's why she's out of sorts. If you're not careful, you're going to have a big sourpuss on your hands. Your Angel will *seem* more like a Grumpy toddler."

I suggested that Melissa slooooow down. "For Lani to really be involved and to enjoy it, she doesn't need so many groups." Melissa was not a stupid woman, she understood exactly what I was saying. And then she admitted something that any Spirited person would understand: she herself enjoyed one by-product of Lani's many activities—the socialization—kibitzing with other mothers, swapping ideas, comparing notes. Melissa was also proud of her little girl, who admittedly was adorable and precocious, and loved watching her mix and mingle. She relished the amusing incidents that happened in the various groups and delighted in sharing these experiences with her family and friends.

"Besides, isn't all this *good*

How to See More Clearly

You may have recognized yourself in one of the stories about parents who have trouble accepting their children's temperament. If so, here's a helpful checklist to improve your sensitivity and powers of observation.

✓ **Self-reflection.** Look at who *you* are, both as a child and an adult. Be aware of your own temperament and of the tapes that run in your head.

✓ **Join a group to see how other children act and react.** It's important to watch other children and to observe the interaction between your child and others.

✓ **Remember that some voices are worth listening to.** Talk with other parents whom you respect. Listen to their observations about your child with an open mind. Don't see everything as a put-down—and don't get defensive.

✓ **Make believe it's someone else's child—what do you *really* see?** Step back. Be as objective as you possibly can. You'll be doing your child and yourself a big favor.

✓ **Have a plan for change.** Take steps to give your child what he or she uniquely needs (see pages 39–40). Remember that change takes time.

for her, Tracy?" Melissa asked. "Doesn't she need to be around other children? And isn't it good to expose her to a variety of experiences?"

"Ducky, she's got years and years ahead of her to learn from life," I replied. "And yes, she needs to be with other children, but she also needs you to respect that she gets tired. You keep wondering, 'What's wrong with her?' when she's out of sorts. She's not being mardy [grumpy] to spite you. She's just telling you, 'I've had enough. And if you thrust another bloody tambourine into my face, I'm going to throw it right back at you!'"

A Plan for Change

In each of the cases above, I tried to first make the parents aware of their blinders so that they could start to see their child (and themselves) more realistically. For some, it's easier to be objective than for others. Melissa, for example, earnestly "tries" to slow down, as I had advised her, and to view Lani's needs as *Lani's* needs rather than as a reflection of her own desires, but she has a way to go. Last I heard, she had been boasting to some other mothers how "good" Lani was to sit through an entire performance of *The Lion King*, so I guess old habits die hard.

If you see yourself in any of these stories, if you hear yourself making certain kinds of statements (see sidebar on page 30), you may be having a bit of trouble accepting your child as he or she really is. If so, you need *a plan*:

1. Take a step back. Honestly look at your child. Have you been ignoring or underestimating her temperament? Think back to when she was a baby. You'll find threads of her personality that you probably noticed from the day she was born. Pay attention to this information, instead of pushing it away.

2. Accept what you see. Don't just give lip service to the idea of loving the child you have—really embrace who your child *is*.

3. Look at what you've been doing that works against your child's temperament. What actions, reactions, things you've said? For example, do you give your Grumpy child enough space? Do you talk too loudly or move too fast for your Touchy toddler? Do you provide enough activity for your Spirited child?

4. Change your own behavior and structure the environment to meet your child's needs. Of course, change takes time. Also, I can't give you a precise road map, because your child is unique. In the next chapter, though, I offer *H.E.L.P.*, a good strategy that will enable you to walk that narrow line, respecting your child for who he is and, at the same time, providing the structure and boundaries within which he can thrive.

CHAPTER TWO

H.E.L.P. to the Rescue: A Mantra for Everyday Moments

I seek your forgiveness for all the times
I talked when I should have listened;
got angry when I should have been
patient; acted when I should have
waited; feared when I should have
been delighted; scolded when I should
have encouraged; criticized when I
should have complimented; said no
when I should have said yes and said
yes when I should have said no.

—Marian Wright Edelman,
The Measure of Our Success

A Tale of Two Mothers

Just as I don't believe there are "bad" children—only children who haven't been taught how to behave and interact socially—I don't believe there are "bad" mums or dads. Certainly, some people I meet seem naturally better at parenting than others, but in my experience (and according to research findings) almost all can learn. That said, let me exemplify this point by telling you about two mothers I know.

A play group is in session. Four adorable toddlers, all around age two, give or take a few months, are scampering amid a clutter of toys and stuffed animals while their mums—women who've known each other since the children were infants—sit in chairs and couches at the perimeter of the room. Of the four, Betty and Marianne were always considered the "lucky" ones. Betty's Tara and Marianne's David were the Angel babies, infants who slept through the night early on, babies who were highly portable, and now, toddlers who easily fit into a variety of social situations, although lately David has begun to whine a great deal. The reason is apparent when you look at the difference between these two mothers. One is tuned in and seems to intuitively know what's best for her child. The other, however well-intentioned, needs a few pointers. You'll probably have no trouble guessing who's who.

Betty hangs back casually while the children play, carefully observing, while Marianne perches on the edge of her seat. If Tara's not quite ready to join the other kids, Betty allows her to get involved at her own speed. In contrast, Marianne pushes David into the fray. When he protests, she says to him, "Now don't be miserable. You *love* playing with Hannah and Jimmy and Tara."

As the children become occupied in play—serious business for toddlers—Betty allows Tara to fend for herself. At one point, one of the other children interferes in Tara's play, but Betty is careful not to rush in. She lets the two work it out; after all, no one is hitting or pushing. In contrast, Marianne is hypervigilant; she doesn't take her eyes off David and acts before any hint of trouble. "Don't do that" comes out of her mouth often, no matter whether the alleged aggressor is David *or* another child.

Somewhere midsession, David begins going to other mothers looking for a snack. His behavior is like that of puppy who knows you have a treat in your pocket. Betty, who never fails to bring something for Tara to munch on, produces a plastic bag filled with baby carrots, reaches in, and hands one to David. Slightly embarrassed, Marianne says, "Thanks, Betty. We rushed out this morning and I didn't have a chance to pack a snack." The other mothers glance knowingly at Betty. This obviously isn't the first time Marianne "forgot."

In an hour or so, as the play period begins to wind down, Tara become a bit cranky. Without hesitation and in a way that doesn't make her little girl feel bad, Betty says, "I'm going to leave now because Tara's getting tired." Seeing Betty pick up Tara, David lifts his little arms toward his mum, too, a gesture, accompanied by whining, that clearly says, "I've had enough as well, Mum." Marianne responds by bending down and trying to cajole David into continuing to play. She gives him a different toy that works for a while. A few minutes later, though, David has a meltdown. While trying to climb into the play car—a feat that he accomplishes easily when he's not so tired—he falls and is now inconsolable.

This little vignette, based on an actual play group I witnessed, highlights an important, and common, difference in parenting styles. Betty is observant, respectful, and sensitive. She plans for contingencies, and she acts quickly in response to her child's needs. Marianne certainly doesn't love David any less than Betty loves Tara. However, she needs a little guidance. She needs H.E.L.P.

H.E.L.P.—An Overview

If you read my first book, you know I'm fond of acronyms, because they help parents keep certain principles in mind. In the busyness of everyday life, thoughts are bloody hard to hold on to; and with babies and toddlers, it's often hard to keep much in mind *or* memory. Therefore, I've come up with an acronym that will remind you of four factors that help create and nurture the parent/child bond, keep your toddler out of harm's way, and at the same time, foster your little one's growth and independence. I call it H.E.L.P., and it stands for:

Hold yourself back
Encourage exploration
Limit
Praise

Good News about Attachment

For most children, the primary "attachment figure" is mum, although anyone who provides continuous and consistent physical and emotional care and demonstrates an emotional investment in a child can also become an attachment figure. These various people are not interchangeable, as anyone who has lost a beloved nanny quickly finds out, and the most recent research indicates that one doesn't detract from or undermine the other. In other words, Mum, don't worry. Though your toddler spends all day with Dad or another caretaker, she'll still run to you when you walk in and want you to kiss her boo-boo.

H.E.L.P. might sound like an oversimplification, but the truth is, the essence of good parenting (and not just for toddlers, by the way) boils down to those four elements. The latest research on what is known as "attachment"—the development of confidence and trust between child and parent—tells us unequivocally that when children feel secure, they are more willing to venture out on their own, better able to manage stress, learn new skills, and relate to others, and more likely to trust that they are competent enough to deal with their environment. The letters of H.E.L.P. incorporate the major factors that lead to a secure attachment.

By *holding yourself back*, you're gathering information. You watch, listen, and absorb the total picture to determine what your child is all about—so that you can anticipate his needs and understand how he responds to the world. You're also giving your toddler the message that he is competent and that you trust him. Of course, if he needs you, you step in to offer a hand—but that's not the same as "rescuing" him.

By *encouraging exploration*, you are showing your child that you believe in his ability to experience what life has to offer and that you want him to experiment with objects, with people, and eventually, with ideas. He'll know that you're there, and he'll glance back to make sure you've stuck around, but by not hovering, you're telling him, "It's okay to venture forth and discover what's out there."

By *limiting* you are properly asserting your role as the grown-up, keeping your child within safe boundaries, helping him to make appropriate choices, and restraining him from situations that are physically or emotionally harmful—because you, as the adult, know better.

And by *praising*, you are reinforcing learning, growth, and behaviors that will serve him as he goes out into the world and interacts with other children and adults. Research tells us that children who are praised appropriately want to learn and enjoy cooperating with their parents. They become more receptive to their parents' input, and not so incidentally, their parents become even more attentive and nurturing in return.

Now let's talk in greater detail about each of the letters in H.E.L.P.

The *H*—Why Hold Back?

Some parents—I call them HELPing parents—are naturally good at holding back. Often, they learned to restrain themselves when their child was an infant. Others need to be taught. They are, like Marianne, well-intentioned parents who want the best for their children but tend toward *over*involvement. They may "shadow" their children, as one parent I know describes the constant hovering—they watch their child's every move. For such parents, it often helps to understand *why* holding back is so important.

Not to toot my own horn, but the mums and dads to whom I taught baby whispering (and, I would hope, those who have read my first book) have usually mastered the *H* in H.E.L.P. by the time their babies become toddlers. That's because many continue to use S.L.O.W., a method I teach for tuning in and determining what an infant is trying to "say." (S.L.O.W. reminds a parent to *Stop, Listen,* and *Observe,* so that they can then figure out *What's up.*) With

S.L.O.W. in mind, these parents learned to restrain themselves instead of rushing in whenever their baby cried; they watched and listened for only a second or two at most. As a result, they became more attuned to their baby's communication. When their children became toddlers, that training paid off. Not only are their children generally better at playing independently, but the parents are more at ease, too. These parents trust their observations; they know who their little ones are, know their likes and dislikes, know what sets them off—and most important, they know when it's time to step in.

Luckily, it's never too late to learn how to hold back (although I'd strongly suggest developing this skill before your child is in high school!). Besides, I'm sure you don't want to risk the consequences of *not* learning: When you constantly step in, prompt, correct, or try to save your toddler from an experience (unless, of course, it's dangerous), you hinder her. You prevent her from developing the skills she needs and inadvertently tell her she *can't* function without your help. What's more, children sometimes become aggravated when a parent tries to take over (see sidebar).

The Five Types: Reacting to Rescuers

All children resent being rescued but show their indignation in different ways:

Angel or **Textbook** toddlers, who are fairly even-tempered, may not protest when you butt in—unless you are a chronic meddler, at which point they'll balk and even say, "Me do."

Spirited toddlers might yell, bang, or bash things.

Grumpy kids might push you away or start throwing things, and if that doesn't work, they wail.

Touchy toddlers might not cry, but they give up; a parent's interference can stifle their curiosity and convince them they can't manage on their own.

Clearly, some children *want* and *need* their parent or other caretaker to interact with them. But the only way to determine this is to hold back and observe *your* child's patterns. Is he naturally inquisitive and daring, or complacent and cautious? Does she crave interaction or prefer to play on her own? Watch, and you'll find out.

Whatever you see, I urge you not to think of yourself as the choreographer of your child's life. A parent's role is to support, not lead. Here are some suggestions that will help you to hold back.

Let your child take the lead. If it's a new plaything, let her operate the toy before you do. If it's a new situation or place, let her climb down from your lap or let go of your hand on her own time. If it's a new person, let her hold out her arms when *she's* ready, not when you are. When she asks for your help, of course be there for her, but give her only as much assistance as she needs, rather than taking over.

Let situations unfold naturally. As you observe your child, your mind might buzz with possibilities: "Oh, I'm sure he's not going to like that toy," or "He's going to be afraid if that dog comes too close." But don't jump to conclusions or second-guess your toddler. Yesterday's tastes and fears may not be the same as today's.

Get out of the way. Everyone hates a busybody or a know-it-all, including toddlers. Naturally, *you* know how to stack blocks without their falling. Of course, you know an "easier" way to get something down from the shelf. You're the grown-up! Equally important, if you do it for him, he won't learn to problem solve. Interference tells your child he can't do it—a message that will stick with him and impact on the way he views all new challenges in the future.

Don't compare your child to other children. Allow her to develop in her own time. I know, I know, this can be difficult, especially if a mother sitting next to you in the park compares her child with yours ("Oh, I see that Annie is still crawling"). Your child will pick up your anxiety almost as fast as it comes over you. And put yourself in her place. How would you feel if you were compared with a coworker, or worse, an ex? She won't like it any better. (More on comparisons at the beginning of Chapter Four.)

Remember that you are not your child. Don't project your feelings or fears onto her. It's true that sometimes the apple doesn't fall far from the tree, but allow your toddler to develop without prejudice, a lesson Roger had to learn (pages 35–37). If you hear yourself making statements such as, "I never liked large groups either," or "Her father was shy, too," you might be overidentifying with your toddler's struggles. Empathy is good, but the way to express it is to *wait for your child to tell you* (by words or actions) what she's feeling. *Then* you can say, "I know what you mean."

The *E*—That Fine Line between Encouragement and Rescue

Sometimes when I explain H.E.L.P. to a mum, especially the part about not interfering, her eyes glaze over and she begins to look confused. I understand her problem. Many parents are like Gloria, the mother of eleven-month-old Tricia. The first time Gloria gave Tricia a shape box, she sat down with her and picked up the pieces herself. "See, Tricia? The square goes here, the circle here," she said as she dropped each shape into the box. Then she started over; meanwhile, Tricia hadn't so much as laid a hand on her new toy. "Now you do it," Gloria said, taking hold of Tricia's hand. Mum placed the square block into her daughter's palm, directed it over the square hole, and said, "Drop it." At that point, Tricia lost interest entirely.

Gloria was clearly having trouble walking that fine line between helping her child learn and hampering her natural curiosity. By *rescuing* Tricia from frustration (which, to be honest, the child wasn't even exhibiting), this mum was acting on her own feelings. Rather than simply encouraging her daughter, she rescued her, which robbed Tricia of the experience.

In contrast, an encouraging parent—a HELPing parent—would have hung back and just watched for a while, waiting to see what her child would do. If she saw *the child* getting frustrated, rather than giving in to her own frustration when the child wasn't doing it fast enough, she would say, "Look, Janey, this block is a square and it fits into the square hole." Janey might struggle for a few minutes. But that's okay; it's how children learn patience and perseverance. Besides, the best motivation for learning is success and the inner joy that such moments generate. By helping a child too much or too early, you take those opportunities from her.

"But how do I know when she is so frustrated that she *needs* me to step in?" Gloria asked. "I know enough to stop her when she's about to put her finger in an outlet. But I'm stymied when it comes to situations like this one where she's essentially safe. How do I know *when*?"

I explained that she should first *ask* Tricia. "If she's having trouble getting the square in, say to her, 'That's okay. I see that you're trying hard. Would you like me to help you?' If she says 'no,' respect her wishes. But if she's still having trouble after a few moments and is getting visibly upset, try to help again: 'I see that you're getting frustrated. Here . . . let me help you.' When the shape finally drops in, cheer for her, 'Yay, you did it. You got it in!' "

The bottom line here is that we don't step in until our child needs us. Knowing your child provides important clues.

Know what frustration looks like on your child. Tricia wasn't very verbal, which meant she couldn't *tell* her mum outright that she was frustrated or literally ask for help. Therefore, I told Gloria, "You have to identify what frustration looks like on Tricia. Does she

---

A Guide to Stepping In

Be an observant, respectful, HELPing parent by being patient, giving your child ample opportunity to explore, choosing age-appropriate toys, and guiding him toward activities. Follow this protocol for stepping in:

✓ Know what *your* child sounds and looks like when frustrated; hold yourself back and observe him until you see those signs.

✓ Start with verbal observation: "I can see that you're having a problem."

✓ Always ask before actually helping: "Would you like me to give you a hand?"

✓ Respect your child if he says, "no," or "I can do it myself," even if it means letting him go outside without a coat. This is how children learn.

✓ Remember that your child actually knows more than you think he does— for instance, when he's cold, wet, hungry, tired, or has had enough of a particular activity or place. Cajoling or trying to convince him otherwise will eventually make him doubt his own perceptions.

make a funny little noise? Scrunch up her face? Cry?" When Tricia does acquire language, it will probably be easier for Gloria to gauge her need for assistance, because emotions will become part of her vocabulary. In the meantime, Mum has to rely on facial expressions and body language. (More on teaching children how to verbally express the language of emotions in Chapter Five.)

Know your child's tolerance level. Some types of children have more perseverance than others, more patience, and therefore, a higher tolerance for frustration. A Grumpy or Touchy toddler might try a puzzle once or twice, but failing to "get it," will move on without giving it a thought. Angel and Spirited types tend to have more staying power. And with Textbook toddlers, it depends upon what else is happening in the environment and where the child is developmentally—when he's learning to walk, for instance, he might not have the patience for puzzles. More than the four other types, Touchy children also tend to lose interest when a parent is too intrusive, which is why the "holding back" part of the equation is particularly critical for them. Tricia was a Touchy toddler. Therefore, Gloria could offer her assistance, but the moment Tricia lost interest, Mum needed to back off.

Know what your child is developmentally capable of. A knowledge of child development can be particularly helpful in determining when to step in, especially with Textbook toddlers, who seem to do everything on developmental cue. But with any type of child, you need to ask yourself, "Is my toddler ready for this activity?" (In Chapter Four, I talk about the importance of staying within your child's *learning triangle.*) I had noticed, for instance, that Tricia had trouble letting go of objects, which is common among toddlers around a year old or less. The child tries to throw or drop something, but it's as if she has glue on her palm, and the object gets "stuck." Asking her to "drop it" may have been outside Tricia's learning triangle, which in turn probably added to her frustration and contributed to her losing interest in the shape box even faster.

A little frustration is a good thing for children. It stretches their capabilities, helps them learn how to delay gratification and develop patience. However, presenting just the right degree of challenge is tricky. If the task at hand is age-appropriate, you're less likely to step in prematurely (rescue), but at the same time, you'll know enough to act before frustration turns into tears or a tantrum. To achieve that balance, look closely at your toddler's world and what's in it.

More about the *E*—Creating *Encouraging* Environments

I always remind parents, especially those whose homes are filled with vast numbers of toys and gadgets featuring buttons and bells and whistles, that it doesn't cost a penny to give your child ample opportunities to develop skills. When these parents insist that their intention is to "maximize our child's potential" and "enrich her environment," I am equally vehement that learning happens anywhere and everywhere. When parents are aware and creative, every moment of every day presents an opportunity for helping their child explore and experiment.

I love meeting the other kind of parents—those who realize that the richest learning environment is right in front of them, just waiting for their children. They manage to exploit opportunities for learning without resorting to a warehouse of very expensive playthings. Bliss and Darren, a couple in their early thirties, live in Los Angeles where a fierce keep-up-with-Baby-Jones current carries many parents in its flow, but these two have managed to swim against the tide. Bliss and Darren keep their children's world simple. Truman and Sydney, age three years and eighteen months respectively, have lots of books, art materials, and construction toys, but they are also happy to play imaginary games with various objects they find around the house—toilet paper tubes, boxes, bowls. The kids spend a great deal of time outside, too, making castles in the dirt, building forts out of scrap wood, splashing in puddles. Truman and Sydney get only two presents from their parents at Christmas, not the carload I've seen under so many American trees.

I had an opportunity to see the effects of such an upbringing

Making Your Home an Exploratorium

Cities everywhere now have "exploratoria" for older children (usually five and up), where they can see the principles of science and physics at work. Do the same in your own home. Tailor the environment to your toddler's physical and intellectual level and make sure that the area is *safe* for independent play. Here are some suggestions—I'm sure you can come up with other ideas on your own.

- Create different play areas inside the house: surround an area rug with a barricade of pillows; place a sheet over the dining room table or a desk and allow your toddler to crawl in; pitch a tent in the den.

- Set up an area outside with dirt or sand, measuring cups and different shapes.

- Provide opportunities in the tub or at the sink for supervised water play (see safety tips on page 111). Have squeeze bottles and measuring cups on hand. On a hot day, give your toddler ice cubes to play with.

- Put on some lively songs and encourage your toddler to make "music" and keep time with cardboard tubes, plastic containers, pots and pans, and wooden spoons.

- Make sure that your toddler has at least some playtime in the crib during the day. That way, he gets to feel safe there and associates his crib with fun and is more likely to be willing to play independently in the morning. Put in a favorite toy, three or fewer stuffed animals, and a "busy box."

when Truman and Sydney came to my office. After watching Truman delight in a set of cardboard blocks, I asked if he'd like to take them home. A smile immediately began to grow on his face. "Really?" he asked. "Thank you," he said sincerely, "thank you."

It's not just that Truman was polite; it was obvious that he was truly grateful for the gift—a refreshing response, to say the least. Many young children nowadays are so inundated with toys that they quickly become immune to gifts *or* novelty. Even worse, because they play only with gadgets that do their thinking for them, they are deprived of valuable opportunities for creating, constructing, and problem solving.

Toddlers, especially, are filled with wonder. They're little scientists in the making. Their eyes and minds are wide open and ready to explore. They don't need an object to stimulate them. At birthdays and holidays, why do you think toddlers often go for the boxes instead of the presents inside? It's because a box can become anything the child would like, while most new toys have to be "operated" in a certain way. Cartons provide hours of imaginative entertainment. Children hide in them, use them to play house or fort. They can jump on them, crush them, and there's no right or wrong way to play with them.

In your kitchen, too, you'll find a warehouse of playthings that almost every child adores: pots and pans, measuring cups, plastic bowls, wooden spoons. A sealed plastic container (secured with tape, please) filled with dried peas is a tambourine. A set of measuring spoons is a rattle. An overturned plastic bowl is a drum and a wooden spoon, the drumstick. Instead of discarding the paper towel or toilet paper tubes, give them to your toddler. Children stay more interested in such playthings because these objects become whatever the child makes of them, not what some manufacturer has designed.

I'm not saying that educational toys aren't worthwhile. Many are wonderful for reinforcing skills. But I am saying that parents nowadays tend to go overboard (or feel guilty if they can't afford so many store-bought toys). It's understandable, of course. Mom-and-pop toy stores have been replaced by virtual child warehouses, gigantic stores that stock everything babies and toddlers need and even more of what they don't need.

So when you focus on the *E* in help, scale back a bit. The raw materials for a rich educational environment are already at your fingertips (see the box on page 52). Encourage your child to explore the ordinary things in his environment, to observe the natural wonders of nature, and allow his growing mind to consider, create, and construct.

The *L*—Living with Limits

Naturally, you'll want to be careful, too. The world is a potentially dangerous place for a growing toddler. Aside from the perils of the environment, your little darling doesn't yet understand the rules of life, and it's up to you to teach him. This is where the *L* in H.E.L.P. is useful. Toddlers need boundaries. You can't give them carte blanche because they don't have the mental or emotional ability to deal with such wide-open freedom. We also need to stress the difference between us and them: we are the adults—and we know better.

There are several different types of limits you must keep in mind now that your child is mobile and his cognitive abilities are growing by leaps and bounds.

Limit stimulation. Parents of infants naturally have to prevent overstimulation, but this is important in toddlerhood as well. It's great for children to get excited, to run around, to listen to lively music. However, toddlers' capacity for stimulation varies, so you need to know what *your child* can handle and for how long. His or her temperament provides a clue. Touchy toddlers, for example, continue to have that low threshold for excitement that marked their infancy. When Rachel, the Touchy two-year-old you met in Chapter One, walks into a room filled with peers, even if they're relatively quiet, she's apt to bury her face in her mum's lap. Or if she goes to the park with her nanny, and lots of kids are running about, she might never want to get out of her stroller. With a Spirited toddler, like Betsy, once she's "turned on," it's hard for her to wind down. And when Allen, our Grumpy toddler, is overstimulated, he cries as if it's the end of the world, which of course only gets him more worked up. Even with Angel and Textbook types, though, too much of *anything* can lead to fatigue, and often, tears. The wise mum or dad slows down the action or leaves the scene before that point. Limiting stimulation is particularly important for any child as you near her bedtime hour (more on that in the next chapter).

Limit choice. When I did a great deal of sleep-in work with infants, I had occasion to observe many families in which there was a toddler-in-residence as well. I was unendingly amused by breakfast scenes much like this one.

Baby Buddy has been fed, and now little Mikey, age nineteen

months, is in his booster chair, ready for his cereal. "Honey," Mum intones sweetly, "would you like Cocoa Puffs, Cheerios, Cap'n Crunch, Rice Krispies?" Mikey just sits there, overwhelmed. He is just starting to say a few words, but lack of vocabulary isn't his problem now. Mikey is confused; he doesn't know what to do with so many choices. I try to be tactful when Mum asks me, "What's wrong, Tracy? Doesn't he understand me? Isn't it good to give children choices?"

"Of course," I agree, "you definitely should give him choices, but at this age *two* are more than enough." Indeed, giving limited choice helps a child feel as if he has some control over his world, as I explain later (pages 219–220), but too many choices are confusing and counterproductive.

Limit undesirable behavior. A child who has a meltdown whenever anyone says "no" is not, as some parents fear, a "bad" kid. Quite the opposite; when I witness such a scene, I say, "Poor little thing. No one taught him about boundaries." Children need to *learn* what's expected of them. The only way that happens is when parents *teach* them. Indeed, helping your child live with limits is clearly one of the greatest gifts you can give your child. I've devoted all of Chapter Seven to discipline, which I prefer to think of as *emotional education*. There I explain my *One/Two/Three* philosophy (pages 227–230): *One*—when a particular kind of behavior, such as hitting or biting, initially occurs—step in at once. *Two* reminds you that if the undesirable behavior happens a second time, you've probably got a pattern on your hands. By *Three*, the third time, you've let it go too far. The reality is that when children's emotions get out of control in any way—screaming, crying, yelling, wild exuberance—it's often hard for them to come back to earth. Granted, it isn't always easy, but it is often possible to nip a tantrum in the bud and to de-escalate rising emotions *if* you pay attention.

Limit anything that's not good in big doses. For most children, television and sweets would be at the top of this list. Numerous studies have been done on each, always concluding that big doses of either one tend to work kids up. Touchy and Spirited toddlers are particularly vulnerable. There may be other activities, foods, certain types of toys, or places that have an adverse effect on *your* child. If so, accept that your toddler doesn't do well in certain circumstances or under certain conditions. Respect his reactions, rather than continually trying to "acclimate" him or her.

Limit potential failure. Although your toddler's abilities are growing every day, don't try to push her. By giving her a toy that's too advanced for her, by expecting her to sit through a movie that's too long, or eat in a posh restaurant that isn't kid-friendly, you're not only putting your child in over her head, you're asking for trouble. As I will explain further in Chapter Four, the same goes for developmental milestones. When, for example, Mum and Dad insist on holding little Juanita's hands to help her "walk," they don't take into consideration the fact that nature has a specific sequence—and timetable—in mind for Juanita. Why try to rush it? Often these are the same parents who call to ask me what to do when Juanita gets up in the middle of the night, stands in her crib, and cries because she doesn't know how to sit down. Perhaps if they had let Nature take its course, or taught her in the day how to get down once she was standing, Juanita wouldn't be having difficulties at night.

Limit your own uncivilized behavior. Toddlers develop skills by repetition and imitation. During every waking hour, your toddler is watching, listening, and learning from your example. It behooves you to pay attention, therefore, to what you're inadvertently "teaching" him. If you curse, don't be surprised if the same words are among the first to come out of your child's mouth. If you're rude, your child will learn to act that way, too. And if you put your feet on the coffee table and munch on chips while watching television, I guarantee it won't be easy to enforce "no food in the living room" and "no feet on the furniture" when it comes to your toddler.

If the above list makes you feel as if you have to be a referee or a policeman all the time, to some extent, you're accurate. Toddlers cry out for boundaries. Otherwise, their interior landscape *and* the world at large is too scary and unmanageable.

The *P*—In Praise of Praise

By far, the most positive teaching comes from affection and praise for a job well done. Affection is something a child can never have too much of. When I was a wee lass, sometimes my Nan would just kiss me, out of the blue. I'd look up and say, "What was that for, Nan?" Invariably, she'd answer, "Just because," and I felt like the most loved and cherished child in the world.

Even the scientists agree that love is the magical element in the parenting equation. When a child feels loved, she feels secure, and she wants to please her parents, and as she gets older, she wants to do right by the world as well.

While there's no such thing as being *too* loving, praise is another matter. It is possible to *overdo* praising a child. The trick is to *praise only for a job well done*. Ask yourself, "Did my child really do something worthy of praise?" Otherwise, your kind words will mean nothing and do nothing, and she will eventually tune out your praise. Remember, too, that the purpose of praise is not to make your child feel good the way hugs and kisses do. It is *to reinforce a task well-done, to compliment good manners, and to acknowledge good social skills, including sharing, kindness, and cooperation.* In short, praise lets your child know that she's done something right or well.

However, parents are sometimes blinded by their own love, and they often confuse the difference between affection and praise. They honestly believe that heaping on the praise bolsters their child's self-esteem. But when there is an *over*abundance of applause or accolades, just the opposite happens: Children don't trust praise that's too plentiful.

Also, when eager mums and dads praise their child too emphatically for a minor triumph, they might find themselves reinforcing the wrong thing. For example, one day Rory pulls his sock off. "Good boy, Rory!" Toni gushes excitedly. The next day, when Rory won't keep his socks on, Toni wonders why. In this case by making too big a deal of Rory's sock-pulling, Toni has given him the impression that he'll be rewarded every time he does it. (Make no mistake; we surely should applaud children's attempts at

Perfect Praise

To avoid giving your child gratuitous compliments, follow these guidelines:

✓ Praise only when the child actually does something good or right. Use words ("Good job!" "Way to go," "Well-done"), a cheer ("Yay"), a high five ("Give me five"), or actions (a hug, a kiss, a thumbs-up, applause).

✓ Praise everyday moments and specific actions ("You're doing a good job with that spoon"), *not* her looks ("You're so cute") or general behavior ("You're so good").

✓ Catch him in the act ("How polite of you to say 'Excuse me,' when you burped," or just as he gives a toy to a friend, "What good sharing").

✓ Praise with thanks ("Thank you for cleaning up/helping set the table").

✓ Praise through rewards ("You were such a good cleaner in play group today. Let's stop and feed the ducks on the way home").

✓ At bedtime, recall something specific about her good behavior during the day ("You were really patient in the shoe store today," or "It was nice that you said 'thank you' to the lady at the bank when she gave you a lollipop").

✓ Model the kind of behavior that deserves praise. Be polite and respectful yourself.

independence, but not go overboard; more about this in Chapter Four.)

Another error parents sometimes make is to praise in *anticipation* of an action. A music class I recently witnessed comes to mind. Like the other mums, Janice was sitting behind eleven-month-old Su Lin. Of the four toddlers listening to a tape of the "Eensy-Weensy Spider,"* only one, not surprisingly the oldest of the bunch, was attempting to imitate the teacher's hand movements. The others, including Su Lin, sat wide-eyed and befuddled, hands in lap. "Good job!" exclaimed Janice as the song ended. With that, Su Lin turned around to look at her mum, with an expression on her face that said, "What the Dickens are you talking about?" Janice meant well, but what was she really teaching Su Lin? Mummy likes it when I sit still!

*Americans, I've been told, call it the "Itsy-Bitsy Spider."

Everyday H.E.L.P.—A Checklist

Keep H.E.L.P. in the back of your mind throughout the day, especially if you find yourself in a sticky situation. Of course, with a toddler that could happen several times a day! Think of each letter and ask yourself . . .

H: Am I holding back or have I been in my child's face, interfering, being too intrusive, rescuing before he needs my help? Remember that the H—holding back—is for the purpose of observation, which is not the same as being detached, rejecting, or ignoring your toddler.

E: Have I encouraged my child to explore or do I hover? There are many opportunities in a day for exploration, any number of which can be thwarted by a parent. Do you, for instance, talk for her when she's playing quietly with another child? Do you do her puzzles instead of seeing if she can manage them on her own? Do you stack blocks for her without first letting her try? Are you constantly directing, monitoring, and instructing?

L: Do I limit or allow things to go too far? Too much of anything is not usually good for toddlers. Do you give too many choices or allow too much stimulation? Do you wait too long before reining in tantrums, aggressiveness, or other high emotions? Do you curtail activities that aren't good in big doses, like eating candy or watching television? And do you allow your child to participate in situations that aren't age-appropriate, which could lead to danger, distress, or feelings of failure?

P: Do I praise appropriately or do I overpraise? Do I use praise appropriately—to reinforce specific acts of cooperation, kindness, or behavior or a job well-done? I've seen parents who say, "Good job" to their toddler when the child just sits there and breathes. Not only are those parents using praise improperly, eventually their words of praise, deserved or otherwise, will mean nothing to their children.

Are You a HELPing Parent?

As I said at the outset of this chapter, some parents are what I call HELPing parents—they instinctively employ H.E.L.P., knowing when to hold back, when to step in, encouraging their child's independence but also imposing limits, praising when praise is due.

These kinds of parents usually have a high tolerance for toddler behavior—and not so incidentally, tend to have toddlers that are easier to handle, regardless of temperament.

HELPing parents are in the middle of the parenting continuum, which traditionally spans the gamut from authoritative to laissez-faire. They are neither strict nor lax, rather a sensible in-between, a balance of the two. Some mums and dads, though, tend to veer to one extreme or the other—they're better at loving than limit-setting or the other way around. Below is a simple self-test that can help you see your parenting patterns. It's not exactly scientific, but these are common behaviors I see in parents. If you answer these questions honestly, you'll get a good idea of where you fall on the continuum.

What's Your Parenting Style?

For each question, circle the letter that best describes you. Be as honest and self-reflective as you can be. Below you will find instructions for tallying up your results.

1. When my toddler is heading toward something dangerous, I
    A. let her find out for herself what will happen
    B. distract her before she reaches her destination
    C. immediately swoop down and pick her up

2. When my toddler has a new toy, the first thing I usually do is
    A. leave him alone; even if he's struggling, I think, "He'll figure it out in time."
    B. wait and intervene only if he seems frustrated
    C. demonstrate how to use it

3. When my toddler has a tantrum in the market because I won't buy her candy, I usually
    A. angrily take her out of the store and tell her she's never ever shopping with me again
    B. stand my ground about the candy and take her out of the supermarket
    C. try to reason with her while she's screaming—and if that doesn't work, I give in

4. When my toddler hits another child in a play group, I usually
    A. pull him away from the child and angrily yell, "No! Don't hit!"
    B. physically restrain my child's hand and say, "It's not nice to hit anyone."
    C. tell him, "That's not nice," and chalk it up to a phase he's going through

5. When my toddler balks at a new food,
    A. I raise my voice, become frustrated with her; sometimes I make her sit there until she eats it
    B. I continue to offer the same food at different times, each time gently coaxing her to try it
    C. I may try to cajole her into eating, but I never force the issue; I just assume she doesn't like it

6. When I am angry at my toddler's behavior, I am most likely to
    A. intimidate him into acting appropriately
    B. walk out of the room until I calm down
    C. swallow my feelings and give her a hug

7. When my toddler has a full-blown tantrum, the first thing I usually do is to
    A. respond angrily and try to physically restrain him
    B. ignore her; if that doesn't work, I remove her from the activity and tell her, "You can't behave like that. When you calm down, you can go back."
    C. try to reason with her; if that fails, I try to cajole her into a better mood by giving her what she wants

8. When my toddler cries because he doesn't want to go to sleep, I usually
    A. tell him he has to—and let him cry it out, if necessary
    B. calm him, make sure that his needs are met, but then encourage him to sleep on his own
    C. pretend to sleep with him or take him into my bed

9. When my toddler acts shy or even slightly reticent in a new situation, I usually
    A. make light of her fears and push her a bit to toughen her up
    B. encourage her gently but allow her to hang back until she's ready to join in
    C. leave immediately, because it's not good for her to get upset

10. My philosophy of child-rearing can best be summed up by saying that I believe in
    A. training my child, making him into someone who fits into our family and into society
    B. providing equal parts of love and limits, respecting my child's feelings but also guiding him
    C. following my child's lead so as not to squash his natural instincts and interests

Where Do You Fall?

To score the self-test above, give yourself one point for each *A* answer, two for each *B*, three for each *C*, and add up your score. Read on for an indication of where you fall on the continuum of parenting styles.

If your score is between 10 and 16: You may be what I call a *Controller*—a parent who leans toward the authoritarian end of the continuum. Controllers are strict, even rigid about standards and have no trouble setting limits for their children or levying punishment for misdeeds, but they tend not to give their children much leeway. Dorrie, for one, has been an ace at setting boundaries for Alicia from the day she was born. It was most important to Dorrie to have a child who is polite and well-behaved in public—and she does. But Alicia, who was very outgoing as a baby, is now somewhat reticent when it comes to trying new things or playing with other children. She's always got her eye on her mum, to see whether Dorrie approves. I have no doubt that Dorrie adores her daughter, but she sometimes doesn't take into account that her little girl has feelings of her own.

If your score is within the 17 to 23 range: You're probably a HELPing parent who exhibits a good balance of loving and limit setting. Your natural instinct is consistent with the letters of H.E.L.P. You're probably a lot like Sari, a HELPing parent I've watched since her son Damian was a baby. Sari was always a keen observer, but she also let Damian make his own mistakes . . . unless he was in danger or about to attempt something that he wasn't ready for. She was a creative problem solver, too, as the story of "Sari, Damian, and the Big, Heavy Glass Pitcher" illustrates (see box on page 63).

If you scored anywhere from 24 to 30: You're probably more of an *Enabler*—a parent who is somewhat laissez-faire and lax about limits. You fear that too much interference will crush your child's

Sari, Damian, and the Big, Heavy Glass Pitcher

One day, when Sari was pouring orange juice into a sippy cup, Damian, then two, said, "Me do it!" Sari knew that giving him the heavy glass jug was out of the question. So she told him, "This is too heavy, but I'll get you your own pitcher." From the cabinet, she produced a small plastic pitcher, poured a few ounces of juice in it, and led Damian to the sink. "This is where you can practice pouring. That way, we don't have to worry about spills or cleaning up the floor." Damian was delighted with the compromise and for the next several mornings pushed a chair over to the sink and said, "Damian pour juice." Within a week or two, he had become quite adept at pouring, so much so that he could handle the increasingly larger quantities of liquid his mum gave him. He was soon able to take the juice carton from the refrigerator, walk to the sink, and pour the OJ right into his little plastic pitcher without spilling a drop. As he explained to a visitor who watched this routine, "This is where we pour things."

natural inclinations. You may even believe that if you discipline your child, you risk losing her love. At the same time, you tend to be a bit overprotective; you might hover rather than allow your child to explore freely. Clarice, for example, is an Enabler. From the time Elliott was a baby, she watched his every move. As he got older, Clarice constantly monitored his play. She is always talking, explaining, showing him something. She is far better at teaching than at setting boundaries. This mum is certainly respectful of her son, but she leans too much in that direction, causing an observer to wonder, "Who's in charge here?"

Not surprisingly, I tend to get more SOS calls from Enablers than from Controllers. Mothers like Clarice, who have trouble setting limits, discover the hard way that their children need more structure and stability in their lives. The calls I get from them are usually about erratic eating habits, sleep problems, or behavioral

What Influences Parenting Styles?

Obviously, I believe (and research confirms) that it's best to be a HELPing parent. People land more toward one end of the continuum than the other for a variety of reasons.

Their parents were that way. You might insist, "I'll never be like them," but they were your role models. Many parents repeat patterns established in their own childhoods. As one particularly smothering mother said to me, "My mother loved me to death, and I intend to do the same thing with this child." It's not necessarily bad to do what your parents did in the past. Just make sure it's appropriate now for you and your child.

Their parents were just the opposite. They discard everything done in their own childhoods, often without awareness. Again, it's best to think through what you want and what will work best. Your parents might not have been all wrong. Therefore, it's better to choose some practices you learned from them and reject others.

They have a particular type of child. To be sure, the type of child you have influences how you react toward him in various everyday situations. As I stressed earlier (pages 37–39), your own temperament may or may not be a good fit for your child's nature. Some kids are more trying, more obstinate, more sensitive, more belligerent than others—and it takes a very conscious parent to handle them. If you're being overly rigid or relaxed in reaction to your child's temperament, ask yourself, "Is this what's best for my child?"

difficulties. On the other hand, mums like Dorrie who have no trouble setting limits tend to have children who toe the line. All the same, a Controller's inflexibility and her rigid standards often compromise her child's curiosity and creativity. Alicia, for one, doesn't seem to trust her own perceptions, so she constantly looks to her mum, not just for approval but to tell her how she *should* feel.

Admittedly, it's hard to be a HELPing parent, to balance loving and limit setting, to know when to jump in, when to hold back, to dole out just the right amount of praise at precisely the right moment, to know when and how to discipline appropriately so that the punishment fits the crime (more on that in Chapter Seven). Then again, you may genuinely *prefer* to operate closer to one of the extremes of the parenting continuum. In any case, if you know where *you* stand on the parenting continuum, at least you'll be able to make *conscious* choices about your own behavior, how you react, and how you treat your child. After all, everything you do shapes your child.

You will read more about H.E.L.P. throughout this book, as I believe it provides an essential foundation on which sound parenting is built. Equally important is the idea of maintaining a structured routine, which I deal with in the next chapter.

CHAPTER THREE

R&R (Routines and Rituals): Easing the Toddler Tug-of-War

The drops of rain make a hole in the stone not by violence, but by oft falling.

—Lucretius

Even the smallest rites of everyday existence are important to the soul.

—Thomas Moore,
Education of the Heart

"What's the Big Deal about Routines?"

That's how Rosalyn, an actress on a soap opera, responded when I suggested that she incorporate more structure into Tommy's and her day. She had consulted me because her one-year-old son cried as if there were no tomorrow whenever his mum left the house.

"What does routine have to do with separation?" she asked, not waiting for an answer. "I hate structure, because day in and day out, everything's the same," she insisted in a droning voice that spoke volumes about her own need for variety and stimulation. In her profession, after all, every day was a new adventure.

"Yes," I said, "but think about your life when you went to the studio every day. Each morning you woke up at the same time, you showered, ate breakfast, and got to work in pretty much the same way. Sure, your lines changed and sometimes new actors were added to the mix, but there were also regulars on whom you knew you could rely, as well as writers, the director, camera people. Sure, every day presented different challenges, but weren't those predictable elements a comfort to you? The truth is, you actually had a structured routine, although you might not have chosen to see it that way."

Rosalyn looked at me. The expression on her face said, "What the devil are you talking about, Tracy?"

I continued, "You were free from the drudgery of pounding the pavement every day, like some actresses have to do. They worry about their next paycheck, maybe even their next meal. But you had the best of both worlds—a steady job and yet one that offered variety and new demands on a daily basis."

She nodded. "I guess," she said reluctantly. "But we're not talking about me; we're talking about a one-year-old."

"It's the same for him. Actually, it's even *more* important in his case," I explained. "His day doesn't have to be boring, but a little stability—and more important, predictability—will make him less anxious. Actually, if you think of it in terms of your own career, maybe it will be easier to understand. You were able to hone your skills because you didn't have to think about what might be coming next. All I'm saying is that Tommy deserves—and craves—the same degree of comfort. If he knows what to expect, he will become more cooperative, because he'll feel as if *he* has some control over his environment, too."

I meet many mums like Rosalyn. They either don't realize the importance of a structured routine, or they think it will cramp their style. They come to me with their children's dilemmas: sleep difficulties, poor eating, behavior problems, or separation anxiety as in Tommy's case. The first thing I do is help them look at *routines* and *rituals*, or as I like to call it, *R&R*.

What Is R&R?

First let me explain what I mean by R&R. Throughout this chapter, I tend to use the words "ritual" and "routine" interchangeably because the two Rs are intertwined. Indeed, whenever you repeat and reinforce an act, you are doing R&R.

Routines structure the way we handle the "givens" in a child's daily life: waking, mealtimes, bath, bedtime. Most of our daily routines are what ritual expert Barbara Biziou (see sidebar on page 70) calls "unconscious rituals"—we tend to perform them without thinking of their significance. For example, a good-morning hug, a wave bye-bye, and a good-night kiss are all rites of connection. You say the same words whenever you drop your toddler off at day care, or you give your child a thumbs-up sign whenever you leave the house—those are ritual acts, too. And when we repeatedly remind children to say "please" or "thank you," we are not just teaching them to be polite, we are reinforcing etiquette, which is a social ritual.

Such day-to-day rites enable a child to understand what's coming next, what they can expect as well as what's expected of them. Their familiarity is both reassuring and confirming to young children. As Biziou observes, "By using rituals, we help ourselves and our children make better sense of the world. They begin to regard even the mundane—a bath or a family dinner—as sacred moments of connection and togetherness." The trick for parents is to become more conscious of these everyday moments and to make them more purposeful.

R&R can mark everyday moments or extraordinary times. I've devoted the first part of this chapter to rituals associated with our daily routines, and the second part to rituals that reinforce family traditions and help us celebrate milestones, holidays, and special other times. But first, let me explain why they're so important.

Why Do Children Need R&R?

Counseling mums and dads of newborns, I always prescribe a structured routine, to give babies a good foundation and to allow parents to rest and revive themselves from the rigors of early parenting.* If your child has been on a structured routine from the day he came home from the hospital, all the better. You've made his life more stable and predictable. But now that he is toddling about, R&R—maintaining a routine, along with other types of rituals—is even more important than it was in infancy.

R&R provides security. A toddler's world is challenging, confusing, and often scary. She is experiencing a time of her life during which the unparalleled rate and breadth of developmental growth is astounding not just to you, but to her. Each day, there are a host of new contests and trials. Danger lurks around every corner. R&R gives your child support as she takes her tentative first steps, bolstering her both in the physical sense and in understanding and managing her emotions and her new social life as well.

---

*In my first book, I offered the E.A.S.Y. routine, a way of structuring a baby's day to include *Eating, Activity, Sleep,* and time for *You,* in that order. Even if you didn't use E.A.S.Y., at this point your toddler's day probably incorporates that natural progression. If not, it should.

R&R cuts down on toddler struggles. Happily cooperating on the changing table is a thing of the past. Your little one is now like the Energizer Bunny; he wants to get up and go and keep going, which means you become the traffic cop, and sometimes, the jailor. Now I'm not saying that we can eliminate the inevitable tug-of-war altogether, but instituting predictable mealtime, bedtime, and play routines will surely diminish the battles. That's because predictability helps children learn what to expect; conversely, a lack of routine leaves them at sea.

For example, I got a call from Denise about her toddler's "sleep problem." At night, she had been giving one-year-old Aggie her bath, then a massage, then reading her two stories, giving her a bit of milk in a bottle, and finally putting her to bed, at which point Aggie would coo a bit and then fall asleep. By the time the night-time routine was completed, though, it was 8 o'clock, and Denise wanted Aggie in bed by 7:30. She decided to eliminate the books. Now, instead of going to sleep willingly as she had done, Aggie screamed. What was going on? Denise forgot that children thrive on routines, not on timetables. Becoming obsessed with trying to save that extra half hour, Denise had changed

---

The Anatomy of a Ritual

Barbara Biziou, author of *The Joy of Ritual* and *The Joy of Family Ritual*, breaks down the elements of a ritual to include:

1. Intention. Every ritual, even those we perform daily and don't think about, has a deeper meaning. For instance, although we may not say it out loud, the purpose of the bedtime ritual is relaxation.

2. Preparation. Some rituals also require ingredients, which should be on hand ahead of time. With children preparation is key and the ingredients are often quite simple—for instance, a high chair for mealtime, a special hand-drying towel for washing up, a book for bedtime.

3. Sequence. Every ritual has a beginning, a middle, and an end.

4. Follow up. Every time you repeat a ritual—whether you do it daily, in the case of everyday routines, or yearly, in the case of special family days and holidays—you reinforce its meaning.

Adopted from *The Joys of Everyday Rituals* and *The Joy of Family Ritual* © Barbara Biziou, St. Martin's Griffin, 2001. All rights reserved.

---

her child's usual ritual—and now both were suffering as a result. I suggested that she reinstate the old bedtime customs and simply start a bit earlier each night. "Miraculously" Aggie's so-called sleep problem disappeared.

R&R helps toddlers deal with separation. That's because R&R helps children anticipate events that repeat daily. Research has shown, in fact, that as young as four months old, children develop expectations. We can use this knowledge to teach toddlers that even though mum leaves, she'll return. In little Tommy's case, for instance, to allay his anxiety, I advised Rosalyn to ritualize her departure, at first leaving the room for just a few minutes. She always prepared him ("Mommy has to go bye-bye for a little while, Tommy"), and then, as she left the room, she said, "Be right back, honey" and blew him a kiss. As Tommy became better able to tolerate his mum's absence, I instructed her to lengthen the time out of the room. Eventually, she was able to leave the house using exactly the same R&R. Doing the same thing each time, saying the same words, helped prepare Tommy and helped him feel more in control. His panic didn't abate immediately, but by creating leaving and reentry routines ("Hi, Tomster, I'm home," accompanied by a big hug and kiss), Tommy soon realized that even though Mum left she would be back. (More about separation in Chapters Six and Eight.)

R&R supports all kinds of learning—physical feats, emotional control, and social behavior. Children learn by repetition and imitation.

What Research Says about Routines

Children develop a conscience when "everyday family life is characterized by routines that enlist the young child's cooperation in rituals like bedtime, story reading, waking, mealtimes, bathing and other recurrent, predictable events. The presence of these routines is one way of making expectations known and avoiding constant confrontations. Children thus learn cooperation . . . in the predictable flow of daily life."

—From *Neurons to Neighborhoods* (see page 16 for complete source)

Rather than parents trying to push or prod their child, by doing the same things day in and day out, learning takes place naturally and organically. Take good manners. Even before a child learns to talk, Mum routinely says, "thank you" when handing her a bagel to gnaw on. In time, Mum's words are replaced by the toddler's first "ta," and later, the real words, "thank you." Ultimately, R&R helps shape children, teaching them not just skills, but morals, values, and mutual respect.

R&R avoids problems by helping parents set clear boundaries and be consistent. Toddlers constantly test parents' limits, and parents often cave under the stress, which only makes their children more manipulative. R&R helps us structure situations and lay out expectations ahead of time—in which case we're less likely to find we have an out-of-control toddler on hand. Let's take Veronica, who didn't want nineteen-month-old Otis jumping on furniture. "When he does," I suggested, "gently correct him. You might say, 'Otis, you cannot jump on the couch,' but also show him an appropriate place to jump—an old mattress you set up in the playroom." Veronica did just that, but the next day, when Otis started bouncing on his bed, she had to repeat the routine. "Otis, you cannot jump on your bed," she said as she led him into the playroom. It took only three or four times for Otis to realize, *Oh, I get it. I'm allowed to jump here but not on the sofa or on my bed.*

R&R helps you prepare your child for new experiences. In Chapter Six, I talk about creating *rehearsals for change*—a set of experiences that gradually foster a child's growing independence. The idea is to introduce your little one to new experiences at home first, increase the challenges bit by bit, and then take the show on the road. So, for example, to prepare ten-month-old Gracie for sitting in a restaurant, her mum made sure Gracie was part of the family dinner routine. She sat in her high chair with her sister and brother at the table and partook of their nightly dinner ritual—lighting a candle, holding hands, and saying a prayer. By being included in this way, Gracie tried new foods, learned how to eat and how to use utensils, and began to understand what kind of behavior was expected at the dinner table. Sitting still for increasingly longer periods was a rehearsal for her later restaurant experiences which, not surprisingly, she handled quite well.

R&R allows everyone to slow down and to make the most mundane moments into times of connection. What could be more special than bath or story time? And if we parents slow ourselves down and imbue these events with intention ("I will use bedtime to connect with my child"), we are also teaching our children by example how to put greater meaning into everyday moments. Such occasions will strengthen the parent/child bond, and at the same time, send an important message to your child: "I love you. I want you to know that I'm here for you."

Raising my own daughters, although I allowed for the unexpected and was far from inflexible, I employed lots of R&R. I kept mostly to a structured routine, even before they were old enough to understand time, so they always knew what came next. For example, when I came in from work, they knew they would have a full hour of my complete attention. Nothing was allowed to cut into *our* time. I didn't talk on the phone; I didn't do chores. Because they weren't old enough to tell time, I set a timer, and they knew that when it rang I had to make dinner and tend to other tasks around the house. They were always willing to let me go, and they helped out in the little ways they could, because they felt so nourished by the sacred time we'd spent together.

R&R Around-the-Clock

Let me remind you that while certain types of R&R are practiced by almost every family I know—a book or story before bedtime—R&R must be tailored to your family. As you read some of the suggestions below, take into account your child's temperament, your own parenting style, and the needs of other family members. As the chart on the next page shows, some parents are better than others at structuring and maintaining routines. Consider *your* schedule, too. Be realistic. If you can't eat with your child every

A ROUTINE INVESTIGATION

Some parents have an easier time than others when it comes to setting up and maintaining a structured routine. Below, I look at how each of the parenting types I identified in Chapter 2 handles this challenge. Where do *you* stand?

	Controllers	HELPers	Enablers
Philosophy	Firm believers in structure and routine.	Know it's important to set up and maintain a structured routine.	Believe that too much structure will cramp child's style and their own spontaneity.
Practice	Good at instituting routines but may make their own needs more important than child's.	Good at instituting routines that accommodate child's needs, those of other family members, *and* the demands of their own day.	Believe that structure is inhibiting. Their day is built around their child; no two days of the week are the same.
Adaptability	Might have trouble adapting to child's different needs or making last-minute changes when needed.	Flexible enough to veer from the routine when necessary and aren't thrown by changes.	At the extreme, fly by the seat of their pants so often they give new meaning to the word "adaptable."
Possible Outcome	Child's needs are sometimes compromised; parent can become frustrated and upset when schedule is not adhered to.	Child feels safe; life is predictable; creativity is encouraged within reasonable limits.	Such a free-wheeling philosophy often translates into chaos. Because parents have trouble doing the same thing one day after another, child never knows what's going to happen next.

night, at least commit to two or three nights of the week. Also, rituals are personal; they are most meaningful when they truly reflect the values of the participants. And you are most likely to maintain those rituals and routines that feel best to you. So while some families might say grace at a meal, yours might not. In some households but not in others, bath rituals are Dad's domain.

Below, I take a little trip around the clock to look at routines that are repeated daily. Though they will change somewhat as your toddler grows, these are the mainstays of family life: waking, eating, bathing, exits and entrances, cleanup, nap, and bedtimes. You won't find any problem-solving ideas here; this chapter is about prevention. By repetition of these acts, by teaching children what you expect, you can often *avoid* problems before they occur.

For each of the following daily routines, I offer suggestions about intention (purpose and goal), what you might need to prepare, the sequence—how to begin, proceed, and end the ritual—and, where it's appropriate, follow up. (In the case of many of the everyday rituals, which occur daily, you don't have to worry about follow-up.) Consistency is key. Remember, too, only *you* can figure out the most creative ways of making R&R both dependable and fun for your family. Put on your thinking cap.

Waking Up. There are only two ways a toddler wakes up—happy or crying. In infancy, waking patterns are determined by temperament. But by the time babies become toddlers, their waking patterns are more a matter of what parents have reinforced and less the child's personality. In fact, good R&R can actually override temperament.

INTENTION: To teach your child that bed is a nice place to hang out and to have a toddler who wakes up smiling, coos, and plays contentedly on her own for anywhere from twenty to thirty minutes.

PREPARATION: Make sure your child plays in her crib during the day. Spending fun time in a crib reinforces the idea not only that it's safe, but it's a great place to play. If your toddler doesn't yet feel this way, put her into her crib once or twice during the day. Have on hand her favorite toys, and in the beginning, stay by her side, reassuring her with your presence. Play peek-a-boo and other games to make it a fun experience. Don't leave the room at first. Use the time to fold laundry in her bedroom, straighten shelves, or do paperwork, so that your presence is felt but you're not physically intervening. Gradually walk away and then out of the room for increasingly longer periods (see also pages 80–82 about exits and entrances).

My Toddler Wakes Up Crying: What's Happening?

When a parent tells me their toddler wakes up crying, it usually suggests that the child doesn't feel comfortable in her own crib. I usually ask these questions:

- **Do you tend to rush in at the first sound she makes?** You may have inadvertently trained her to cry when you don't come fast enough.

- **Does she also display anxiety— wailing at the top of her lungs, wrapping her arms tightly around you when you come to get her?** This is a sure sign that the crib has become a dreaded place. Take steps to change that (see below).

- **Does she have periods during the day when she enjoys playing in her crib?** If not, it might be a good idea to include them in your play routines (see "Preparation" on page 75 and Leanne's story on pages 254–262).

FROM BEGINNING TO END: In the morning, try to gauge how long it takes your child to go from cooing and playing on her own to crying. Walk in *before* she gets to the crying stage. If you have your own schedule to attend to, you might have to go in sooner. Or if you know a diaper needs changing, by all means, don't wait.

Go in cheerfully and make a big deal out of greeting a new day. Some parents have a wake-up song, or a special greeting, such as, "Good morning, my little pumpkin. I'm sooooo glad to see you." The ritual ends with your taking him out of the crib, with both of you excited to start the day.

TIP: Whatever you do, don't give your child sympathy if he cries in the morning. Pick him up, hug him, but please don't say, "Oh you poor thing!" Act jolly, as if you're happy to start the day. Remember that children learn by imitation.

Mealtimes. Toddlers are notoriously fussy eaters—a fact that concerns many parents who consult me (I cover how and what to feed children in Chapter Four). "Back off," I tell such anxious parents. "Concentrate more on making the mealtime routine consistent than on making your toddler eat." I assure you, your child won't die of malnutrition—numerous studies show that despite occasional lapses in appetite, otherwise healthy toddlers manage to eat a sufficient amount and balanced selection of food *if their parents don't push them* (see pages 112–127).

INTENTION: Think of meals as a way of teaching your toddler what it means to sit at a table, use utensils, try new foods, and most important, eat with the family.

PREPARATION: Serve meals at approximately the same time every day. Whereas babies are little eating machines, toddlers are often just the opposite. They're too busy testing out the world and making their way in it. Hunger isn't the same motivating drive it once was, but we can help them tune in to this and other bodily needs by letting them see that "the next meal" is just around the corner.

Allow your toddler to participate in family dinners at eight to ten months, which is usually the time he's able to sit and take solid foods. Have a special eating chair for him, a booster seat that you put on a regular chair, or a high chair. The important thing is that being in his "eating chair" lets him know it's time to (hopefully) sit still and eat. If you have older children, have them eat at the same time. It's great if you can join them at least a few nights a week; even if you don't actually eat with them, have a snack. Your presence will give the occasion the feel of a "family dinner."

FROM BEGINNING TO END: Hand washing is an ideal premeal ritual that lets a child know it's time to eat. As soon as your child can stand on his own, invest in a small, sturdy step stool, so that he can reach the sink without your help. Let him watch as you wash your hands, and then give him the soap and encourage him to try. A little hand towel hung on a hook or bar next to the sink should be designated as his special hand-drying towel.

Start the meal with grace, candlelighting, or simply saying, "You may begin." Have conversation, just as you would at a dinner with adults. Talk about your day; ask the children about theirs. Even though your toddler can't answer at first, he'll begin to understand the give and take of conversation. And if he has siblings, he'll learn a host of lessons by just listening.

Consider the meal over when your child stops eating. Many parents, undoubtedly anxious about proper nutrition and adequate food intake, try to sneak an extra bite into a toddler's mouth, or they coax and cajole him, even though he turns his head away. Even worse, some follow him into the den and try to shovel in a few more spoonfuls while he's playing (see Shannon's story, pages 274–277). Remember the intention of this ritual: to teach your child mealtime mores. One doesn't play while eating.

End the meal with whatever practice feels right for your family. Some families say a final prayer or blow out the candles. Others take a moment to thank the preparer of the meal. A suitable ending might simply be the act of taking off your child's bib accompanied by the words, "Dinner's over. Time to clean up!" Once your toddler can walk and carry, she can also bring her own (presumably unbreakable) plate to the sink. I also like to get children in the habit of toothbrushing after meals. Start as soon as you've introduced solid foods.

> **TIP:** *To get your child used to the idea of brushing her teeth, start with her gums. Wrap a soft, clean terrycloth around your index finger and rub her gums after eating. That way, when her teeth come in, she'll be accustomed to the feeling. Buy a soft, baby toothbrush. Your toddler will probably suck on it at first, but eventually she'll learn how to brush.*

Follow-up: Keep up mealtime R&R no matter where you go. When you take your child to another house to eat, to a restaurant, or if you go on an extended trip away from home, maintain as much of the above as possible. This will make your child feel secure and reinforce everything she's learning about mealtimes. (More about taking your child into the "real world" in Chapter Six.)

Bath Time. As much as some infants dread a bath, toddlers often dread getting *out* of the tub. A consistent bath-time ritual can go a long way toward avoiding that struggle.

INTENTION: If it's an evening bath, the intention is to help your toddler relax and get ready for bed. If it's a morning bath, which is less frequent among families I know, the purpose is to get your toddler ready for the day.

PREPARATION: Announce to your toddler in a cheery voice, "It's time for your bath!" or "We're going to have a bath now!" Run the bath, and put cups, squeeze bottles, duckies, and other floating toys into the tub. If your child doesn't have sensitive skin, you might want to put bubbles in, too. Thinking back to my own daughters, I remember more toys in our bath than in our toy box! Also, have two washcloths on hand, one for you, one for her.

> **TIP:** *Always run your cold water tap first and then add the hot. To prevent your toddler from accidentally turning on the hot water and scalding herself, buy a faucet cover that goes over the hot water tap, or, if it's a two-in-one handle, one that goes over the whole apparatus. Also, use a rubber tub mat to prevent slipping, and set the thermostat on your hot water heater at no higher than 125° F.*

FROM BEGINNING TO END: Put your child in, or if she's old enough, let her climb in on her own. (Be careful, of course; tubs are notoriously slippery.) I always like to sing a song while bathing. "This is the way we wash our arms, wash our arms, wash our arms. This is the way we wash our arms, so early in the evening. This is the way we wash our back, wash our back," and so on. It helps the child learn her body parts and often stimulates her desire to wash herself.

Because most toddlers hate to see a bath end, don't lift her straight out of the tub. Instead, start taking the toys out of the tub first. Then pull the plug, let the water out, and say, "Uh-oh, water's going down the drain. Bath time is over!" End with a good snuggle in a fluffy towel.

> **TIP:** *Even though you may have more confidence in your child's ability now that she's a toddler, under no circumstances should you ever leave her alone in the bathtub. (For safety tips, see page 111.)*

Exits and Entrances. All children go through a stage when it's hard for them to separate from their parents, even if mum just goes into the next room to make dinner. Clearly, some toddlers take it harder than others, but it also depends on the parents. If they work every day, leaving the house and returning at predictable times, and have done so since the child was a baby, it's often easier for their toddler to get used to the routine and to know what to expect. It's a bit more difficult when one or both parents leave and return to the house in a more erratic pattern. At the same time, I've also seen children who seem to have adjusted to a parent's absence suddenly become fearful.

INTENTION: To make your child feel secure, knowing that when you leave, you'll also return.

PREPARATION: Introduce your child to the idea of your leaving. If you start around six months and proceed gradually, by eight months she will probably play on her own for up to forty minutes. You can also help your child get used to the idea of your ducking away by first playing peek-a-boo with her. Such game playing reinforces the idea that even if she can't see you, you're still there. Don't attempt this when your child is tired or cranky, however. And if your child is initially scared and starts crying, wait until later, or even another day, and try again.

When you get to the point of being able to leave the room, make sure you leave her in a safe situation—a crib or playpen—or under someone else's watchful eye. Each time you exit, say the words, "I'm going to [the kitchen/my room]. I'll be there if you need me." But come right back when the child calls you, so that she learns she can trust you. If you have an intercom or a walkie-talkie, talk into it while you're in the other room just to reassure her, or call into her: "I'm only in the kitchen, honey." Go back and reassure her if necessary. Build up these times away, spending increasingly longer periods out of your toddler's view.

When you do leave the house, whether you're going on an errand for fifteen minutes or to a full day of work, be honest. Don't say, "I'll be right back" if you're planning to be gone for five hours, or worse, "I'll be back in five minutes." Even though toddlers have no concept of time, when a few days from now you promise him that you'll take him to the park in "five minutes," he's going to get upset, because he'll think that's a very long time.

FROM BEGINNING TO END: When you leave, use the same words and gestures each time. "I'm going to work, honey bun," accompanied by a big hug and kiss. It's fine to say, "We'll go to the playground when I get back," but be careful not to promise what you can't fulfill. It's also important to know what is most soothing for *your* child. For example, it helps some children to go to the window and wave, but others get more upset because it prolongs the leaving process.

Admittedly, there's a fine line between honoring a child's feelings ("I know you don't want me to go . . .") and stating the reality (". . . but Mummy has to get to work."). Remember, it's often not the leaving that upsets a child; it's *how* you leave. If you keep going back and forth, you're reinforcing the child's anxiety. You're telling him (indirectly): "Your crying will bring me back to you."

> **TIP:** *For your own peace of mind: If your child is upset when you leave, call the sitter from your car or when you get to work. I assure you, most children are fine within five minutes after Mum exits.*

When you return, walk into the house saying the same words each time: "I'm back," or "Hi, honey, I'm hooooome." Always greet your toddler with lots of hugs and kisses and say, "Mummy has to change her clothes now, so I can play with you." (If you recall, TV's Mr. Rogers started every show by changing his shoes, a ritual that said to the children in his audience, "This is our time together.") Then take at least an hour to be with him—make it your special time.

Some mums also like to call ahead, so that the sitter can say to the child, "Mummy's on her way home." The sitter can also bring the child to the window when you're about to pull up (that's assuming you don't live in Los Angeles where the traffic makes it hard to give anyone a precise ETA!). Interestingly, many children whose parents work regularly cue into rituals not necessarily intended for them. In my own house, for example, Sara knew that in the late afternoon, whenever Nan put a kettle on, I was on my way.

TIP: *Never bring a gift home when you return. You are the gift.*

Cleanup. Because toddlers often have trouble with transitions, I like to incorporate cleanup routines throughout the day. In my groups, for example, even with children as young as eight months, we always had "cleanup" before doing music, which was a more settled activity. Besides, it's never too early to start learning responsibility and respect.

INTENTION: To teach a child responsibility and to instill in him respect for his own and other people's belongings.

PREPARATION: Your toddler should have a box, several hooks, and if possible, some shelves in a closet that he can reach *on his own.*

FROM BEGINNING TO END: When your child comes into the house, say, "Time to hang our jackets." You go to the closet and hang yours, and he will follow suit. After he has been playing in his room, and it's time to either eat or get ready for a nap or bed, say, "Time to clean up now." At first you'll have to help. In my groups, I say, "I'm putting things in the box," and then they imitate. Understand that your child might come up to the box and try to take more toys out, but just keep saying, "No, we're putting things *in* the box now. We're cleaning up." He learns what cleanup is through constant reinforcement of this ritual.

FOLLOW-UP: Wherever your toddler goes, whether it's to Grandma's, to a play group, or to cousin Nell's, reinforce this cleanup ritual.

Naps and Bedtime. There's nothing quite so delicious as book reading and snuggle time before bed. Parents usually love it as much as toddlers do. Then comes the moment of getting your child off to sleep. Some children need more support than others—sleep is a skill children must *learn* (see page 255). But even if your toddler is a "good sleeper" who goes down for naps and to bed with relative ease, it's important to maintain consistent bedtime rituals. Sleep problems can crop up suddenly as your child becomes increasingly mobile, typically between the first and second year. Dreams can plague her sleep, as well as impatience. She wants to get back on her feet! I deal with sleep dilemmas in Chapter Eight, but here are some suggestions for sleepy-time R&R.

INTENTION: At nap time and in the evening, your goal is to help your child calm down, going from the rigors and excitement of play to a more relaxed state.

PREPARATION: End stimulating activities, like TV or play. Put toys away (see the preceding cleanup ritual) and announce, "It's almost time for bed." Draw the curtains and pull down the shades. To help your child relax physically, incorporate the evening bath as part of the nighttime ritual—as well as massage if your child enjoys it.

FROM BEGINNING TO END: After bath and jammies, say, "Let's go and choose a book." If your toddler is between eight and twelve months and hasn't yet developed reading "favorites," choose a book for her. Decide ahead of time how many books you're willing to read (or how many times you'll read the same one) and tell her. Stick to it—otherwise, you're asking for trouble (more about that in Chapter Nine).

Beyond the above givens, families tend to tailor this ritual to their and their children's taste. Roberta and her little girl Ursula sit in a rocking chair every night, with Ursa's favorite bunny nestled between them. Roberta reads the story, they cuddle a bit, and then Ursa slips easily into her crib. Deb's son Jack has his "blankie" and story time, usually a favorite tape accompanied by a picture book. When Jack jumps off Deb's knee and wants to play with his truck, she gently reminds him, "No toys, Jack—it's bedtime."

Some toddlers also have a bottle or breast before bed. If it helps the child relax, that's fine—as long as he doesn't *need* a bottle or breast to sleep (see Leanne's story on pages 254–262). (Besides, it's bad for children's teeth to take a bottle of milk to bed.) At nineteen months, Dudley still wants his bottle, but his mum lets him have it downstairs. That way, he has the familiarity and security of the bottle but is still able to fall asleep without it. Dudley also has other comforting rituals. He waves goodnight to the moon and stars out the window. And if Daddy is not home, he kisses Daddy's picture.

The bedtime ritual should end when you put your child into his crib. Some parents are able to leave the room immediately; others stick around a few minutes to put a reassuring hand on their toddler's tush, sing a lullaby, or give a back rub. If you know your child, you know what settles him. (See Chaper 8 for tips about getting a reluctant child to stay in bed once the ritual is over.)

Special-Occasion R&R

As I said at the outset of this book, innumerable occasions arise in a family's day, week, or year that can be enhanced by conscious rituals. As with everyday rituals, an important aspect is personal meaning. What works for one family may seem empty to another. Also, some families have special needs. In her book, for instance, Barbara Biziou describes "Gotcha Day," to celebrate the day an adopted child came into the family. I'm sure you have meaningful traditions that are unique to your clan as well. Below are some of the most common special occasions.

Family "Togetherness" Time. Whether you do it once a week or once a month, it's important to have regular times of togetherness in a family, a time when you can share ideas, emotions, or simply have time for fun. Some parents incorporate traditions from their own families, others make up their own, still others do a combination of the new and the old.

INTENTION: To foster cooperation, communication, and connection.

PREPARATION: If you have children four or older in addition to a toddler, you might want to make this into the more formal "family meeting" ritual created by Biziou, which allows for sharing and forgiveness, as well as fun activities. If it's just you, your partner, and your toddler, simply set aside a few hours a week during which you are all together. Let Biziou's family meeting ritual inspire you, but scale the ritual to toddler-size. You can incorporate several of its elements even with a very young child—for example, the "talking stick" is a good way for a toddler to learn patience and listening skills.

FROM BEGINNING TO END: Start with an announcement: "This is our special family time." Light a candle to signify the ritual's beginning, taking care to keep the flame out of your toddler's reach. Even if you don't embark on a full-blown family meeting, you can still designate this as "sacred" time and space that neither responsibilities nor concerns can invade. Don't compromise this ritual by answering phones, attending to chores around the house, or dealing with adult matters. This is a time to be with your toddler—it can be a meal, a trip to the park, or an hour or two in the living room, talking, playing, singing songs (hopefully, not watching TV). Blow the candle out to signify the end.

FOLLOW-UP: If you have a very young toddler—say a one-year-old—this idea may sound silly. "He won't understand it," you insist. Well, that may or may not be true. I do know that by repeating this family togetherness ritual, your child will not only come to understand its importance, but also look forward to it.

Dad Time. As I said in the Introduction, although fathers nowadays are certainly more hands-on than in previous generations, the mums I talk with still feel that the men in their lives—granddads as well—have a long way to go. In part, it's territorial. Some mothers simply don't want to relinquish the reins, or they inadvertently discourage Dad from participating (see sidebar). In part, it also can be a matter of availability. If Dad is out of the house all day at the office and mum is at home, there's no way he can make up that difference. But even in households where Mum works, Dad is more often the "helper" than a real parenting partner. (In cases where there's a stay-at-home father, the tables may be turned, but I've rarely seen it.)

In families where the children have a more equal balance of parent time, it's because Dad makes a real effort to spend separate time with his child or children, and Mum supports him in it. It may not happen when Junior is born. Fathers are sometimes skittish about handling infants; toddlerhood is often the first time they really feel comfortable as caretakers. Martin, for instance, was a bit of a distant dad when Quinn was born. But he now delights in taking his eighteen-month-old son to the park every Saturday morning. Mind you, he's a big Lakers fan, so he schedules these trips early, to avoid cutting into game time. Still, it gives his wife, Arlene, a break, and just as important, allows Martin to really get to know Quinn firsthand, not through Arlene's eyes. Interestingly, Martin was a bit reluctant the first time he took Quinn out on his own. Only by

---

Making It Hard for Dad

Many mothers unintentionally compromise their toddler's comfort with their fathers because they:

Tell Dad what to think: Greta and Dad are playing with a toy vacuum. "She doesn't want to play with that now," Mum says. "We already put it away." It's important for Dad to establish what Greta likes and doesn't like.

Criticize Dad in front of the child: "That's not how to put her T-shirt on."

Send the child a message that it's not safe to be with Dad: She hovers when Dad is with Greta. If Greta cries, she immediately "rescues" her from Dad.

Make him the bad guy: Whenever Greta won't go to sleep, Mum sends Dad in to settle her down. When Greta misbehaves, Mum says, "Wait 'til your daddy gets home."

Are reluctant to give up the nurturing role: Dad is reading a story to Greta, and Mum comes in, picks her off Dad's lap, and says, "Oh, I'll finish the story."

---

actually *doing* it was he open to making this a weekly ritual. Many fathers are like him.

INTENTION: To help a child have a separate connection with his father.

PREPARATION: Some planning and even negotiating may be necessary between Mum and Dad, especially if both parents are working. Iron out kinks in the schedule ahead of time. Once Dad commits to this time, however, nothing should stand in his way.

FROM BEGINNING TO END: Let the child know that this is his special time with Dad. As always, saying the same words and doing the same things each time help mark the beginning of this ritual. Martin, for instance, says to Quinn, "Okay, buddy, it's time for us to go," at which point he whisks Quinn off his feet and puts him on his shoulders. Quinn, who is only a year old, instinctively knows that Daddy time is different from Mommy time. Martin loves to sing, so on the way to the park, he belts out a little made-up song: "Daddy and Quinn, Quinn and Daddy, goin' to the park, because it's Saturday." Quinn can't sing along with words, but Martin says he's already beginning to hum along in Quinn-talk. They stay at the park for an hour or so, at which point Martin tells Quinn, "Okay, buddy, time to go home. Time to rest!" When they get home, Martin makes a big deal out of taking his sneakers off. Then he takes Quinn's sneakers off. The trip to the park is over. Now it's time for a nap.

Daddy time needn't always be playtime, though. It's good for Dad to take over aspects of the daily routine as well. Most popular among fathers seems to be the evening bath. Other men love to cook breakfast. The point is, just about anything can be Dad time as long as it's Dad's intention to make it a regular, recurring event.

Family Milestones. Birthdays, anniversaries, and other special family days are all good reasons to celebrate. But here are two points of caution: don't overwhelm your toddler with a too big or too fancy or otherwise inappropriate celebration, and don't limit your celebrations to events in which your toddler is the star. In other words, it's good for even young children to step out of the limelight and learn how to honor other people, too.

INTENTION: To help your toddler understand the significance of a particular milestone without the usual emphasis on material acquisitions.

PREPARATION: A few days before the event, let your toddler know that a "big day" is coming. He has a limited understanding of time, so too much advance notice will be anticlimactic. If the occasion is his birthday, invite only a few close relatives. A good rule of thumb is to have one friend per year of age. So if your toddler is turning two, invite two pals. Many parents don't stick to that guideline, but try to at least limit the number of children to those your child plays with often—his play group buddies.

If the occasion is to mark someone else's big day—say, a sibling's or grandparent's birthday—help your toddler understand the meaning of this special day. Encourage him to make something for it—a drawing, a Play-Doh object, a card that he dictates to you and signs with a scribble. If your toddler is too young for arts and crafts, suggest that he give away one of his toys to the person ("It's Nana's birthday, would you like to give her this dolly?"). Another great gift for a grandparent is to teach your toddler to sing (or clap to) "Happy Birthday."

FROM BEGINNING TO END: When parents of a one-year-old throw a big barbecue, I know it's more for them than for their child. The best child-centered birthday parties are loosely structured and short. They begin with free play, end with food and cake and the blowing out of candles. No matter what the occasion is, though, try to limit the celebration to two hours. I know many parents who hire clowns and entertainers of all sorts for toddler parties, but give me a break. Toddlers don't need entertaining. A mother recently told me about a celebration for a one-year-old at which the child ended up crying and had to leave her own party! If you hire an entertainer, at least make sure the person sings songs that are familiar to the children.

If you keep in mind that the purpose here is not only to celebrate milestones, but to give children a sense of family connection, and to begin helping them learn manners and generosity, it will guide your actions. If the party is for little Susie, make sure that Susie says "thank you" or at least you say it for her every time someone hands her a gift. If the party is for a sibling or other relative, or if it's a Mother's Day bash, make sure that Susie does or says something thoughtful to the celebrant.

FOLLOW-UP: If the party is for the toddler, it's never too early to begin teaching her how to send thank-you notes. Even if she can't read, write, or verbally express herself, you can write the note for her, read it aloud, and let her "sign" it with a scribble. It should be short enough for your toddler to comprehend:

Dear Grandma,
Thank you for coming to my party. I love my new doll. Thank you
for bringing it.

> *Love,*
> *Mabel*

Holidays. It's wonderful to see many families nowadays attempting to give their children holiday experiences that retain the original meaning of the holiday (which, after all, actually means "holy day") and make these times less materialistic. Admittedly, it's not easy to battle the rampant materialism of our culture.

INTENTION: To celebrate holidays with more of an emphasis on the reason for the holiday and less on the presents one gets.

PREPARATION: Buy a picture book that explains the holiday and read it to your child. Think of ways that your child can participate in the holidays other than by getting gifts—decorating, making presents for other people, helping to make cookies. Use the holidays as a time to remind children to get rid of toys they no longer use and give them to needy children.

FROM BEGINNING TO END: Let's take the winter holiday season (although these principles apply to any holiday). Whether you celebrate Christmas, Hanukkah, or Kwanza, start the day at a house of worship or with friends. Before any other festivities, have a time of storytelling and reflection. When children are brought up with spiritual values, they become surprisingly sensitive to the needs of others. Help the children learn restraint, too, perhaps by allowing only one present to be opened on the eve of the holiday. In any case, limit the number of gifts your toddler is given.

Follow-up: See the follow-up for Family Milestones, on page 89. Children should write thank-you notes for holiday gifts as well.

R&R Forever

Parents who create rituals and routines for their children describe them as an "anchor" for daily life and for their own values. These events and practices stay with the child, even as he or she takes developmental leaps and becomes increasingly independent. It's not just the rituals themselves; it's the way parents think about them. R&R brings a kind of consciousness to both everyday life and to special occasions that keeps parents and children on a more even keel. In subsequent chapters, I look at other types of family rituals as well, among them rituals that mark developmental changes (weaning), ease transitions (a new baby), even those that help children manage their emotions (time-out). By taking time to perform these rites and thereby slow down the busy pace of life, rituals not only help us connect, they can make any and every moment more special.

CHAPTER FOUR

Nappies No More: Striding toward Independence

Comparisons are odious.

— Popular fourteenth-century saying

It is good to have an end to journey toward; but it is the journey that matters, in the end.

— Ursula K. Le Guin

Sooner *Isn't* Better

I recently dropped in on Linda, whose infant daughter, Noelle, was only a month old. During my visit, her fifteen-month-old, Brian, had a play date with Skylar, his best friend. Naturally, because I was in the process of writing this book, I paid particular attention to the toddlers (and as luck would have it, little Noelle was fast asleep during the first hour I was there).

As we watched the boys, Linda explained that she and Sylvia, Skylar's mum, had met in a parenting seminar when they were both pregnant and were delighted to discover that they lived so close to one another. As was the case today, whenever one of the women had an appointment or an errand to run, the other usually watched the boys. Consequently, their children had spent time together literally since birth. Linda turned to me at one point during the play session and explained, almost apologetically, "You know Skylar does everything first. That's because he arrived three weeks earlier than Brian." Then, with more than a hint of anxiety in her voice, she quickly added, "But Brian is coming along nicely, don't you think?"

Sadly, I encounter lots of parents like Linda. Instead of enjoying every stage and staying *in the moment*, they constantly weigh their child's progress, they fret, they try to make their child "go" faster. They tend to compare their children with other children. Whether it's a kiddie class, a playground scene, or a play group in someone's living room, everyone seems to be in a contest. The mother whose child walks first, boasts; those whose toddlers aren't yet walking, feel bad. They'll ask, "Why isn't Karen doing that yet?" or, like Linda, they'll make excuses: "He was born three weeks later."

Only recently, I was at the birthday party of two one-year-olds, Cassy and Amy, who were born on exactly the same day. Cassy was toddling about quite efficiently, while Amy was barely able to pull herself into a standing position. However, Amy was already able to name objects and call her dog by name. Just as important, she knew that the big rumbling vehicle coming down the street was a "truh" (truck), just like the toy "truh" she had at home. Watching

Amy, Cassy's mom asked me, "Why isn't Cassy talking yet?" Little did she know, but only moments before Amy's mother had questioned me as well: "Why isn't Amy walking?" I explained to each woman that when a child zooms ahead in physical development, she often lags somewhat in language development and vice versa.

Comparisons are only part of the problem which actually starts in infancy. Parents view normal developmental occurrences as their child's accomplishments: "Look he's holding his head up." "Oh, he can roll over." "Now he can sit up." "Oooh! He's standing." Such comments are ever bemusing to me because those milestones aren't really *accomplishments*. Rather, each is Nature's way of saying, "Pay attention: Your baby is getting ready for the next step."

Admittedly, some of the pressure heaped upon parents nowadays comes from grandparents. A statement like, "Why isn't Lucia sitting up yet?" from a parent or in-law is enough to send some mothers or fathers into a tailspin. Even worse are comments like, "Don't you think you should be propping her up so she learns how to sit?" Goodness me! That implies not only that little Lucia must be slow, but also that Mum and Dad aren't doing enough.

Of course, it's normal for parents and grandparents to be excited about toddlers' growing abilities. And some degree of comparison

No Showing Off

"Watch," Proud Mother said to her out-of-town guests. "He can clap now." Then, when the poor little dear just sat there, she said dejectedly, "Oh, he did it this morning."

Children are not circus performers. Parents shouldn't ask them to do tricks for their grandparents or for adult friends. Proud Mother's son may not have understood his mum's words, but he surely heard her tone of voice and saw the disappointment on her face when he didn't respond on cue.

Children do exactly what they can do, *when* they can do it. If they can clap, they'll clap. They don't purposely hold back. By asking your child to do something he might have done once, you're setting him up for failure and disappointment. And if by chance he does perform on cue, he may get applause, but then you're appreciating him for how well he does tricks rather than applauding who he is.

is natural and even desirable *if* you observe other children through noncompetitive eyes. It can certainly be reassuring to see for yourself what a large variety of behavior and growth patterns exist within "normal" ranges of development. However, when parents become *too* invested in comparisons or they try to speed up the process by "training" their child, they're doing their toddler a great injustice. Instead of giving the little one a so-called head start, they're likely to give him anxiety.

To cut down on contests and avoid parental pushiness, I run my toddler play groups very loosely. I have a format (see page 202)—for example, I incorporate at the end of every session music, which is a lovely, calming way to close. But I categorically stay away from anything that smacks of teaching, because the purpose is socialization, not education. From what I've heard and observed of other classes, however, this is not always the case. In some kiddie groups, instead of teaching parents to watch for a sign that their child is ready to walk, the instructor directs mums and dads to hold their children in an upright position, allegedly to strengthen their legs and thereby get them to stand sooner.

The problem is that while some children will start standing (because it's their time), others won't. Trust me, ducky, a parent could spend a whole bloody hour, week after week, pulling her child up, but her toddler will plop right down the moment she lets go unless he's ready to stand. Instead of accepting this, his parents then buy a gadget or device designed to make a child walk "sooner." However, readiness has nothing to do with calisthenics *or* contraptions.

What happens next is even more distressing. When Junior plops down, Mum and Dad are disappointed. The other children in the class are "ahead" of him. And how do you think that makes Junior feel? At best, he's confused: *Why are my parents pulling me up all the time and looking so sad about it?* In worst-case scenarios, it's the beginning of a lifelong pattern that could damage his self-esteem: *I'm not meeting my parents' expectations, and I'm not loved for who I am, so I must not be very good.*

The truth is, by the time children are three, they all pretty much do the same thing—no matter what their parents have done *for* them. (So much for head starts.) Development follows what I call a *natural progression*—it automatically happens. Some children develop faster than others physically, while others make quicker mental or emotional strides. Whatever path they take, they are probably following in their parents' footsteps, because rate and pattern of development is largely a genetic phenomenon.

It doesn't mean that you don't play with your child or encourage her. It doesn't mean you refuse to help her when she shows interest in a new skill. It *does* mean that you have to be an observant guide, rather than a pushy teacher. I'm all for making children independent, but you need to give your little one the *time* to get ready. You must allow her body and mind to take the lead, rather than trying to goad her to "excel."

In this chapter, I will help you gauge what signs to look for, when to step in, and what you can do to guide your child's natural developmental course toward his or her increasing independence. We cover a lot of ground here—mobility, play, eating, dressing, and potty training. (In the next two chapters, I look at cognitive, emotional, and social growth.) As you read through each section below, I once again exhort you to remember the mantra H.E.L.P.

H.E.L.P.

Hold yourself back: Wait for your child to show signs of readiness before rushing in.

Encourage exploration: Give your child opportunities according to his readiness—so that he attempts new challenges and stretches his repertoire.

Limit: Stay within his "learning triangle" (see pages 106–110), taking care never to allow your child to attempt something that leads to extreme frustration, a heightened emotional state, or danger.

Praise: Applaud a job well done, a new skill mastered, and admirable behavior, but never go overboard.

Toddler on the Loose—Waaaaatch Out!

The driving force of toddlerhood is mobility. Your little one is on the go and wants to keep going. In his mind, everything else—including food and sleep, unfortunately—impedes his progress. But think of the wonder of it all: Within the first nine or ten months of his life, your child has already transformed from a helpless lump with little control over his limbs to a toddler who can scoot 'round the house on whatever will carry him—his knees, his rear, or his feet. What's more, his growing physical prowess gives him a new vantage point. The world looks different when you can sit up, even more so when you stand up. And, my friends, when you can walk without anyone's help, you are then able to move toward things you like and away from things that scare you. In other words, you're on your own!

Bear in mind that each step in the developmental ladder happens slowly and in its own time. After all, a child doesn't really "sit" at eight months. All along, his body has been maturing, his limbs strengthening. It usually takes two months or so for him to go from the point of sitting precariously on his own, to being able to pull himself into a sitting position. The same is true of crawling. From the time your

The Crawling Conundrum

It has long been recognized that some children go straight from sitting to standing. Today, their ranks are growing. The reason, scientists believe, is that now babies spend less time on their tummies, a by-product of concern about Sudden Infant Death Syndrome (SIDS).

Prior to 1994 when the "Back to Sleep" campaign was launched, most babies were put to sleep facedown, and wanting a better view of the world, they learned to flip over—a precursor to crawling. But now that parents are routinely advised to put babies to sleep on their backs, little ones don't need to flip from front to back.

Two recent studies, one here and one in England, conclude that many back-sleepers (one-third in the U.S. study) don't roll over or crawl on schedule and some skip the crawling stage altogether. But don't worry if your child is one of them. By eighteen months, there is virtually no developmental differences between crawlers and noncrawlers—and both start walking at the same age. Nor is there any validity to the once-held belief that crawling is necessary for brain development.

child first starts "swimming" on his tummy and kicking his legs, he is practicing the *components* of crawling. It will take another four or five months for all the necessary pieces to finally fit together.

The chart on pages 100–103 shows *milestones of mobility*— typical developments that transform babies into toddlers. Needless to say, while your child's physiology matures, so do his sense of self and his social awareness, his ability to handle stress and separation. We can't pretend that the various areas of development have nothing to do with each other. Still, physical capability is a good place to start. The state of your child's body determines whether your child can sit at a table and eat, what kinds of toys he can handle, how he conducts himself around other children.

As you read the chart, bear in mind that early control of muscles runs in families. Although about half of all babies can toddle by thirteen months, if you or your partner walked late, chances are your child will progress through these stages later than her friends, too. Some children catch up; others lag behind for a few years. At two, your child might not be as agile as some of his peers who are able to jump and run, but by age three, the differences, if any, will be minimal.

No matter what your child's individual rate of development, along the way there will be falls and disappointment and even some regression. If she falls hard and hurts herself today, it stands to reason that she may be a little skittish about getting up tomorrow. But not to worry—she'll soon pick up where she left off. As she gets steadier on her bare feet, encourage her to experiment on different kinds of surfaces—it will improve her motor control.

TIP: If your child falls, don't rush in without first judging whether she's really hurt. Your anxiety can hurt her, too—by scaring her and shattering her self-confidence.

You'll notice that I rarely mention "typical" ages for the various milestones. That's because I want you to pay more attention to the *process* than the end result. Even if your child is "late," he is probably right on schedule for him. We adults have to do things in our time, too. Think of yourself at the gym, for example. In order for you to master a new piece of equipment, your muscles, your coordination, and your brain all have to get the hang of it before you look like you know what you're doing. In the same way, if you start a new aerobics class, the movements will seem alien at first, to both your mind and your body. You may be a quick study and catch on easily, or you may need more practice than your classmates. Twelve weeks later, it will be hard to tell who had a slow start.

The same is true of your toddler and each new developmental plateau he attempts. If you watch carefully, you will see the signs of his readiness and be able to encourage his natural progression. Respect who he is—rather than getting anxious or trying to rush him, realize that he's right where he should be. If you feel that your child is way behind others in his group, or that even after holding back he doesn't seem to be responding, bring up your concerns at the next visit to your pediatrician. A routine milestone check will indicate if there is any problem.

One final point: *Developmental leaps upset the apple cart.* I am

---

An E-mail from a Wise Mother

One way that we were able to deal with the "terrible two's," as they have so ineptly been labeled, is to call them "the terrific two's." I thought of my son, Morgan, as having PMS 'round the clock for a year and was able to identify with his tantrums, meltdowns, and "poor" behavior. I thought of myself during PMS and how helpless I feel, how hormonal I am, and how my emotions are up one minute and down the next. Just think, being two years old and having no idea why you feel the way you do and all these people getting mad or frustrated with you and you can't explain how you feel or what you really want because you have no stinking idea how to feel better! I'm 32 and know what I'm going through, and still feel as though I can't handle it. I cannot even begin to imagine how a toddler feels. So we would just pray and love Morgan through it all. We had given him a lot of nurturing beforehand and so to love him through the frustrations, to redirect him when he was in danger, to reason with him as best we could, and to support each other through it all was just another simple progression.

thrilled to receive e-mails like the one in the sidebar on page 98—that mum certainly has a great attitude. Still, I often hear comments from parents who view toddlers' changes as if they're bad: "He used to sleep through the night. Then he started to stand up, and now he can't get himself down. What's wrong with him?" Nothing's *wrong*. Your child is getting older and more independent. He may get confused at times, but it's up to you to give him opportunities to use his newfound skills (see Tip below).

> **TIP:** *Spurts of unprecedented mobility often cause sleep disturbances. Your child's limbs are alive with movement, much the same way yours are after a workout. She's not used to it. Your toddler may start waking up at night, stand up in her crib and cry out for you because she doesn't yet know how to get down. You'll need to teach her . . . during the day. Put her in her crib for part of an afternoon play period (you should be doing this routinely anyway—see pages 75–76). When she stands up, take her hands, place them on the vertical bars of the crib, and with your hands on top of hers, gently slide them down. As her hands go lower, it will cause her to bend her knees and sit. After only two or three times, she'll get it.*

The reality is, toddlers go through phases. Just when you've gotten used to your child's being one way, he'll do something else. Truth be told, the one and only thing that you can expect from your toddler's life is change. You can't control it, and you can't (and shouldn't want to) stop it. But you can change your attitude toward it. Think about how change can upset an adult—someone gets a new job, a relative dies, there's a divorce, a new baby arrives. Now imagine what it's like to be a toddler! Appreciate both the nature and speed of change in your little one's life, and most important, put a positive spin on it. Instead of exclaiming mournfully, "Oh my God! He's different now," embrace the wonder of it all.

Milestones of Mobility

Feat	Stages Children Go Through	Tips/Comments
Sitting	If put into position, sits unaided, steadied by her own arms, but balance is precarious; posture is stiff and robotic, like a baby Frankenstein monster minus the stitches.	Place cushions around her for safety.
	Reaches for a toy without falling over.	
	Rotates her body from side to side.	
	Gets herself into a sitting position without anyone's help.	
Crawling	Practices "swimming" on his tummy and kicking—movements that he'll use in crawling.	
	Figures out that by squirming, he can move himself.	
	Using his feet to push off, he crawls backwards.	This stage can be very frustrating; if he tries to get a toy, he travels farther from it.
	"Creeps"—a kind of forward wriggling motion.	Once he starts moving, make sure electrical outlets are covered and cords out of reach; don't leave a child under two unattended (see sidebar on page 105 and other safety tips on page 111).
	Gets up on all fours and rocks.	

Feat	Stages Children Go Through	Tips/Comments
	Finally gets arms and legs to work together.	Children who prefer crawling to walking zoom around the house on all fours. If your child skips this stage, he'll be none the worse for it (see sidebar on page 96).
Standing	In infancy, exhibits a stiff-legged reflex that then disappears.	
	In fourth or fifth month, she delights in "standing" on your lap, your hands securely tucked under her armpits.	
	Pulls herself up.	When she is able to pull herself into a standing position, offer her your fingers to help her be a bit more steady on her feet.
Cruising	Walks holding on to furniture or someone's hands.	If he has been cruising for two months or more and is still not quite confident enough to let go, try moving objects he normally holds on to—say, a chair and a table, a little farther apart. Then, in order to keep going, he has to brave that gap on his own.
	Lets go, first with one hand.	

Feat	Stages Children Go Through	Tips/Comments
Toddling	Look, ma! No hands! Walks tentatively on her own but falls over if she loses momentum.	Once your child starts toddling, keep the floor uncluttered and make sure there are no sharp edges where she can clunk her head. As she gets steadier on her bare feet, encourage her to experiment on different kinds of surfaces—it will improve her motor control.
	Gains increasing control of her muscles and is better able to handle that still-oversized head of hers; she won't have to watch her feet as she toddles.	Keep a careful eye on her at all times, making sure, for instance, that whatever object (chair, stroller, push toy) she leans on isn't so light she can tip it over.
Walking	After a month or so of toddling, logging in several miles of practice can expand his repertiore:	Clear the decks, ducky. Like Pinocchio, your little one has turned into a real boy (or girl)!
	Walks *and* carries a toy.	If you have any glass doors, now is the time to cover them with Plexiglas—a child who walks, but still can't stop easily, can run right through a glass door.
	Walks and can look up.	
	Can reach above his head while walking.	
	Can turn, walk up and down a slope, squat down and get back up with little effort.	

Feat	Stages Children Go Through	Tips/Comments
You Name It! (Running, jumping, spinning, kicking, dancing, climbing . . .)	He can jump, spin, and dance. He runs constantly, even plays "chase" with his friends.	He has no sense of what's safe and what's not, so you need eyes in the back of your head.
	Tears about the house *and* attempts to climb into and onto everything.	Give him climbing opportunities but point out what he cannot climb on— like your living room couch. (More about keeping him *off* the couch on page 72).

Playing on Their Own

Play is truly the business of toddlerhood. It's where a great deal of learning and mind stretching take place. There are all sorts of play— solo or with other children (read about play dates and play groups on pages 199–205), indoors or out, with toys or with items found around your household. Play builds motor skills, improves your child's mind, and prepares him for the world. Toys and activities must not only be age-appropriate (see below), but also playtimes must be structured to encourage your child to amuse himself independently, and when it's time to do other things, to help him stop playing.

By the time your child is eight months old, she should be able to play independently for forty minutes or so. Some children are naturally more independent than others, some more clingy. If your child is nearing a year and still needs you by her side constantly, it may be separation anxiety (which is normal for toddlers anywhere from eight to eighteen months). But you also need to ask yourself if you've *allowed* her to become independent. Do you carry her everywhere? Do you always sit with her when she's playing? Do you need your child more than she needs you? And are you therefore inadvertently giving your little one the message that you don't trust her to be on her own? (See sidebar on page 104.)

Start now to send a different message. If your child is playing on the floor, for example, raise yourself up onto the couch. Gradually, move farther and farther back. Busy yourself with something else so that you don't focus exclusively on her. After a few days of this, finally move yourself out the door. Begin to build up the time that your child can play independently, knowing that you're in the next room. (Also introduce a security object if she doesn't already have one; see pages 174–176 and 267–271.)

Some parents have just the opposite dilemma; their children have trouble stopping play to leave a play group, to come to the table, or to get ready for bed. Children need to know how to delineate their play time—to appreciate that some activities involve stimulation, imagination, sensation, even getting dirty, as play often does, and others involve sitting still, being quiet, or cuddling, such as meals and bedtime. The children who seem to understand this are those whose parents give play periods a predictable structure—a beginning, a middle, and an end.

Building Trust

The dictionary includes the following definitions of "trust"—confidence, firm belief, reliance, care, expect, consign for care. Each meaning of the word sheds light on various aspects of the parent/child connection. We are the caretakers of our children, and we need to build their trust in us so that they, in turn, can trust themselves.

Trust is a two-way street. Fostering your child's ability to play on her own lets her know that you trust her. But you first must build her trust in you:

- Anticipate change and think about it from the child's perspective.

- Make separations gradual.

- Don't place more responsibility on your child than she can handle.

- Don't ask your child to do things she can't yet achieve.

Beginning. Initiate fun time by announcing, "Now it's time to play." Of course, you may not be able to do this each time, because so much of a toddler's day is about play, but as often as possible, make note in some way that play is starting. This replicates what happens in the real world as well—at other kids' houses or in day care and preschool—so you might as well get your child used to it.

Middle. During play periods, keep the number of playthings to a minimum. For instance, when you give your child blocks, don't give him the whole set at first. A one-year-old can handle four to six initially, an eighteen-month-old, ten to start. By the time he's two, he's ready for a whole set because by then he can build a tower and knock it down. Also, get rid of toys no longer played with (see sidebar on page 107).

End. Toddlers have no concept of time, so it won't do you (or her) any good to say, "In five minutes, you'll have to stop playing." Instead, give her a verbal and visual warning. As you take out the toy box for cleanup, say, "Playtime is almost over." However, if she's very involved, don't just whisk her away. She might be in the midst of trying to figure out whether the square block fits into the round hole, and you ought to respect her need to finish. At the same time, remember that you're the adult; you have to set boundaries. If your child continues to resist stopping or refuses putting her toys away, acknowledge her feelings, but be firm: "I can see that you don't want to stop now, but it's dinnertime." Finally, engage in a cleanup ritual (see pages 82–83).

Signs of Potential Danger

Never leave a child unattended before the age of two. Put him in a crib or playpen, or leave another adult in charge. After the age of two, *if* you know that an area is childproof and you've watched your child playing there before and know he's not prone to dangerous risk taking, trusting him on his own for short periods builds his confidence. He may also wander out of the room you're sitting in. No matter how competent or cautious your child is, however, it's always time to investigate if you hear:

• Nothing but quiet

• Sudden crying

• Odd rifling around

• A loud bang, followed by a sudden cry

TIP: If you know that your child has trouble leaving an activity or ending a game, set a timer for the end of play period and tell her, "When the buzzer goes off, we have to [whatever your next activity is: eat, leave for the park, get ready for bed]." When the "control" belongs to an object, you don't have to assume the unpleasant role of nag.

Your Toddler's Learning Triangle

Naturally, play is not just a matter of when but also *what*. I suggest that parents always stay within their toddler's *learning triangle*—that is, present physical and mental tasks which the child can manipulate and get pleasure from *on her own*. Activities and toys should be age-appropriate, so that they stretch your toddler's abilities but aren't so demanding that her play frequently ends in frustration or tears. That is not to say that we don't challenge children, only that we present *reasonable* difficulties and opportunities for problem solving that they can handle and situations that are safe. Granted, a little frustration is good—it's how we all learn—but too many defeats cause children to give up. If you want to know what falls within your child's learning triangle, look at what she can *do*.

She can sit. She will be happy as a little clam when she's poised on the floor of your kitchen, exploring your pots and pans, or outside on the grass, examining individual blades or twigs within reach. Her manual dexterity is markedly improved by now, and she has better hand-eye coordination. In fact, where she once used her mouth to explore the world, now her hands are her most useful instrument. She can glance at an object, reach for it, and shift it from one hand to the other. Favorite activities include games of patty-cake and peekaboo, rolling a ball, turning the pages of a cardboard book. She also has her pincer grasp down pat, which means that she's likely to find tiny bits on the floor that your vacuum cleaner left behind. She will delight in using her fingers as a tool, for exploring, poking, feeling. Although she can pick things up, she doesn't quite have the hang of dropping them. This is the time to begin to enforce limits with actions if not with words (see Tip on page 107).

He can crawl. Your child is gaining better control over all his muscles by now. He can point and gesture, open and close things, shake his head, clumsily toss a ball, and put one block on top of the other. He likes busy boxes—things that have buttons, dials, levers—and toys that respond, like a jack-in-the-box, which a few months ago might have startled him. He can now drop things as well as pick them up. Because he can get around, you're likely to find him rifling through a cabinet you've (hopefully) childproofed (no sharp objects, nothing breakable, too heavy, or small enough to be swallowed). He has a short attention span, though, and will change quickly from one toy to another, because he's more interested in getting places than in doing any one thing. He loves to knock over the tower of blocks you built for him, but he may not have the patience to wait for you to stack more than two! A simple game of hide-and-seek helps him begin to understand object permanence—the idea that just because he can't see something (or someone) it doesn't mean it's not there. He loves to make noise with things, and he can now coordinate both hands and thus bang a spoon on a pot. Outside on a sunny day, splashing in a bucket of water (with you at his side to keep him safe) gives him both the sounds and the sensations he craves. But no matter what objects you give him, with his increasing mobility and curiosity, it will *seem* as if he's only interested in whatever can harm him or your house. Therefore, this is the time to make sure that your home and yard are accident proofed (see box on page 111).

Clean House!

The numbers of toys in most kids' rooms nowadays is shocking. Besides buying too many in the first place, parents never get rid of toys that are no longer interesting to the child or developmentally appropriate. Put unused toys in the attic for future children or donate them to a shelter. I prefer the latter, especially if you involve little ones in the process. It's never too early to help children see the benefit of good deeds. Make a ritual out of it, perhaps by marking a date every three to six months on your family calendar as "Toy Giveaway Day." If your child is too young or too reluctant to help you sort through everything, do it when she's in bed. She probably won't notice that a particular toy is gone. If she does, bring it back—it must have been one of her favorites.

TIP: *Whether your child is heading toward an outlet, a hot pot, or a valuable, don't simply warn her ("You'd better not touch* *that")—take action. Remember that at this stage, actions speak louder than words. You have three choices: (1) distract her ("Look, honey! A doggie!"); (2) interrupt her (sometimes calling her name is all it takes); or (3) whisk her away altogether. Give a simple explanation: "That's dangerous," or "That's hot," or "That's Mommy's dish, not a toy."*

Boy Toys? Girl Toys?

I've noticed in my toddler group that mothers of boys—less so mothers of girls—have very definite ideas about what toys are gender-appropriate for their children. For instance, Robby, age nineteen months, loved the dolls in the play box, but his mother, Eileen, would invariably intervene when he picked one up. "That's for little girls, honey." Poor Robby looked crestfallen. When I asked Eileen about it, she explained that her hubby would be upset if he thought that his son played with dolls.

Rubbish, I say! Just as we encourage children to play with toys that teach them new skills and stretch their minds, we ought to encourage them to go beyond gender stereotypes. When a boy plays with a doll, he learns to be nurturing. When a girl plays with a fire truck, she learns about excitement and activity. Why should either of them be denied a full range of experiences? After all, when today's toddlers grow up, they will need to be both caring *and* capable.

She can get herself into a standing position and cruise. Your toddler has a totally new perspective because she now sees the world from a standing position and her cognitive skills have improved as well. She may offer you a cookie and then pull it back and laugh—her first understanding of teasing. She may drop things from her high chair just to see what happens and also to watch your response. She finds it endlessly amusing to simply get herself into a standing position. She is further rewarded because now she can reach for things at a higher level. Your valuables, which she always found interesting, are now *accessible* to her as well. Beware! Again, safety is key: as your child tugs on various objects to pull herself up, she and the object can easily topple over. With her increasing sense of autonomy, she's likely to pitch a fit if you step in, so it's particularly important to remember the mantra H.E.L.P. Watch her but don't interfere unless she asks you to participate or is heading toward danger. Provide the opportunities for her to explore her new physical prowess. Put the music on and let her dance. The best playthings are sturdy toys that she can hold on to, with pieces that turn, open, and close, so as to give her a chance to use her newfound dexterity. You can now introduce her to a swing set, but be careful. Use a baby seat at first until she learns how to hold on and has better balance.

He can toddle. At first, when your child walks fast, he will have trouble stopping. Once he is fairly steady on his feet, though, give him toys that he can pull or push. (Given earlier, these toys are sometimes faster than the child is and he ends up splat on his face.) After he's been toddling for a month or more, lifting, fetching, and carrying will keep him busy and happy, and not so incidentally, improve his balance and hand-eye coordination as well. Give him his own little bag or a backpack into which he can endlessly pack and unpack his favorite toys and tote them wherever he goes. He now shows a clear preference for certain objects or activities over others, because he understands so much more. Grasping, among other new ideas, the concept of "mine," he may be more possessive of his playthings, especially in the presence of another child. But he can also become your little assistant. For the bedtime ritual, I say, "Choose your book, and then we can get you in the tub." He can get his jammies from a low drawer, lay out the towel, and put whatever toys he wants into his bath. Though he can turn on the faucet, I don't advise encouraging this. He might be tempted to do it when you're not around and scald himself. If you have a swing set in the backyard or there's one at the park, be careful. Sometimes the seats are exactly at head height, and a toddling child can run right into them.

She can walk well, climb, jump, and run. She'll be quite good with her hands by now, too, so give her lots of opportunities to screw and unscrew, bang, build, and pour. Encourage her physical experimentation by giving her a foam mat to bounce on and roll about. At this stage, she also will begin to problem solve—say, move a step stool toward a cabinet when she spots a toy that's too high to reach. She can help with simple chores, too, like salad making, or carrying silverware or a plate (plastic, please) to the table. Give her thick crayons and she's more likely now to scribble than to eat them, which she would have done at an earlier age. She will be able to manipulate easy wooden puzzles as well, the kind with large pieces and a little peg on the top that makes it easier for her to handle. Because her mind is also developing at lightning speed, she is more confident and inquisitive. What seems "destructive" or "bad" is actually her curiosity. She wonders constantly, *What would happen if I . . . throw this, squash it, tear it, stomp on it? Will it bounce? Can I knock it down? What's inside it?* It's time now to hide the telly-clicker (you Yanks call it a "remote"); otherwise, you'll find it reprogrammed. She also might decide to use your VCR slot as a letter box to post a piece of toast. Instead, give her replicas of anything she sees grown-ups use, like a toy vacuum cleaner or a child-sized car. But she's also able to pretend now, so she might pick up a stick and make believe she's vacuuming the floor, or she'll pretend to "munch" on a block as if it's food. She'll also put a telephone receiver to her ear and have a mock conversation (even if she's only babbling). My Nan had a toy telephone next to the real one, and whenever the real one rang, she'd hand us the toy phone. It was a wonderful way of keeping us busy while she talked. Your little one will continue to be possessive about her own stuff, but now is also a good time to start teaching her to take turns and share (see pages 195–198). Water play and sandboxes are terrific at this point. Get out the old baby tub you've stored in the garage or attic, and fill it with water or sand. For water play, never leave your child unattended (see box on page 111). Give her squeeze bottles, cups, and jugs (pitchers!) to enhance the experience. For sand play, cups and jugs are good too, as well as a spade and pail.

TODDLER SAFETY

The expression "into everything" sums up toddlerhood. The good news is that almost anything is fascinating to your child. The bad news is that almost anything is fascinating to your child—including electrical outlets, the slot in your VCR, Grandma's delicate figurines, air conditioner vents, animals' eyes, keyholes, bits of dirt, and the contents of the cat box, to name a few. Thus, while it doesn't take much to amuse your toddler, it takes a lot to keep him safe. Purchase a first-aid kit. Look around you and use your common sense. Here's what to avoid and how to do it:

- Tripping/falling: Keep rooms reasonably uncluttered; place corner guards on sharp corners; install window guards and gates at the top and bottom of stairs; place nonslip mats in the bathtub or shower and under area rugs on bare floors.

- Poisoning: Install safety locks on any cabinets containing medicines or poisonous household substances; even mouthwash and cosmetics should be out of reach. (Your child won't die from eating pet food, but you might want to keep it out of reach, too.) If you think a poisonous substance has been ingested, call your doctor or 911 before doing anything. Keep a bottle of Syrup of Ipecac in the house, to induce vomiting in case of poisoning.

- Choking: Remove mobiles from the crib; keep button-sized batteries and anything else that can fit through a toilet paper roll out of reach.

- Strangling: Shorten curtain and blind cords and electrical cords, or use pegs or masking tape to keep them above your child's reach.

- Drowning: Never leave your child alone in the bathroom, and certainly not in the tub, nor in a kiddie pool, pool, or even a bucket; install toilet-seat locks.

- Burning: Keep chairs, foot stools, and ladders away from counters and stoves; install stove knob-guards; cover the bath tap with a guard or wrap it with a towel; keep water heaters at 120 degrees to avoid scalding.

- Electric shocks: Cover all outlets and make sure every lamp in your house has a bulb in it. I advise all parents to take a CPR course. If you've taken one that focused exclusively on infant emergencies, you need a refresher class on toddlers. Young children require different types of maneuvers than infants when administering CPR and handling other emergencies—for example, dislodging an object caught in the throat.

From Feeding to Eating

Although food is low on your toddler's list of priorities—he'd much rather be scuttling about—this is the period of life when children make the monumentally important step from feeding to eating. Where your baby once contentedly suckled your breast or nursed on a bottle, as a toddler he can eat solid food. He grabs at the spoon when you feed him, and because he's able to pick up small bits of food without your help, thank you very much, he's on his way to becoming an independent eater.

Nutrition is a relatively simple issue in infancy, when breast or bottle supplies whatever your child needs. But as she matures, she not only needs solid food to keep her going and growing, she also needs to learn how to eat on her own. This is complicated by the fact that her preference for various foods, her appetite at any given moment, and her capacity will change from month to month, even day to day. Add to that the fact that you might have your own issues about food, and it's not surprising that this journey can be a bumpy one. How it goes depends on three factors: *The atmosphere* (your attitude toward food and the climate it creates in your home), *the eating experience* (the social and emotional pleasure—or distress—of mealtimes), and *the food* (what your child consumes). I describe each of these elements below: As you read, keep in mind:

> *You* control the atmosphere and the eating experience, but life will be a lot easier if you remember that *your child* controls the food.

The Atmosphere. Parents whose children are "good eaters" tend to go with the flow. They create an atmosphere of fun and ease at mealtimes. They never force a particular food or insist that a child who isn't hungry continue eating. No matter how picky their child is, these parents know that eating should be a pleasurable experience. Manners are taught, but food preference is *not* something kids learn—as in "He's got to learn how to eat his vegetables!" In order to create a welcoming atmosphere in your home, examine your own attitudes about food. Answer these questions:

WHAT WAS EATING LIKE IN YOUR FAMILY OF ORIGIN? Every family has a food ethos—pervasive attitudes about eating and what it means—and children are greatly affected by it. As a result, ideas about food unconsciously pass from one generation to the next. There might be great joy and delight around food, or anxiety; an attitude of abundance or one of scarcity; a sense of ease ("eat only until you're full") or an aura of tension ("finish what's on your plate").

Be aware of your own baggage. If you grew up in a family where mealtimes were tense, even punitive, you may unconsciously create a similar climate in your own home—which will certainly not contribute to your toddler's enjoyment of food. If you were forced to finish every morsel, you might attempt to employ such strategies now—and I guarantee it's not the way to go.

ARE YOU ANXIOUS ABOUT YOUR TODDLER'S EATING HABITS? From the time that humans began hunting and foraging, elders were responsible for putting food into babies' mouths. But they couldn't *make* their children eat, and neither can you. Perhaps you consider it "bad mothering" to have a child who doesn't eat well. Or you might have been painfully thin in childhood or suffered some sort of eating disorder in adolescence. If you bring any of these anxieties to your toddler's mealtimes, there's a good chance eating will become an ongoing struggle, with your little adventurer wanting to climb out of his high chair rather than be fed. The more you try to force a new food, or encourage him to eat "just a few more bites," the more he will perceive this as a way to seize control, and believe me, he'll win. In fact, there's a good chance that food will become an issue for the next several years.

Despite your child's now more active lifestyle, he won't always be in the mood to eat, nor will he necessarily like what you put in front of him. So instead of obsessing over uneaten food, look at your child. If he's alert, active, and happy, he's probably getting whatever nutrition he needs. Studies show that even babies have an innate ability to control their caloric intake. A few days of noneating are usually offset by good eating days. It also helps to look around you and talk to other mums. Many children are so-called picky eaters in their second and third years of life. Still, they and their parents live to tell amusing stories about it.

WHAT ARE YOUR OWN FOOD PREFERENCES AND HABITS? If you don't like bananas, you're not going to enjoy giving them to your child. If you were a picky eater, or still are, chances are your child isn't going to have a robust appetite either. Or if you're the kind of person I am, who likes to eat the exact same thing for months, don't be surprised when your child insists on a daily regimen of Cheerios and yogurt. Children also can be just the opposite of their parents— one of mine is a picky eater, the other not. Either way, though, it's important for you to be aware of your own "stuff" around food. I can remember walking into the house one day, and my Nan was feeding Sara brussels sprouts. I wanted to gag, but Nan shot me a hard glance. Knowing that my reaction would affect Sara, Nan said, "Tracy, would you fetch me my sweater? I think I left it upstairs." I purposely stayed upstairs a few minutes, to give Sara time to finish.

HOW DO YOU FEEL ABOUT YOUR CHILD'S BECOMING AN INDEPENDENT EATER? The transition from feeding to eating can be a welcome prospect for some parents, a disturbing occasion for others. Certainly, lots of mothers (most often, they're the ones who do the feeding of babies) can't wait until their child is independent at mealtimes. They've done their stint at breastfeeding, and spooning mush into their toddler's mouth quickly loses its appeal. However, some women need to be needed. Because they relish the intimacy of nursing, they unconsciously tune out when the baby of the house starts sending signals that say, "No more breast (or bottle)," or "I want to eat like a big girl now."

I urge you to look at your attitude because if your child senses that you don't want to let go, it will surely affect her strides toward autonomy. Indeed, from the moment she first tries to grab the spoon from your hand while you're feeding her, or when she asks for a sip out of your glass or water bottle, she is telling you, "I want to strike out on my own." It behooves you to present her with a series of skill-building opportunities so that she can eventually feed herself. But if you're one of those parents who fall into the I-don't-want-to-let-go category, you need to do a bit of self-searching. What, exactly, are you holding on to? And why? Is there another area of your life (for instance, your partner or your work) that you're avoiding or don't find satisfying? Look in the mirror and ask yourself, "Am I trying to keep my baby dependent because there's something else I don't want to face?"

Remember that life with a toddler is ever-changing and evolving. One minute your child is totally dependent on you, the next he won't let you do anything for him. This was particularly hard on Carolyn, who felt rejected by her ten-month-old, Jeb, her third child. Long after Jeb had begun to lose interest in nursing and had started to grab the spoon from her, Carolyn continued to spoon-feed him on her knee, because this made her feel close to him; it was reminiscent of breastfeeding. But Jeb

---

Feeding Alert!

Overanxious parents can turn children into anxiety-ridden noneaters. It may mean that your child is picking up your concerns about food, or that you're making her stay too long at the table if she:

Holds food in her mouth without chewing

Repeatedly spits food out

Gags or vomits

---

wasn't having any of it. He would squirm off his mum's lap and try with all his might to wrest the spoon from her hand. Every mealtime became a battle. I explained to Carolyn that as much as she wanted to hold on to the past and those quiet moments of nursing, she couldn't. Her "baby" was a baby no more, but a toddler with a mind of his own and more sophisticated physical capabilities. Rather than see this natural progression as a rejection of her, she needed to realize that Jeb's behavior was only his way of asking for what he wanted: independence. She had to give in. "You're right," she acknowledged, "but it makes me so sad. With my older children, I cried when they went off to school and yet I felt happy that they skipped into the classroom without clinging or even looking back."

I can certainly empathize with Carolyn and other mums who try to hold on. But the proverbial bottom line is this: mothering is different from smothering. At many points throughout our children's lives, we are called on to give them the gift not only of loving them, but also of letting go.

The Eating Experience. As I pointed out in the previous chapter (pages 77–79), mealtime R&R is vitally important. Sitting at the dinner table helps your child understand what big people do at mealtimes and what's expected of him. In fact, the eating experience is just as important as *what* he eats. And the more he is exposed to the social nature of eating, the better he'll become at sitting still, feeding himself, and enjoying the communal occasion. Eating is a social skill, and by watching you and siblings, if there are any, your child will learn patience and manners as well.

START EARLY TO INCLUDE YOUR CHILD. As soon as she can sit up, she's ready to join the family at the dinner table. And the first time she grabs a spoon from you, that's your cue to encourage her to eat on her own.

DINE WITH HIM. Even if you're not hungry, have a snack—some cut-up vegetables, a piece of toast—and sit at the table with him. It makes mealtime more of an interactive process than if you were just sitting there, trying to get food into him. It also takes some of the focus and pressure off him. You're in it together!

DON'T PUT A WHOLE BOWL IN FRONT OF HER. . . . unless you want it in your lap or splattered all over the kitchen. Instead, put some finger foods (see below) on the tray for her to pick up on her own. Put the bowl on your plate, and feed her while she's attempting to feed herself.

HAVE FOUR SPOONS ON HAND, TWO FOR HIM AND TWO FOR YOU! When they first eat solid food, toddlers bite down on the spoon and grab it. Give him the first spoon. Then use the second one for the second mouthful. Before you know it, he'll be banging the first one and grabbing the second. That's where spoons three and four come in handy. It's kind of like a conveyor belt, replacing one spoon after the other as he grabs each one.

TRY TO MAKE MUCH OF HER MEAL INTO FINGER FOODS. It will not only free you up, it will make her feel more like a "big girl" who's feeding herself. Don't be surprised when most of what she eats goes on the floor. She's learning, and for the first few months, not much may end up in her mouth. Prevention is worth a pound of cure. Invest in a large bib with a pocket that catches food. Put a tarp under her seat or high chair. Believe me, if you don't react to her messiness, which is all part of her exploring this new world of solid food, she will probably grow out of the finger-painting-with-her-food stage faster than if you keep trying to stop her or keep her clean. By fifteen to eighteen months, most toddlers can handle a spoon. Don't intervene—unless she tries to stick the spoon into her ear!

DON'T PLAY FOOD GAMES AND DON'T ASSOCIATE FOOD WITH PLAY. Everything you do sets an example for your child. So if you play "airplane," for example (put food on the spoon and say, "Here comes the foooood"), when he later eats at other houses or in a restaurant, he'll think it's okay to have food flying through the air. If you give him a toy to amuse himself during meals, he'll think mealtime is synonymous with playtime. Or if you put on TV to distract him, he may behave better, but he won't really know what he's eating and he won't learn from the experience.

Time for a Sippy Cup? Think H.E.L.P.

- **H**old back until he wants a sip from your glass, cup, or water bottle.

- **E**ncourage him to experience drinking on his own, but know that until he masters the skill of controlling the flow, all the liquid will come out of the sides of his mouth.

- **L**imit the mess by putting on a vinyl bib or covering him in a tarp. Limit your own frustration by remembering that he needs practice. (Some parents feed toddlers in their diapers, but I don't recommend it. Civilized people eat in clothes, and as we'll see in Chapter Six, what we teach at home, toddlers expect to do elsewhere.)

- **P**raise only when he manages to actually drink the liquid. Don't say "good job" when he merely holds the cup up and everything comes spilling out.

ENCOURAGE HER EFFORTS AND PRAISE HER APPROPRIATELY WHEN SHE EXHIBITS GOOD MANNERS, BUT WHEN SHE DOESN'T, DON'T TAKE IT PERSONALLY. Remember that your child wasn't born with table manners; she's learning. Surely, you should teach her to say "please" and "thank you," but don't become a school mistress. She will learn mealtime etiquette mostly by imitation.

Let him get up when he's finished. You can always tell when your child has lost interest in eating. First, he'll turn his head away and clench his lips together. If he's eating finger foods, he might start throwing pieces on the floor or smashing things more vehemently than usual (some smashing is normal). If you make him sit there and keep presenting bites of food, I assure you he will soon kick, try to wiggle out of the chair, or cry. Don't let it get that far.

The Whole Milk and Nothing but the Whole Milk!

Between a year and eighteen months, whether your child has been on formula or breast milk, introduce whole milk. Toddlers should have at least 24 ounces a day for vitamins, iron, and calcium. Start with one bottle a day for the first three days, two bottles for the next three, and finally, three bottles a day. Cheese, yogurt, and ice cream can substitute for whole milk. Common allergic reactions include excess mucus, diarrhea, dark circles under the eyes. If your child is allergic or if you want to give soy milk, talk to a nutritionist or your pediatrician.

The Food. As I pointed out earlier, this is your child's domain. Of course, you need to help her make the transition from feeding to eating by giving her opportunities to learn how to eat on her own and to enjoy the same kinds of food the rest of the family eats. Unfortunately, though, all of this is happening at precisely the same time that your child is learning that she has a separate self, that she can move about on her own, and most important, that she can say "no." And the fact is, you can lead your child to a gourmet meal, but what goes into her mouth is ultimately up to her. You may be surprised to learn that toddlers need fewer calories than you think: 1000 to 1200 a day. Most of that will come from the 16 to 26 ounces of breast milk or formula that they consume—and after a year to eighteen months, whole milk (see sidebar)—even as you introduce solid foods. Here are other points to keep in mind.

WEAN AS A PREVENTIVE MEASURE. Most American pediatricians routinely suggest that you wean your baby at six months. Rather than watch the calendar, I suggest that you watch your child and start solid foods (see sidebar) sooner rather than later. First of all, if you wait too long, your child may become so accustomed to down-

ing liquids he will reject solids; getting him accustomed to chewing will be a much more troublesome process.

Also, weaning can help prevent sleep disturbances. Indeed, I often get calls from mothers whose six- or seven-month-old— a child who normally sleeps straight through—has started waking in the middle of the night. To calm him, his mother offers him her breast or a bottle (neither is a recommendation I'd make, but we'll deal with that in Chapter Eight, pages 254–262). If the child only "snacks" for a few minutes, I strongly suspect that his waking is either the result of anxiety or a bad dream—he's suckling for comfort. If he takes a full feed, though, he probably needs more calories.

Granted, sleep disturbances caused by increased mobility and newfound fears are common and unavoidable during the toddler years. However, sleep disruptions caused by a lack of calories *can* be prevented. If you notice that your child is eating more often during the day, take that as your cue. Instead of nursing him

The What and When of Weaning

Some parents in this country (and some books as well) are confused by the term *weaning*. They think it means to take baby off the breast. In actuality, weaning is the transition from a liquid diet to solid foods. Your baby is probably ready to wean when:

✓ **She is five or six months old.** Though babies of previous American generations were weaned as young as six weeks (still a common practice in Europe), the American Academy of Pediatrics now recommends beginning the process at around six months. By then, your baby can sit up and control her head; her tongue protrusion reflex has disappeared; her intestines can digest more complex solid foods; and allergies are less likely.

✓ **He seems hungrier during the day, nurses more or has an extra bottle, and/or wakes up in the middle of the night and takes a full feed.** This suggests that he needs solid foods because he's not getting sufficient calories from breast milk or formula.

✓ **She shows an interest in food that you're eating.** She might watch you intensely and then, with an open mouth or a reaching gesture, ask for a taste. Or if you're chewing, she might try to poke her finger into your mouth. (In other cultures, moms chew foods and then give it to their babies.)

Food Allergies

It is estimated that 5–8 percent of babies and young children under the age of three have true food allergies. Likely culprits include citrus, egg whites, lamb, berries, some cheeses, cow's milk, wheat, nuts, soy products, carrots, corn, fish, and shellfish. This doesn't mean that you don't present any of these foods; just be aware of potential reactions. Allergies are often inherited, but sometimes crop up even when there is no family history. Some studies indicate that 20 percent or more children grow out of food sensitivities, but it's not because their parents de-sensitize them by giving them more of whatever food they react to. In fact, the opposite often happens: the food allergy becomes more dangerous, and rather than growing out of it, the child has a lifelong problem.

By introducing only one new food per week, if any sign of allergies appears, you'll know what caused them. If your child seems to be sensitive to a new food, stop serving it immediately and don't reintroduce it for at least one month. If he still shows a reaction, wait at least a year and consult a doctor.

Adverse reactions to food are quite serious, the worst being anaphylactic shock, an allergic reaction that affects several organs simultaneously and can be fatal. Milder symptoms usually appear first and might become worse in time.

✓   loose stools or diarrhea
✓   rashes
✓   puffiness or swelling in the face
✓   sneezing, runny nose, or other cold-like symptoms
✓   gas pains or other symptoms of stomachache
✓   vomiting
✓   itchy, watery eyes

more often or giving him an extra bottle before bed, provide the additional calories he needs in the form of solid food.

> **TIP:** *There are lots of high-quality baby foods to be bought, but if you want to make your own, steam or boil fresh vegetables and fruit, and use a food processor or blender to puree them. Freeze in ice-cube trays, which will give you handy one-ounce portions, and the next day transfer the cubes to a plastic bag and defrost as needed. Never add salt to a toddler's diet.*

Remember that weaning is a gradual process. On pages 122–123, I offer "From Liquids to Solids: A Six-Week Starter Plan," which is a sample weaning routine, beginning at the age of six months. It is meant only as a suggestion. I find that most babies digest pears easily, which is why that's the first food I usually introduce. However, if your pediatrician suggests starting your child on rice cereal, by all means do.

You'll see that I only add one new food per week, which is always introduced in the morning (see sidebar on food allergies). The following week that food moves to the midday meal, and a new food is added for lunch. By the third week, your child will be eating solid foods three times a day. In the subsequent weeks, increase the amounts as well as the variety. Keep a food log, noting the date and amount of every new food you introduce. It will help both you and your pediatrician in case problems occur. (On page 124 are my suggestions for foods to introduce each month. If you follow them, simply note the dates and amounts next to each food, and presto, a food log!)

Introduce finger foods early. Purees are fine, but as your child begins to expand her diet and demonstrates that she can tolerate various foods, give her the same fare in a more adult form—foods she can eat on her own that require a bit more work than mushy substances. For example, once you see that she can eat pears, give her peeled, slightly cooked pears cut up into small pieces. Now that she's got that highly effective pincer grasp, she can not only pick up food but also pop it into her mouth. Once she realizes this, she'll delight in feeding herself. You want her to get used to the texture. Even without teeth, a child as young as seven months can "gum" certain foods and safely swallow them. Or give her bite-sized pieces that literally melt in her mouth.

Cut finger foods into tiny bits, ¼-inch square or slightly larger for very soft foods. With vegetables, such as carrots, broccoli, or cauliflower, as well as crunchy fruits, like pears and apples, you need to parboil them first. The possibilities are endless. Most of what you serve for dinner can be converted for your toddler. Some ideas include: Cheerios, small pieces of pancake or French toast, most vegetables and soft fruits (such as ripe berries, bananas, peaches), small bits of tuna, cooked flaked fish, bits of cheese.

From Liquids to Solids: A Six-Week Starter Plan

Week/Age	7 A.M.	9 A.M.	11 A.M.
#1 26 weeks (6 mos)	baby wakes, feed breast or bottle	4 teaspoons of pears; finish on breast or bottle	breast or bottle
#2 27 weeks	breast or bottle	4 teaspoons of sweet potatoes (or any new food); finish with breast or bottle	breast or bottle
#3 28 weeks	breast or bottle	4 teaspoons of butternut squash (or any new food); finish on breast or bottle	breast or bottle
#4 29 weeks	breast or bottle	$1/4$ of a banana (or any new food); finish on breast or bottle	breast or bottle
#5 30 weeks (7 mos)	breast or bottle	4 teaspoons of pureed apples; finish on breast or bottle	breast or bottle
#6 31 weeks	breast or bottle	4 teaspoons green beans, 4 teaspoons of pears; finish on breast or bottle	breast or bottle

1 P.M.	4 P.M.	8 P.M.	Comments
breast or bottle	breast or bottle	breast or bottle	Start by introducing only one food in the morning; pears are easy to digest.
4 teaspoons of pears; finish on breast or bottle	breast or bottle	breast or bottle	Pears move to lunch meal; new food introduced in morning.
4 teaspoons of sweet potatoes; finish on breast or bottle	4 teaspoons of pears	breast or bottle	Former new food moves to lunch, now solids are given three times a day.
4 teaspoons of sweet potatoes, four teaspoons butternut squash; finish on breast or bottle	4 teaspoons of pears; finish on breast or bottle	breast or bottle	Quantity increased at midday meal.
4 teaspoons of sweet potatoes, 4 teaspoons of pears; finish on breast or bottle	4 teaspoons of butternut squash, 1/4 banana; finish on breast or bottle	breast or bottle	Quantities increased at lunch *and* dinner.
4 teaspoons of butternut squash, 4 teaspoons of apples; finish on breast or bottle.	4 teaspoons of sweet potatoes, 1/4 banana; finish on breast or bottle	breast or bottle	As new foods are added, two are given at each meal; quantities also increase, depending on child's appetite.

Food Introduction Record

6 Months	7 Months	8 Months	9 Months	10 Months	11 Months	One Year
apples	peaches	brown rice	avocado	prunes	kiwi fruit	wheat
pears	plums	bagels	asparagus	broccoli	potatoes	cantaloupe
bananas	carrots	bread	zucchini	beets	parsnips	honeydew
acorn squash	peas	chicken	yogurt	egg-free pasta	spinach	oranges
butternut	green beans	turkey	ricotta cheese	lamb	lima beans	watermelon
squash	barley		cottage cheese	mild cheeses	eggplant	blueberries
sweet potatoes			cream cheese		egg yolks	raspberries
rice			beef broth		pink grapefruit	strawberries
oats						corn
						tomatoes
						onions
						cucumber
						cauliflower
						lentils
						chickpeas
						tofu
						fish
						pork
						veal
						egg whites

TIP: Until your child is one year old, just in case he's allergic, avoid egg whites, wheat, citrus (other than pink grapefruit), and tomatoes. After your child is a year old, you can add shredded chicken, scrambled or hard-boiled eggs, and soft berries to the list of finger foods, but until at least eighteen months, continue to be careful about nuts, which are hard to digest and easy to choke on, as well as shellfish, chocolate, and honey.

MAKE APPETIZING BUT EASY-TO-PREPARE FOODS FOR YOUR TODDLER. Although toddlers are anything but discriminating when it comes to food, it's never too early to introduce a child to the joy of variety and adventure. While I wouldn't suggest that you spend hours slaving over a hot stove for a meal your child might dump on the floor, be creative. Cut bread into shapes or place food on the plate in the form of a face. Try to give your toddler healthy food and a balanced diet, but *never* force her to eat or engage in a struggle. If you have a child who likes only two or three different items, use them to smother other food. Say applesauce is a favorite—try it on her broccoli. And if that doesn't work, remember that she won't die from lack of variety or too few vegetables (fruit has many of the same nutritious elements).

Can My Child Be a Vegan?

Parents who are vegetarians themselves often ask if it's okay to put their baby or toddler on a vegetarian diet. Especially when dairy products and eggs are eliminated, most vegetarian diets fall short of the minimum daily requirements. Also, vegetables are high in bulk but may not give your child enough vitamin B, calories from fat, or contain enough iron, which children need for growth. To be on the safe side, check with your pediatrician or health care specialist; you may want to contact a nutritionist as well.

LET YOUR CHILD EAT IN ANY ORDER AND IN ANY COMBINATION. Who says applesauce comes after chicken, or that you can't dip fish into yogurt? Children learn the rules of eating by sitting at the table, and they'll eventually imitate them. But in the beginning, let your child eat the way she wants.

NUTRITIOUS SNACKS ARE FOOD, TOO. Before you worry about your child not eating enough, consider what he eats between meals. Some children can't down a big meal in one sitting; they do better at "grazing" throughout the day. That's fine, especially if you give your child healthful snacks, like slightly cooked vegetables or fruits, Goldfish crackers, or bite-sized pieces of toast with melted cheese on top. Children naturally gravitate toward carbohydrate snacks, like biscuits, but it's also a matter of how *you* present the food. If from the get-go you make healthful foods sound special and appetizing ("Mmmm . . . I've got apples for you"), your child will look forward to them. At the end of the day, when you add it all up, you might be surprised to see that he's getting more nutrients than you realized.

EARLY ON, ALLOW YOUR CHILD TO BE PART OF FOOD PREPARATION. When your child reaches the "me do" stage, you can't beat 'em, so it's best to join 'em. Children as young as fifteen months can help mix, rip lettuce into pieces, decorate cookies, prepare snacks. What's more, cooking develops fine motor skills, and most important, encourages your child's *relationship* to food.

Sample Menu

This is just a guide; it's not God's law. I have a one-year-old in mind here, but what your child eats depends on her weight, temperament, and stomach capacity.

Breakfast
¼–½ cup cereal
¼–½ cup fruit
4–6 ounces either formula or breast milk

Morning Snack
2–4 ounces fruit juice
cooked vegetable or cheese

Lunch
¼–½ cup cottage cheese
¼–½ cup yellow or orange vegetable
4–6 ounces formula or breast milk

Afternoon Snack
2–4 ounces juice
4 crackers with cheese

Dinner
¼ cup poultry or meat
¼–½ cup green vegetable
¼ noodles, pasta, rice, or potatoes
¼ cup of fruit
4–6 ounces formula or breast milk

Before Bed
4–8 ounces formula or breast milk

AVOID LABELING ANY FOODS AS "BAD." You know what they say about forbidden fruit. Children whose parents religiously avoid cookies and other sweets often crave such treats and tend to turn into little beggars once they get out of the house. And don't assume that your child is too young to understand. Believe me, if you demonize certain foods, he will pick up on it.

NEVER BRIBE A CHILD OR CAJOLE HER WITH THE FOOD. Too often, a parent whose child is about to touch something off-limits or become cranky tries to stave off a meltdown with, "Here, have a cookie." Not only is that parent rewarding the behavior (see Chapter Seven for better ideas about handling such situations), but the adult is also setting up the child to see food as barter, not a pleasurable commodity. Every human has a lifelong relationship with food. By paying attention to how and when we offer our children food, we will foster their love of eating and their appreciation of good tastes and allow them to enjoy the social interplay as well.

Dressing for Success

My coauthor and I considered subtitling this section "Dressed to Kill," because that's probably how you feel when your toddler runs away, T-shirt over his head, and promptly knocks over a treasured family heirloom. To be sure, the days of no-hassle diapering and dressing are usually over once a child learns how much fun it is to be in motion. Lying on a changing table just doesn't do it for most toddlers. Some will have out-and-out meltdowns over the prospect. Here are some ways I've seen parents head off potential problems:

Get everything ready first. Preparation is key. You don't want to waste time fumbling with these things while your toddler is squirming. Take off the top of the diaper cream, lay out the nappy, and have the wipes close by.

Pick the right time. Your child shouldn't be too hungry, too tired, or too involved in play. If he's just about to complete something he's working on and you swoop down and whisk him away, he's not going to be very happy.

> **TIP:** *Many parents allow toddlers to play in their pajamas after breakfast, but calling them in later to get dressed can be confusing, especially if a child is involved in play. She hears, "It's time to get dressed," but in her mind, she already is! I recommend including "getting dressed" as the end of your breakfast ritual. The child finishes the meal, brushes her teeth, and changes from pajamas into play clothes in order to get ready for her day.*

Announce what you're doing. As you know, I don't believe in ambushing children or taking them by surprise. Let your child know what's happening. "It's time to get dressed now," or "I'm going to change your diaper now."

Don't rush the process. As much as you may want it "over with," being in a hurry won't make dressing any easier or faster. With Touchy, Grumpy, and Spirited toddlers, in fact, you're really asking for trouble if you rush. Instead, reframe; see this as a good opportunity to connect with your child. After all, dressing is a very intimate act. Research suggests that children whose parents make direct eye contact have fewer discipline problems later on. This is a natural time to look into each other's eyes.

Make dressing fun. Talk to your child when you're diapering or dressing. Continue to explain what you're doing. One good way to amuse and explain is to sing: "This is the way we put on our shirt, put on our shirt, put on our shirt. This is the way we put on our shirt so we can go out playing." Use your own words; make up your own melodies. One mum I know was good at spontaneously reciting simple poems to fit the occasion: "Roses are red, violets are blue, now I'm putting a shirt on you!" You know by now what distracts your child; pull out all the stops. If he starts to squirm or cry, this is the *only* time I recommend trying to cajole. I first try a form of peek-a-boo, by bending down and popping up, "Here I am!" If he tries to turn over, I say in a lighthearted voice, "Where are you going," and I flip him back. If he starts crying, you might then try to distract him with what I call a "no-no toy"—an item that you give him as a treat only when you're changing or dressing him. Excitedly proclaim, "Ooh, look at what Mum's got!"

(I know I always admonish parents to "start as they mean to go on," but this is one exception. Though you allow your toddler to examine your heirloom watch while diapering, he won't later consider it one of his playthings. Children seem to know that no-no toys are just for the changing table. Besides, diapering and dressing difficulties are usually a short-lived stage. Great-grandma would be happy to know that her watch was being used to help the two of you get through it more easily.)

> **TIP:** *Buy loose clothes with elasticized waists, big buttons, and Velcro closures. Shirts that can be buttoned or zipped are easier, too. If you buy T-shirts, make sure the opening for the head has buttons at the side, or is big enough or stretchy enough to slip on and off easily.*

Let the child participate. Somewhere between eleven and eighteen months, your child will begin to show an interest in taking her clothes off (usually by tugging on a sock). Praise and encourage her effort: "Good for you, Big Girl. Now you can help Mummy get you undressed."* To ensure success, roll her sock halfway off her foot and pull the toe out a little to give her something to hold on to. Then let her tug off the last little bit. With a T-shirt, you take her arms out, and let her pull the shirt over her head. As she becomes more adept, let her do more of it on her own. Make a game of it. "I pull this sock off, and now it's your turn. You pull the other one off."

Somewhere around age two (give or take a few months), your

---

*Don't go overboard with praise. Remember the mother (page 57) who made such a big deal about her toddler's pulling off his sock that it soon became his favorite activity. He couldn't understand why his mother, after initially going nuts at his accomplishment, was upset because he was pulling his sock off at every possible opportunity.

child will also show an interest in putting clothes on. The first tries are usually with socks. Just as you did before, encourage and minimally assist; get the sock halfway onto her foot, and let her pull it up. When she has mastered that, fold the top of the sock over the heel and have her put her toes in and then pull it up all by herself.

Take the same steps with a T-shirt. At first, help her pop the T-shirt over her head, hold the sleeves out, and let her slip her arms into them. Eventually, she'll get the hang of doing it herself. If a T-shirt has a design on the front, point out that the picture goes in the front. Even solid T-shirts have labels; show your child that the label goes in the back.

E-mail from a Wise Nanny

A few years back, I nannied for a two-year-old and a three-year-old. The elder suddenly started being difficult about getting dressed in the morning. It constantly became a struggle, until I made him feel as though it was his choice in getting dressed. For example, I would ask him if he would like to put on his left or right sock first, making the whole process an interesting ordeal for him and his idea in the first place. It took longer in the beginning but became a game for us both, eventually.

Consider alternatives if the prospect of being on the changing table elicits a strong negative reaction. Diapers can just as easily be changed on floors or couches. I've also seen parents try to diaper while the child is standing, but I'm not a big fan of that. It's harder to get a secure fit, and your child is more likely to run off before you've finished.

Break up the tasks into smaller pieces. A mother usually knows what upsets her child. If it's typically stressful to change your little one's diaper or dress him, prepare yourself. Sometimes, getting through these trying moments is a matter of having your own coping skills in check. I am reminded of Maureen, who knew that whenever it was time to dress Joseph, her Spirited toddler, she was in for a struggle. Invariably, Joseph tried to roll over or run away, or he would grab hold of his T-shirt, making it difficult for Maureen to get it over his head. For the previous week, she had tried fighting Joseph, but that only made her little boy more resistant, and the dressing nightmare got worse. Likewise, cajoling him didn't help.

So this wise mum broke the process down, attempting only one piece of clothing every fifteen minutes. As long as she didn't keep Joseph still for too long, and she announced the goal at each step ("We just have to get your T-shirt on"), he could handle dressing. Within a month, he became surprisingly more cooperative.

Admittedly, this was a last-resort strategy. If your child is like Joseph, respect that getting dressed is uncomfortable for him—at least for now. Stretching out the process in this way might help him feel more comfortable. Yes, luv, it *will* take up more of your time and force you to start getting ready earlier. But particularly with reluctant dressers, if you rush, you'll have a battle on your hands several times a day. Believe me, by honoring his needs, your child will get through this stage of difficulty faster than if you fight him every step of the way.

Give your child a say in the matter. Your newly autonomous toddler doesn't like dressing, both because it immobilizes her and also because she's not in control. Although dressing isn't optional (see below), you can offer limited choice as to when, where, and what:

When: "Would you like to get dressed now or after I wash the dishes?"

Where: "Would you like me to change your diaper on the changing table or the floor?"

What: "Would you like to wear your blue T-shirt or your red one?" (If she doesn't know her colors, make it simple, by holding two shirts in front of her: "This shirt or this one?")

Needless to say, if you've been chasing your child around the house for an hour, or if she's having a tantrum, such a rational approach won't work. It's best that you take to heart my next point:

Remember that you know best. Whatever diversions you employ to make your child more cooperative, whatever tricks you use to make the process easier, the bottom line is that your child doesn't really have an option when it comes to diapering and dressing. Hanging about in a soiled diaper can lead to a rash. Eventually, you have to put your foot down, and your child *has* to cooperate or at least give in when his diaper needs changing.

When mothers or fathers allow their toddlers to run about naked and rationalize, "He won't let me dress him," I'm inclined to groan. Getting dressed, like eating, also has a social component to it. We don't go out unless we have clothes on. Point this out to your child: "We can't go to the playground until you get dressed." Even at a pool or at the beach: "You can't go back to play until you get a dry bathing suit on."

> **TIP:** *Don't change your toddler in public. Just because he can't talk yet doesn't mean he considers dressing a spectator sport. After all, would you like to change your clothes in the supermarket, in a park, or at the beach in full view of other people? I think not—and neither would your child. If you can't duck into a rest room, go to your car. If you have no other option, at least use a blanket or jacket to cover him.*

Have an ending ritual. Even if you simply say, "All dressed!" or "Now we're ready to go to the park," this lets the child know that the ordeal is over. He sees the cause and effect: *I stayed with it, I'm dressed, and now I can play.*

Encourage your child to participate in the care of her clothing. Install hooks for pajamas, bathrobes, jackets, and other often-worn items so that she can retrieve and put away certain clothing on her own. Children love to throw dirty clothes in the laundry basket, too. Such care rituals teach your child that some clothes are put away for another day while others go into the wash.

Dressing is a skill that your child will continue to perfect. What I've done above is given you some tools to help him get started. You'll need to be patient and to take your cues from him. When he struggles, help him. But when he says, "Me do," let him. Even if you happen to be in a rush one morning, if he has learned to put on even a few items all by himself, you can't expect him to go backwards. Unless you want to do battle with him, don't try to take over. Instead, be a bit late this time and learn that next time you'll have to plan your schedule differently. As I repeatedly point out, toddlers can't tell time, and they certainly don't care if you're late. They care only about their independence.

The Final Frontier: Nappies Nevermore

Space may be the final frontier on *Star Trek*, but in your house, getting rid of diapers is the final boundary your toddler will cross as he makes his way across the great divide that separates babies from children. At the same time, if you're like many Americans I meet, this issue will also be marked by confusion. When I first came here, I was surprised to discover that potty training was such a highly charged subject. Parents often hit me with a barrage of questions: *When do we do it? How do we do it? What kind of seat is best? What kind of irreparable harm might we do if we start too early? If we start too late?*

What is most amazing to me is the number of children here who are still in nappies at age three or four. Granted, I don't believe in pushing little ones into doing anything their bodies aren't ready for them to

---

Potty 101

Physical readiness for toilet training depends partially on your child's sphincter muscles. Mums out there know what body part I'm talking about, especially if they had to do Kegel exercises after childbirth. For you dads, next time you go to the loo, try to stop your pee in midstream—your sphincter muscles help you do it. It was once believed that these muscles didn't mature until the age of two, but research is now divided on the subject. In any case, training is both a matter of physical readiness *and* practice. With handicapped children who had no control, we were able to train them by gauging the right times to put them on the toilet. In that case, guidance combined with practice overrides immaturity.

---

do, but at the same time, we need to present opportunities for children to learn. Sadly, too many parents are confused between two issues: behavior that needs to be taught and natural progression (developmental milestones that automatically happen). For example, hitting is absolutely *not* part of the natural progression of toddlerhood and yet some parents will excuse the behavior: "Oh, he'll grow out of it." No, he won't, luv. *You'll have to teach him.*

In reality, most childhood accomplishments are a combination of two factors, physical maturity and parental guidance. This is easy enough to understand when it comes to building a tower with blocks. When your child has matured to the point of being able to hold a block and place one on top of the other, he can theoretically build a tower. But if you never give him a few blocks to get started and allow him to experiment on his own, he'll never learn.

It's the same with going to the loo. A three- or four-year-old whose parents keep waiting for him to come 'round on his own already has control over his sphincter muscles (see sidebar on page 133), but he might never show an interest in "going potty"

Have a Seat, Sonny!

I prefer the type of potty seat that goes on top of yours, rather than the freestanding units that one has to empty. The former are easier to carry if you're traveling, too. But with both, be careful. Children can easily slip through or get wedged in, either of which can be a scary experience to a child who already has fears of being swallowed up by the bowl! Use a small step stool as a footrest; your child will feel more anchored if his feet aren't dangling.

---

unless he's given the right kind of guidance, encouragement, and sufficient opportunities to learn. And it's his parents' job to teach him.

There are almost as many theories out there on toilet training as there are families. As always, I advise a moderate approach, whereby parents encourage rather than pressure the child. You must be observant and arm yourself with information so as to identify the best "window" for starting potty training—when your child's body and mind are ready and yet *before* the inevitable toddler/parent power struggles begin. For most children, the optimal time to begin is between eighteen months and two years. That said, however, I urge you to look at *your* child. Let the acronym H.E.L.P. be your guide.

H—Hold back until you see signs that your child is ready. When my girls were young, I never asked anyone, "At what age do I potty train?" Instead, I *watched* my children. Going to the loo involves a sensation. If you watch carefully, you will notice when your toddler becomes aware of that sensation. Some children stop dead in their tracks. They stand very still, seem to focus, and then suddenly move on. When pooping, they might strain or get red in the face. Some children will go behind a couch or chair to do it. Or they will point to their diaper and say, "Uh-oh." Watch for your child's signs. By twenty-one months, most children become aware of their bodily functions, but it can happen as early as fifteen months. (Girls often mature before boys, but that's not written in stone.)

E—Encourage your child to connect bodily function with words and actions. Once you see that your child's awareness is developing, expand her vocabulary. For instance, when she points to her diaper, you say, "You're wet. Do you want me to change you?" If she tugs on her pants and starts to pull them down, say, "Let me change you now. You have a doody in your diaper."

Whenever you change her diaper, make a point of telling her straightaway, "Oh, this is really wet. It's full of pee." Or if she poops, let her see you flush it down the toilet. I realize that with disposable diapers, you'd normally just wrap it up and toss it in the trash, but now might be a good time to change that practice, so that your child actually sees where the poop goes. If you're not modest, you also could allow your child to accompany you in the bathroom and explain, "This is where we make wee-wee [or use whatever language is comfortable in your house]."

Now is the time to introduce the actions as well. Invest in a freestanding minipotty or a potty seat (see sidebar on page 134) and start by having his doll or favorite stuffed animal go to the bathroom. If he seems receptive to trying it himself, start by putting him on first thing in the morning, shortly after waking up.

Talk to him; distract him with a toy or a game of patty-cake. Another good time to try a short sit on the potty is around twenty minutes after he's had a drink. In any case, make the situation fun, not stressful. Again, read to your child or amuse him with a toy or game of patty-cake. Distracting him in this way makes him relax and he's more likely to go to the bathroom. In contrast, if you just sit there with him and wait, he's going to take it as a demand.

L—Limit your child's time on the potty. No more than 2–3 minutes at first. If you make the potty a stressful experience, you're in for a battle. Therefore, take a deep breath and limit your *own* frustration with the process as well. Relax and your child will, too. *This is not about getting your child to perform—it's about teaching him*. If he pees or poops, great. Congratulate him (see below about praise) and give words to what just happened: "Good job. You did a wee-wee in the toilet." When you take him off, say "All done." If he doesn't go, don't act disappointed. In a very matter-of-fact way, take him off the toilet and say nothing. Finally, limit your child's distress by not putting him on the toilet (a) too often; (b) when he wakes up in a bad mood; or (c) any other time when he is resistant.

Potty-Training Apparel

What does the well-dressed baby-in-training wear? Here are a few points to remember:

- **Diapers.** Disposable diapers are so absorbent nowadays that children don't always recognize when they're wet. Although cloth diapers are more work, in the long run they may not be because your child can recognize when he's soiled or wet and may get out of nappies earlier.

- **Training pants.** Like disposable diapers, training pants are very absorbent. As soon as your child starts to recognize where he goes potty and the sensation that goes with it, and is able to hold it in until he gets there, he is well on his way. You may want to skip the training-pants stage all together.

- **Big girl/boy underwear.** When she is going on the potty at least three times a day, try out some "big girl" (or "big boy") underwear during the day. If she has an accident, don't make a big deal. And never scold! Just change her, wash her bottom, and put on a fresh pair of undies.

P—Praise the Lord and pass the toilet paper! Praise your child wildly when she actually deposits something in the toilet bowl—*not* when she just sits there. This is the *one* time I give you permission to engage in pure, over-the-top, loony praise. "Hooray! You peed in the toilet!" I'd shout and clap like a seal when one of my girls was successful. "Now let's flush it . . . bye-bye, pee." It doesn't take a child long to view this as a great game. I'm sure more than once mine thought, *Hey, Mum's really lost it, but this is fun!* By the way, lots of praise, but please, don't *over*explain. For example, I've heard mothers say, "Good, now this is where you pee-pee every time." Instead, keep your compliments fun, lighthearted—and at your child's level.

The Four Essential Ps of Potty Success
(Pardon the pun, luv, but I just couldn't resist.)

Potty—One that fits his size.

Patience—Never rush the process or look disappointed when he doesn't pee or poop; all children progress at their own speed.

Practice—Your child needs as much as he can get.

Presence—Sit with him and cheer him on.

If you take the initial plunge (sorry—another bad pun) slowly, you'll get to know your child's habits, and your child will more likely be open to the experience. Remember too that your child's personality plays a big role in how receptive he is. Some children are gluttons for the reward of seeing their mother or father go bananas and rejoice in their toilet success; others could care less.

A Final Word about Independence

Your toddler grows constantly, little by little. I urge you to be patient with her growth. Both of you will be happier if you trust the

process, rather than trying to rush it. Welcome each new development and patiently ride out the more difficult stages. Recognize the
difference between what you can guide and what Nature controls.
Sometimes your child's strides toward autonomy will seem sudden
and dramatic, like the moment she first pulls herself up to a standing position. But every day, even when you don't notice the more
subtle changes, her body will become progressively stronger, her
coordination greater. Meanwhile, she is also accumulating experience, taking in new sights and sounds, building on every skill that
she acquires. While all this is going on, her intellect is developing
as well. Her mind, like a little computer, downloads and sorts
through every bit of information that comes her way. Although she
has been *communicating* with you since birth, now she will be able
to literally talk the same language. In the next chapter, we'll take a
closer look at how this incredible process develops and further ce-
ments the parent/child bond.

CHAPTER FIVE

Toddler Talk: Maintaining a Dialogue through T.L.C.

Words are the most powerful drug
used by mankind.

—Rudyard Kipling

Listen or thy tongue will keep thee
deaf.

—American Indian proverb

Continuing the Dialogue

If being a baby is like traveling in a foreign land (an analogy I often use), being a toddler is like being an exchange student. You start to learn the language by being there, soaking up bits of conversation, at first understanding more than you can say. You can get through the day a lot better than visitors who have been in the country for only a week. And you're less likely to get a plate of pasta shoved under your nose when you ask where the loo is. However, you haven't been living there all that long, so you don't know many words beyond the basics. And you still get a bit frustrated when you want something or when you try to express a more sophisticated idea. Luckily, though, toddlers have the benefit of ever-present guides who speak the language, know the country and its customs, and can help them improve their vocabulary and make sense of it all—they're called *parents.*

We are our children's tour directors during the amazing process by which they learn to talk and become active members of the family and participants in life itself. Language is not just the key to communication, it opens up a world of independence and activity. It enables a toddler to ask questions

---

When Will My Child Talk?

The rate of children's language development is determined by various factors. As we discussed in Chapter One, nature and nurture work together. Some factors include

- Exposure to language and interaction with talkers (constant conversation and eye contact encourage children to talk)

- Gender (girls seem to develop language skills earlier than boys)

- Other developmental gains taking precedence (communication skills may lag when a child starts to walk or expand her social repertoire)

- Birth order (younger children whose siblings tend to speak for them may talk later; see sidebar on page 150)

- Genetic disposition (if you or your partner were late talkers, your child might be, too)

Note: *Sometimes children who start to talk also have setbacks if there is sudden change in the household—new nanny, new baby, someone is sick, parent travels or goes back to work.*

("Whassat?"), make demands ("Cookie"), assert himself ("Me do it"), put ideas together ("Daddy all gone. Mommy stay"), and of course, refuse to cooperate ("No!"). Through language, he learns what's expected of him ("Excuse me") and other social graces, such as politeness ("Please") and gratitude ("Thank you"). He can enlist others in his endeavors ("Mommy, come") as well.

It doesn't happen overnight. Language development, like your child's increasing physical prowess, is a slow and steady process. Each new step builds on the one before it and makes ready for the next. First, they gesture, to identify objects or to request them. The babbling sounds of what I call *Banguage* (baby language) are actually a precursor to first words. "B-b-b-buh buh buh" becomes "bah," and later, "bottle." That is why talking to children is so important—they learn by repetition.

Even scientists can't explain the intricate processes that enable children to mimic sounds, turn sounds into words, give meaning to words, put words together, and finally, use words to make complex thoughts. One thing we do know for sure is that parents don't actually *teach* children how to talk as much as show them. Moreover, like all developmental processes, your child starts getting ready to talk long before that first word pops out of his mouth, which is admittedly very exciting but certainly *not* the first time you're able to communicate with him.

In my first book, I stressed the importance of dialogue: talking *with* infants, instead of *at* them. Your child talks in her native Banguage, using her body and voice to express her needs; you talk in yours—the Queen's English, French, Korean, Spanish, or whatever you speak. You listen, you converse with her, she listens to you. You respond to her and respect her as the separate little being she is. You get to know her, begin to understand Banguage yourself, and therefore become better at meeting her needs. And she begins to learn your language as well. As she approaches her toddler years, the dialogue continues. And now it is time to dispense a liberal dose of T.L.C.

What Is T.L.C.?

Children of all ages need "tender loving care," but I have another meaning in mind that will help you guide your child through the critical years of language development. The letters serve as a reminder of the key elements of communication: **T**alk, **L**isten, **C**larify. Below is a quick summary of T.L.C., followed by detailed descriptions of each component and what it involves. Naturally, the three parts are not separate entities; they work together. In every dialogue with your child, you talk, listen, *and* clarify, even when you don't think about it. My goal is to illuminate the process. (Beginning on page 151, you will find specific suggestions as the various stages of language development unfold.)

T.L.C.: A Bird's-Eye View

Talk about everything and anything. Describe your day, his activities, things in the immediate environment.

Listen attentively to both your child's verbal and nonverbal expressions so that he feels heard and also learns how to be attentive himself.

Clarify by repeating the correct word or expanding on ideas and without scolding or making your child feel that his speech is "wrong."

T—Talk. Speech builds a bridge between parent and toddler. As I pointed out earlier, the magic of language is that parents don't actually have to teach children to speak; they learn when we talk to them. Yes, we help children learn their colors and names of objects and shapes, but the greatest "instruction," even for concepts such as those, takes place organically, in the give-and-take of everyday activities. Research bears out that toddlers whose parents talk to them during mundane activities have larger vocabularies at age three than those who hear less daily conversation. And the effect of integrating conversations throughout the day follows them into school, where they continue to do better than their peers on reading comprehension.

Most of us are aware that there are two kinds of Talk, nonverbal and verbal. *Nonverbal* connections include loving looks, a pat on the hand, a hug, a kiss, hand-holding, affectionately tousling your child's hair during a car ride. Though no words are spoken, your child can feel that you acknowledge his presence, that you're there for him, that you care. *Verbal* expressions, which include "parentese" (see sidebar on page 144), take the form of a constant running dialogue, songs, word games, stories, and books. The trick is to be conscious throughout the day of the importance of talking with your child—when you're walking to the playground, preparing dinner, getting him ready for bed.

You don't have to wait until your child can respond. Even when your little one babbles on, uttering a string of gobbledegook, you can converse with her. Instead of ignoring utterances you don't understand, encourage her by throwing in a few well-placed phrases, such as, "You're absolutely right," or "I totally agree." Just as when she was a young baby you (hopefully) put words to her nonsense syllables. Imagine her in her high chair when she's just finished eating. She says, "Googagababaga," and you respond with a question: "Do you want me to get you down from the table?" Or if she's chattering and it's almost time for her bath, you might say, "Oh, you're ready for your bath?" Such everyday dialogue not only helps translate Banguage into English, it acknowledges your child's earliest attempts at communication and validates her efforts.

Parents who haven't been at this since their child's infancy—many feel "silly" talking to babies—often ask me, "But *what* do I talk about with a toddler?" Talk about his day ("We're going to go to the park"), talk about what you're doing ("I'm cooking our dinner now"), talk about whatever is in his natural environment ("Oh, look at the doggie"). Even if you think it's over his head, believe me, he probably understands more than you realize.

Besides, there's no way to precisely know when a child grasps a new concept. Think of the last time you learned something new. You read, studied, asked questions, went over the material again and again. At some point you said to yourself, *Oh, I get it. This is what it means.* It's the same for your child and his acquisition of language.

You also need to figure out what kind of Talk is most effective with *your* child. Depending on your child's temperament and what else he is working on developmentally, you might have to change your approach. For example, where a Touchy toddler responds well to hugs, a Textbook toddler who is just starting to walk might try to squirm out of your arms, because he's more interested in exploring. Or where an upset Angel toddler might sit still for a logical explanation about why she can't have ice cream before dinner, trying to reason with a Grumpy toddler often results in louder crying. Instead, you might have to distract her. And when dealing with your Spirited child, if you notice that he gets very frustrated when he's trying to make something known, it will only escalate his distress if you pick him up, point to various objects, and say, "You want this? Is this it? Or is it this? You want this?" Instead, put him down and say, "Show me what you want." (By the way, that's a good practice to remember with *any* toddler who is struggling to get a message across.)

Parentese Spoken Here

A type of verbal expression that researchers call "Motherese" or "Parentese" has been proven very beneficial to the development of young children's language skills. Scientists suggest that Parentese may be Nature's way of helping children learn how to talk, because caretakers of all sorts—mothers, fathers, grandparents, even older siblings—tend to automatically lapse into it when they're around young children because it gets their attention. Anyone who speaks Parentese:

- Is playful and animated

- Looks directly into the child's eyes

- Speaks slowly and has a singsong quality to her voice

- Enunciates clearly

- Emphasizes one word in the sentence ("Did you see that *kitty*?")

- Repeats words frequently

By the way, my view of Talk does not include television or computers. A toddler who spends a lot of time in front of the TV might be able to sing a Barney song because he can imitate what he's heard, but the best language instruction takes place during the daily interaction between you and your child. As for computers, which admittedly *are* interactive, no one knows yet how they affect young minds. That doesn't stop the software industry from designing programs for the three-and-under crowd, of course, so it may be tempting. (According to one research firm, the demand for baby titles is the fastest-growing segment in the youth-software market.) I personally don't like to see a child under three sitting at a computer, but I realize that many parents buy into the notion that it prepares children for a technological world and can accelerate learning. I believe that children adapt to technology without our help. Besides, there's no proof that early computer use is beneficial. However, if you have a computer and have bought an educational program, at least sit at the keyboard *with* your child. Also, limit computer time; view it as only one of many learning tools.

That said, I go back to my strongest suggestion: hold a running conversation from the moment your child awakens. You can't talk *too* much to your child (except when she's trying to calm down or fall asleep). It's what young children need; it's how they learn. On pages 146–147, I've given you a "script" taken from my own day with a toddler. It is meant merely to show you the ongoing opportunities for talking. Base your own script on your personal style and what goes on when you spend time with your child.

L—Listen. With a toddler (as with a baby), listening means paying attention to both his words *and* his body language. It will be easier now to listen to your child, as her cues are more obvious. At the same time, her needs are also more complex. She's no longer content to snuggle in your arms these days. She wants to explore, figure out what things are and what she can make them do. Even before she can say the words, pay attention to her signals. If you respond to her cues, she will trust her body's cues (for instance, hunger) and her ability to affect her environment (asking for a toy on a high shelf).

Listen to her talk to herself in the crib or when she's playing independently. Left on their own, children tend to practice new sounds or new words, and later, to talk about what happened in their day. Eavesdropping on your child's conversations with herself will help you figure out where she is developmentally and how much she understands.

Everyday Dialogue

Below are some highlights of a day I spent engaged in conversation with a toddler. The trick is to break down into short sentences what you do each moment of the day.

Morning

Good morning, Viola, my sweet flower! Did you have a good sleep? I missed you. Okay, let's get up. Ooh, you need your nappy changed. You're wet. Can you say "wet"? That's right: wet. Let's change you and make you clean and comfy. Would you like to hold the cream while Tracy changes you? Okay. All done! Let's go say hi to Daddy. Say, "Hi, Daddy." Okay, now we can go eat our breakfast. I'll put you in your chair. Up we go! Let's get your bib. What should we have? Do you want banana or apple? Tracy's making your cereal. This is your spoon. Mmmm . . . isn't it good? All done. Let's fill the dishwasher. Do you want to help? Yes? Okay . . . then you put this in. That's right—in it goes.

Errands

We need more food. We have to go shopping. Let's go for a ride. We'll get your shoes. Let me get your coat on. Here we are in the car. Can you say "car"? Car. Good for you! We're driving to the store. Let me lift you into the cart. Ooh, look at all the vegetables. Do you see the yellow bananas? Can you say "banana"? Banana. Good. Here are some green beans. Let's put them into our cart. Okay, all done. We have lots of food now. Let's go to the checkout counter. Tracy has to

What's more, by modeling attentiveness yourself, you're also teaching your child how to listen. Turn the TV off before attempting a conversation. Make sure that you're not on the phone (see sidebar on page 148) or reading the paper while answering your toddler's questions.

Help your child develop listening skills, too. Turn the radio or stereo on and make a point of saying, "Let's listen to music." Point out the sounds of everyday life: dogs barking, birds chirping, trucks rumbling down the street. This helps him tune in to what his ears are telling him.

Finally, listen to *yourself*, and if necessary, adjust your delivery. The tone and pitch of your voice, the cadence of your speech, your habits of communication can be conducive to your child's pay the nice lady. Do you want to say hi to her? Thank you. Bye-bye! Look at all our bags. We have to put them in the car. Bye-bye, store!

Playing

Come on, now, let's go play. Where's your toy box? Oh, you want to play with your doll? Can you say "doll"? Doll. Good job! What shall we do with the dolly? Shall we put her in the pram? Should we cover her? Let's put a blanket on her to keep her warm. Uh-oh, dolly is crying. Pick her up and hug her. Is dolly all better? Oh, dolly is hungry? What shall we give her? Does dolly want a bottle? Can you say "bottle"? Yes, bottle. Look, dolly is getting tired. Do you want to put her to bed? Let's put her back into the toy box to sleep. Good night, dolly. Can you say "good night"?

Bedtime

Let's get ready for bed. First, choose a book. Oh, you want this one? Good choice. Can you say "book"? That's right: book. Good job. Come and sit on my knee. Let's turn the pages. The name of this book is *Brown Bear*. Can you find the brown bear? Good job. Can you say, "bear"? Let's turn the page. Can you find the bluebird? Good, that's the bluebird. All finished now. Let's put the book away. Night-night, book. Say, "night-night." I'm going to lay you down. But first give Tracy a hug. Mmm, I love you. Here's your blankie. Night-night, God bless. If you need me, just call. See you in the morning.

---

listening—or not. For example, you may be accustomed to bossing people around at work, and you use a similarly sharp tone at home. You may talk too loud or too softly. Or you talk in a monotone. I've seen some parents who state two very different ideas as if they're interchangeable—for instance, "Put this on the table, Molly" and "Don't push, Molly. Gabby was there first." Because everything sounds the same, their children often have trouble discerning meaning and emotions. Even worse, you might be a screamer, which definitely causes toddlers to tune out or cower, neither of which makes for good dialogue.

Finally, I must add that the hectic pace of most modern parents' daily lives makes listening an even greater challenge. Because we're so rushed, we rush our children. We want to come up with solutions before we actually hear what they have to say. Just as a harried parent tends to rely on a prop (see page 255), like a pacifier, to silence a crying baby, busy parents of toddlers are inclined to turn on the TV. The children zone out, and before you know it, they don't know how to listen either. (This is most apparent when they hit adolescence!)

Phone - Attention = Interruption

It drives me crazy (and I have no doubt other adults feel this way, too) to be on the phone with a friend who is simultaneously admonishing her toddler, "Now, Benjamin, don't climb up there." Toddlers (and older kids, too) are opportunists when they don't have your attention, and phone calls, in particular, seem to send a signal: *Mmmm . . . Mum's on the phone—I need her.* My daughter's favorite mischief was getting into the coal scuttle whenever the phone rang.

The truth is, luv, most phone calls can wait until your child is napping or in bed. If the phone rings, don't be afraid to say, "Johnny's up. It's not a good time to talk." If it's absolutely urgent, at least prepare your child by telling him, "Mommy has to talk on the phone now." Give him a favorite toy or activity to keep him busy. Keep the call short and you just might make it through without interruption.

To sum it up, listening is a surefire way to build your child's self-esteem. It is also the foundation for trust, problem solving, and conflict resolution. It is a particularly important skill in today's world, which is full of distractions. By listening, you show your child that you're there—in the moment—aware of him, interested, and concerned.

C—Clarify. This reminds us to take an extra few minutes to confirm and/or expand on what our children say. How toddlers hear things and what they first say are quite different. We need to encourage them to use the right word even when they have their own special way of expressing an idea. When my Sara said, "Boo ta-ta," I'd say, "Oh, you want a bottle of tea?" (In England, we give children diluted tea the way American mums offer juice to their babies.) We also need to help toddlers understand the social aspects of talking, the etiquette of communication. For example, when a child talks too loudly, we say, "This is a time to use our quiet voice." Conscientious parents clarify all day long, often without giving it a thought. At the one-year-old birthday party I mentioned in Chapter Four (pages 92–93), each time our little talker, Amy, said "truh," one of her parents inevitably reinforced it: "Yes, that's a truck."

Whether your toddler makes up her own words, or as Amy is starting to do, has a Banguagese version of a real word, to decipher what she means, listen carefully and look for clues in context. Then venture a guess and clarify. Don't copy *her* word for the object, though. *Repeat the word correctly.* For instance, your child points out the window of the car and says, "dah." Because you've been listening and you see that there's a dog on the sidewalk, you know that she means "dog," so you say, "Yes, honey, that *is* a dog. Good job! Dog. Maybe we'll see another dog soon." In that way, you reinforce and praise. You can also *rephrase her statement as a question*: If she says, "buh," you say, "Do you want your bottle?" Both methods serve to correct a child without implying that she's wrong, or worse, shaming her.

Another form of clarifying is to *expand*: When she calls a dog by name, you add, "Yes, that's a black-and-white dog." When she asks for her bottle, you say, "Are you thirsty?" You're confirming that she has connected

---

Clarifying Nonverbal Emotions

You don't have to wait for your child to say words in order to clarify. Your little one sends the following nonverbal cues to tell you how he feels. He'll then look at you for a response. Use his cues and the context to "read" him and then clarify for him: "I can see that you're [angry, sad, proud of yourself, happy]."

Cues that mean I'm unhappy, unwilling, or angry:

My body is stiff.

I throw my head back.

I throw myself on the floor.

I bang my head.

I bite hard on something, like the sofa.

I cry/scream angrily.

Cues that mean I'm happy and likely to cooperate with you:

I smile and/or laugh.

I coo contentedly.

I clap.

I bounce the top of my body, from the waist up, and jiggle for joy.

---

an appropriate sound to an object, reinforcing her use of language and going a step further, too. Soon, "dah" will become "dog," and "bah" will morph into the more adult-sounding "bottle." And though it may be months or even a year before she understands the meaning of "black," "white," or "thirsty," or can put together longer phrases, such as "black-and-white dog," or "I'm thirsty," you're helping program her little computer for more complex ideas and descriptions.

When a child who is beginning to talk seems to be groping for a word, by all means give it to him. Likewise, when your child is using words that only you understand, it's a good idea to help a long-distance grandparent or a stranger understand ("She's asking for her bottle"). However, when he's old enough to finish his own sentences or make himself understood, don't speak for your child.

And here's something else clarifying does *not* mean: overloading your child with information. Some achievement-oriented parents, eager to expand their child's knowledge, often give too much information. I'm reminded of the old joke in which a three-year-old asks his mum, "Where did I come from?" and the woman quickly launches into a detailed explanation of the birds and the bees. The confused child, not understanding a word his mother has said, retorts, "But Johnny is from Philadelphia."

Second Children/Slow Talkers?

Second children often talk later than firstborns because their siblings clarify *for* them. In our family, Sophie would babble, look at me, and then, if I didn't respond quickly enough, she'd turn to Sara, as if to say, *Doesn't she get what I'm talking about?* Then Sara would interpret: "She wants a bowl of cereal."

As long as Sara continued to decode her sister's baby talk, Sophie never needed to use real words. When I realized that Sophie wasn't learning to talk, I said to Sara, "You're a really good sister [which was true *some* of the time], but you have to let Sophie ask me herself."

Once Sara stopped talking for her, Sophie went from almost no words to full sentences in a very short time. As it turned out, she had acquired more language skills than we ever imagined—she just chose not to use them. (More on sibling relationships in Chapter Nine.)

I've seen countless real-life examples of overexplaining as well. Only recently, I was at a child-friendly restaurant. A mother was standing at the cash register, paying the tab, and her toddler was staring longingly at the candies on display. "Candy," the little boy said. "No, you may not have that candy," said Mum in a very schoolmarmish tone. "There's a lot of dye in those candies, and it might give you a sugar rush." Give me a break! (A better approach would have been to divert him from the candy altogether and to offer him a healthful choice instead: "Look, honey. I have a banana and apple in my bag. Which would you like—banana or apple?" More about this in Chapter Seven.)

T.L.C. Tips
Some Important Reminders

Do . . .
Pay attention to nonverbal as well as verbal signals.
Look your child in the eye when you talk *or* listen.
Talk in short, simple sentences.
Encourage your child to express himself by asking simple, direct questions.
Play word games in which you and your child interact.
Exercise restraint and patience.

Don't . . .
Talk too loudly, too softly, too quickly, or too anything for that matter.
Shame your child for not pronouncing words correctly.
Talk on the phone when your child is talking to you.
Busy yourself with household matters at designated "child times."
Interrupt your child.
Use the TV as a baby-sitter.

Banguage and Beyond

Though "the books" report that most children say their first word by one year, some do, some don't, and some have acquired twenty or more words by then. Some children pass systematically through the stages outlined below, while others (typically, children with older siblings—see the sidebar on page 150) say very little until eighteen months or later, and then suddenly start talking in full sentences, as if they've been saving it up.

Children pick up on parents' anxieties about language—at worst, it can silence them—which is why it's critical to accept your child's particular rate of development. I provide some age-by-age guidelines (see box on page 164), because I know that parents always wonder whether their toddler is within "normal" range. All the same, I can't be too forceful in stressing that *there is tremendous variation in language acquisition.* Let your child be the guide that really matters. His progress can be smooth and continuous or happen in jumps and spurts. Instead of obsessing about what's typical for a particular age, determine for yourself *by observation* what stage he's in.

Surprising Research

Babies love sounds. In experiments where sucking produced a sound, babies *as young as one month old* suck harder in order to keep the sound on. Eventually, they get bored, but when a new sound is produced, they perk up and suck fast again. They can hear even subtle differences in sounds. In fact, unlike adults who can only distinguish sounds in their own language, babies can initially distinguish all sounds, a talent that disappears at around eight months.

He speaks Banguage. Babies actually come into the world with an ability to distinguish sounds (see sidebar). Your child's fascination with sounds is his ticket to the world of language. He babbles incessantly at first. He is not just playing, mind you, he is experimenting, seeing what noises his tongue and lips can make. Interestingly, even as he babbles, he will do so in the tones and cadence of your own language. A babbling nine-month-old in this country will sound "American" compared to, say, a baby from Sweden, who tends to babble in a singsong lilt, very much like his parents' language.

Your child's nonverbal language improves now as well, and you will experience a genuine give-and-take (or tug-of-war) between you. His face is more of an open book—he beams with joy, he wears his accomplishments proudly, he pouts when he's sad, and he tells you with his devilish expression that he's up to no good. He understands a great deal now, far more than he can express. He will be more able to read *your* facial expressions, too. A stern look or a change of tone might be enough to stop him dead in his tracks or will make him even more determined to defy you!

Say, "Where's Enrico?" and he will point to himself. Ask, "Where's Mommy?" and he'll point to you. He can wave bye-bye when someone leaves, shake his head to indicate "no," and open and close his palm, which is Banguagese for "I want that!" When he points at something, it may be to draw your attention to an object or to tell you to give it to him. Either way, give the object a name. "Yes, Enrico, that's a cat." Sometimes, identifying an object is enough to satisfy his insatiable curiosity, and that's all he wants you to do.

Throughout the day, listen to your Banguage-speaking child, respond to his nonverbal cues, talk to him in real words, and also give meaning to the sounds he makes. When he says, "Mm, mmm, mmmm, muh," put a word to his babble by saying, "Mm, mmm, mmmm, muh . . . mommy." This is an early form of clarifying.

Use hand puppets and soft dolls to enhance conversations. Buy nontoxic books with cardboard pages, because he'll want to taste the book as well as listen to the story. When you read to him, name objects ("See the pretty flower?"). After a few weeks with the same book, ask him to show you the pretty flower. He will love the sound of nursery rhymes and word games, too.

You'll be surprised at how quickly he learns, for example, the "How Big?" game. One day, as you ask, "How big is Bobby?" pull his arms overhead and show him the response, "So big!" A short time later, he won't need your help with the answer. Help him learn his body parts, too. Ask "Where's Bobby's nose?" point to it and say, "Here it is," and before you know it, he will point to it, too. My Nan used to play "Cheeky, Cheeky, Chin" with my girls and me when I was a wee lass, pointing to parts of the face and reciting in a rhythmic, singsong voice, "Eye, nose, cheeky, cheeky, chin . . . cheeky, cheeky, chin, nose, eye." Even a game as simple as peekaboo teaches children an important rule of communication: you take turns. And one day your child will grab a blanket and hide his face or dip behind a chair, as if to say, "Come on . . . it's time to play!"

You will have to continually reinforce the meaning of words and ideas, especially if danger is involved. For example, if your child approaches a teapot, you say, "Careful, Tammy. That's hot."

She'll go about her business, but a few moments later might go for the teapot again. It's not that she doesn't understand you; she doesn't remember. Simply say, "Remember ... that's hot." The more a child hears something repeated, the more she'll remember it. In England, children learn that teapots are hot a lot earlier than in America, because they see them every day and all day long!

She can say a few words. Mastering various sounds will make it easier for your toddler to then learn her first few words, which can start to happen as early as seven or eight months, or as late as eighteen. The first sounds babies throughout the world make are the consonants *d*, *m*, *b*, and *g*, and the "ah" vowel; *p*, *h*, *n*, and *w* come a bit later. Babies will combine these first sounds to make "dada-dadada" or "mamamamama."

It's interesting to note that the words for "mother" and "father" are strikingly similar across cultures, too: mama and dada, mati and tati, and so on. Parents naturally assume that their child is finally "calling" them, but Alison Gopnik, Ph.D., Andrew N. Meltzoff, Ph.D., and Patricia K. Kuhl, Ph.D., authors of *The Scientist in the Crib*, raise an interesting point: "It's not entirely clear whether babies say 'mama' and 'dada' because that's what their beloved parents call themselves or whether parents call themselves 'mama' and 'dada' because that's what the babies say anyway."

The authors also point out that research over the last twenty years has shed fascinating light on babies' first words. Babies do, in fact, say "mama" and "dada" (of course, that doesn't really address the issue of which came first!). In addition, they say a lot of words that grown-ups don't notice, perhaps because we don't expect them, words like "gone," and "there," "uh-oh," "more," and "what's that?" Psychologist Gopnik, who did a number of experiments designed to find out what babies mean when they use such words, discovered that they use "gone" to describe objects disappearing, "there" to note success (dropping a block into a bucket, pulling off a sock), and "uh-oh" for failure (spilling something or falling down). I was amused, but not surprised, to learn that British babies say, "oh dear" or "oh bugger" to note their mishaps.

At first, words have idiosyncratic meanings that only your child (and her older siblings—see sidebar, page 150) can decipher (like my Sara's "boo ta-ta"). It may or may not mean what *you* think it means, which is why it's so important for you to watch and listen carefully, so that you can discern the meaning from context. Eventually, though, she will begin to understand the real meaning of the word and apply it to a number of situations. That's some accomplishment. It's one thing to say a word, quite another to use it correctly to name an object and to realize that, despite their obvious difference, two objects can have the same name. Amy, for instance, who learned to say "truh," was also able to recognize that the big, noisy vehicles chugging down the street had the same name as the toys she played with at home. Not surprisingly, a child's grasp of this incredibly complex idea—that words stand for things—often occurs at around the same time that she indulges in imaginary play, which also requires her to understand symbolic representations.

When your child is at this stage, her mind is expanding rapidly. She's like a computer, and you have to help input new data. She is trying to make sense of what her newly acquired vocabulary actually means. It can be frustrating at times, for both you and your child. She may know exactly what she wants and not have the word for it. Help her by naming whatever she points at. Or she may use a word, such as "cup," and you think she wants to *see* the cup on the

---

What? No Dada?

Much to his father's dismay, a toddler will suddenly start to call everyone, from his uncle to the deliveryman, "Dada." Being able to mimic a word doesn't necessarily mean the child understands it. Until he makes that cognitive leap, "Dada," like many first words, will have a special meaning to that child. But it will take a while for the word to stand for the guy who comes home every night and chases his boy around the living room.

Some fathers have a slightly different complaint. As one recently said to me, "Alexandra can say 'Mama,' so why doesn't she say, 'Dada,' too?" As it turned out, Alexandra hardly ever hears the word "Dada" because everyone calls her father by his first name. "And how is your daughter to learn to say *Daddy*," I asked, "unless she hears you called it?"

---

shelf and play with it, but she's actually thirsty. If you think she's just asking for the cup, give it to her. If she protests, say, "Oh, you must be thirsty." Pour some water into it and give her a drink.

Children's earliest words vary, although other favorites include *drink*, *eat*, *kiss*, *kitty*, *bath*, *shoe*, and *juice*—all are objects in toddlers' everyday lives. Sometimes your budding wordsmith will grasp a word immediately. But remember that just as an adult has to hear a word more than once, reread its definition, and see it in use several times in order to really learn it, so do most toddlers need a bit of practice with their first words. My philosophy is the same as with food: Give it four or five times to get her used to it. Don't act frustrated if she doesn't repeat the word; just accept that she's not ready.

Start to name emotions as well. Show her a picture and say, "This little girl looks sad." Or, "Can you see which child is sad?" Ask what makes her sad. Point out that people sometimes cry when they're sad. See if she can make a sad face. (Also see page 222.)

> **TIP:** *React appropriately when your child expresses an emotion. When a parent thinks a toddler's "pout face" is cute and therefore responds by laughing or hugging her because she looks so adorable, that's confusing to the child. Even worse, soon you won't know whether she's pouting to express unhappiness or to get your attention (see also pages 232–233).*

Remember that *everything* is interesting to a toddler; every new experience adds to her learning. Give words to the things and activities throughout the day (see my script on pages 146–147). Speak to her constantly, in short sentences: "Look, there goes a red car." Your child also will be able to respond to simple questions ("Where did you put your teddy bear?") and one-step commands ("Bring your shoes to mommy"). She will feel important and proud when she solves simple problems and executes commands successfully. Give her lots of opportunities in everyday moments: "Bring me your book about the rabbit," "Put the toys you want into the tub," "Pick out a book."

He plays the name game. All of the naming and the conversations you've been having for the last several months will suddenly pay off with a virtual explosion of words. If you've been keeping a diary of first words, you probably listed around twenty or thirty, but now you're likely to lose track as your child seems to point to every-thing *and* name it. Within two or three months your child's vo-cabulary can increase from twenty words to over two hundred (and by the time he's four, to over five thousand). Whatever he doesn't know, he'll ask you to identify. And whereas you once couldn't count on his ability to remember new words, now he will astound you with his recall.

Scientists put forth a number of theories as to what causes the sudden word spurt. Most agree that it signifies a new stage of cog-nitive development and that a child needs to have learned between thirty and fifty words before it happens. Clearly, any child who plays this name game already recognizes that objects in his envi-ronment have names and has learned to ask, "Whassat?" He's also likely to pick up everything he hears, and I mean *everything*. Watch what you say, lest you want to hear your little darling exclaim, "Dammit!" (or worse) instead of "uh-oh!" I, who often exclaimed "Jesus Christ!" when I was frustrated, had no idea that Sara even noticed. One day in the supermarket, a woman in front of us dropped a bottle of bleach, and as it crashed onto the floor, Sara chimed in with a very loud, "Jesus Christ!" I wanted to crawl under the counter.

Your child will probably start putting words together in simple, two-word sentences: "Mommy, up," "Give cookie," "Daddy bye-bye." You might even hear him talking to himself while he's engaged in play or right before bedtime, as he's falling asleep. We take language for granted because it so effortlessly slips out of our mouths. But think for a moment what a feat this is for your toddler—that he knows enough not only to use more than one word at a time, but to put the words into the right order and to use them to process his thoughts out loud.

> **TIP:** *Sometimes children go through an echolalia stage—incessant copying of whatever they hear. Instead of answering a question*

such as, "Do you want Cheerios or Cocoa Puffs?" they repeat, "Cheerios or Cocoa Puffs." Although I certainly believe in encouraging children to speak, in this case, a better approach would be to simply ask your child to point to the one he wants.

Many children now begin to categorize objects as well. For example, if you put a group of toys in front of them and ask them to put some in your right hand and some in your left, they will figure some way to sort them out—all the cars in one pile, all the dolls in another. And whereas your toddler might have once called all four-legged animals "doggies," he now realizes that there are also "cows" and "sheep" and "cats," too. A good game to reinforce this understanding is to ask him to name all the animals he knows, or all the animals that live in the zoo or on a farm.

Despite the torrent of words that pours out of your child's mouth, this can be a frustrating time as well. He may have trouble pronouncing certain words. He may get stuck in midconversation and not know what to call something. He will ask lots of questions. And one of his favorite words will be "No!"

> **TIP:** *"No!" is not necessarily a sign that your toddler is obstinate. In fact, he might not even know what it means. Young children often say "no" because it's a word they hear so often. Therefore, one way to cut down on this seeming negativity is to watch your own cascade of nos. Another is to make sure you talk and listen to your child and give him the attention he needs.*

This is the time to start teaching manners. When she asks for something, remind her, "Say please." Say "please" *for* her at first. As you hand the object to her, say "thank you" on her behalf as well. Do this fifty times a day, repeating the same sequence, and it will easily become part of her social discourse.

> **TIP:** *If you've taught your toddler to say, "Excuse me," when she interrupts a conversation, when she does it, don't tell her, "Wait a minute until I finish." First of all, she doesn't know what "a*

minute" means. Second, you're sending a mixed message. After all, she followed your rule and then you changed it by asking her to wait. Instead, praise her for being polite and listen to what she has to say. The other adult to whom you're talking will understand.

At this stage, when your child is beginning to expand his vocabulary and express ever more complicated ideas, "clarifying" is vitally important. Though I never suggest sitting down to "teach" a child, try to structure playtime so that he has opportunities to manipulate shapes and work with colors. Don't start quizzing him on his colors; rather, point them out casually—the yellow banana, the red car. Color matching games are good, too. Give him a red shirt and say, "Can you find some red socks to go with it?" Children can match colors before they can name them. Also introduce concepts like "soft" and "hard," "flat" and "round," "inside" and "outside." Using such words helps your toddler see that objects have particular qualities.

He will still enjoy playing certain "baby" games and reciting nursery rhymes that date back to when he was younger, but now he understands so much more. He will start to repeat them, even recite them on his own. He loves rhythm and repetition. Children also adore music and learn words of songs fairly easily. It's even better when there are gestures to accompany the words—kids

---

Curling Up with a Good Book (and a Grateful Toddler)

Even babies love to "read." Start a child early, and books will become her friends. Don't just read books, change your tone and act out the characters and story. Talk about them, too. The best kind for children under three have:

A simple story line: Younger children like to identify objects, but as they get older, they can follow the sequence of a simple story.

Durability: Especially for children under fifteen months, make sure the print is nontoxic and the pages cardboard.

Good illustrations: Bright colors and clear, realistic illustrations are best for young children; as they get older, they can handle fantasy creatures.

love to mimic adult motions as well. Good choices include: "Wheels on the Bus," "Eensy-Weensy [Itsy-Bitsy] Spider," and "I'm a Little Teapot" (a favorite in my country).

Counting games are great, too, and will help improve your child's understanding of numbers. Recite, "One, Two, Buckle My Shoe," or the "Five Little Monkeys" poem: "Five little monkeys jumping on the bed, one fell off and bumped his head, four little monkeys jumping on the bed . . ." and so on.

Take extra care to tune in to your child now. As always, let him take the lead. Talk about things he's interested in—what he looks at and what he plays with. Words associated with his daily routines are learned first. Also ask him questions that help him develop his memory and think about things in the past and future ("Didn't we have fun in the park yesterday?" "Grandma is coming to visit to-morrow. What should we cook for her?"). Most important, by engaging happily in conversation, you give your child the sense that communication is a wonderful and valuable skill.

She's a full-fledged talker. Sometime between two and three, your child will know scores of words and talk in three- and four-word sentences. She may make many grammatical errors, saying "childs" instead of "children," or "I felled down" instead of "I fell," but don't worry: you're not her English teacher. She will learn the correct form more by imitation than by your correcting her. By this time she has grasped the importance of language as a social tool, as a means of expressing herself and of getting her way. She can use words, play with them, delight in them. Reading, reciting poems, singing songs are adored pastimes and will continue to hone her language skills. Her pretend play becomes more involved now, as she weaves narratives into her actions. Give her dress-up clothes and attend her tea parties. Provide lots of different kinds of props, in fact, like a doctor's stethoscope, a briefcase, and other items grown-ups use. You can give her crayons and she will draw with them or tell you she's "writing." In reality, her scribbling *will* look more like writing now than it did a few months ago.

Some young children begin to enjoy alphabet books at this age, but don't sit down and try to *make* your child learn her letters. Remember our little H.E.L.P. mantra: hold back until *she* shows an interest in learning. The most important thing is not to have her identify letters visually, but to recognize the sounds they make. You can make a game out of it: "Let's look for things that start with the letter *B*. Buh, buh, buh . . . I see . . . a ball! What do you see?"

By now, if you've included books as part of her bedtime ritual (and if not, why haven't you?), your child will relish reading. Don't be surprised if she asks for the same one every night for many months. If you try to skip a few pages, she'll pounce on you: "No, that's not the way it goes. Next comes the part about the chicken!" In time, she might even inform you that she's going to "read" it to you. And sure enough, she has memorized every page.

To Talk or Not to Talk

Children are an endless delight as they begin to acquire language—and sometimes, as my story about Sara in the supermarket illustrates, a source of deep embarrassment. Toddlers who do best have parents who give them lots of T.L.C.—they talk, listen, and clarify. They spend time with them. They don't talk baby talk—otherwise, their toddler learns how to *mis*pronounce words. They are patient, allowing the child to develop at whatever rate is comfortable for her. And as thrilled as they are with their child's progress, they don't make her perform like a trained seal ("Oh, sing your new song for Auntie Mabel").

As the chart on page 164 indicates, it's important to be aware of red flags that might indicate hearing loss or a developmental delay. But there are also instances in which there is nothing organically wrong with a child, and yet he or she doesn't begin to talk on schedule. Recently, Brett, a very astute working mother, told me of such an experience. Jerome, then fifteen months old, wasn't trying to form words as most of his peers were. Brett wasn't alarmed; she knew that there are huge variations in the way children develop. All the same, her gut told her something was "wrong." The mystery was solved when Brett happened to come home early one day from work. Knowing that this was the time Jerome and his nanny were usually at the park, Brett drove there directly from the office.

Observing the interaction between her little boy and his loving and very attentive caretaker, Brett realized what was missing. The nanny played with Jerome but didn't talk to him very much. And when she did, it was very quietly and in monosyllables. As much as Brett loved the nanny, she knew she had to find someone else who would engage in animated conversation with her son. Within days, literally *days*, after the new nanny began spending time with Jerome, he quickly started to form words.

Are Two Languages Better than One?

I'm often asked about foreign languages and whether it's a good idea to expose children to more than one. If two languages are spoken in your home, why not? Although sometimes language development is delayed initially, studies indicate that bilingual children are better at cognitive tasks later on. Between ages one and four, children are most receptive to learning more than one language. If they're spoken to in a grammatically correct fashion, they can learn the two simultaneously and will be fluent by age three. So if you and your partner have different native tongues, each should speak in his or her own language. And if you have a nanny who doesn't speak English well, it's better for her to talk in her mother tongue as well.

The moral of this story is to make sure not only that you have an ongoing dialogue with your child, but also that other adults in her life do the same. If you wonder whether your baby-sitter or nanny is talking to your child, or whether she's getting enough conversation at day care, it's simple enough to find out. Have the sitter or nanny come while you're there and observe. I don't believe in so-called nanny-cams, though. It sends a bad message to "spy" on the person to whom you entrust the care of your child. Besides, I believe one has to be present and involved to observe. Do the same with day care. One couple, who had recently enrolled their child in day care, went to the center three days a week until they were satisfied with the level of care and conversation. In either situation, be truthful with the care provider: "I just want to make sure that you and Katie talk a lot." It's your right to insist. Indeed, not talking to a child is like not feeding him. One starves the body, the other starves the brain.

I've also seen instances in households where Mum talks to the child incessantly and Dad says he "doesn't know how." One woman told me that when her husband complained, "Charlie doesn't like me," she said, "That's because you don't talk to him. How else are you two going to get to know each other?" Dad's reply was, "Well, I'm not much of a talker." Relating the story to me, his wife admitted, "It's true. I talk for both of us."

As far as I'm concerned, that's unacceptable. Dad, you need to start talking to your child long before you can play touch football with him. Take over the book-reading routine at night. A book is a great conversation starter. So don't just read it; talk about it. At other times of the day, talk about whatever you do. Let's say you're planning to wash the car on a Saturday morning. Say, "Billy, look, I'm getting ready to wash the car. See? I'm putting soap in the bucket. Now I'm filling it with water. Do you want to feel the water? Let's put you in your stroller so you can watch. See Daddy wash the car? See all the soap suds? Look at the water splash. It's cold." And so on and so on. No matter what the subject—work, chores in the garden, the Knicks game—talk about what happened, what's happening now, and what will happen next. The more you talk, the more natural it will feel and the easier it will be.

As I've repeated throughout this chapter, *everyone* dealing with a budding talker must keep that conversation flowing. As the *From Neurons to Neighborhoods* (see page 16) report concludes: "The more children are talked to, the more they themselves talk and the more elaborate that talk becomes." Before you know it, your little foreign exchange student will be so fluent that her Banguage will have become a distant memory. As you'll see in the next chapter, your child is going to need these language skills as she ventures forth from the security of her family into the real world.

Speech Development: What to Look For

I present this chart because I know parents like to gauge where their children are. However, there are tremendous developmental variations from child to child; I caution you to use these as *broad guidelines* only. Remember, too, that many so-called late talkers usually catch up by age three.

Age	Speech Milestones	Red Flags
8–12 months	Although some children begin to say "mama" or "dada" as young as 7 or 8 months, by a year most can attach these terms to the right person. They can also respond to one-step commands ("Please, give it to me.").	Child does not respond to her name; she doesn't babble either long or short groups of sounds, does not look at people who talk to her, or is not pointing at or making sounds to get what she wants.
12–18 months	As first words, child says simple nouns ("dog," "baby"), the names of special people, and a few action words or phrases ("up," "go"); may be able to follow one- or two-step commands ("Go to the living room and get your toy.").	Child does not say a word or two, even unclearly.
18–24 months	Child may be able to say as many as ten different words, as well as a great deal of gibberish.	Child does not say more than a few words clearly; by twenty months cannot follow simple request ("Come to Mummy"); does not respond to simple questions with a "yes" or "no."
24–36 months	Child has a word for almost everything; combines words into sentences to express thoughts and feelings; although grammar may be less than perfect, vocabulary is quite extensive; child can carry on actual conversations with adult.	Child uses fewer than fifty words and produces no word combinations; can't understand different meanings (up/down) or follow two-step commands; doesn't notice environmental sounds, like a car horn.

CHAPTER SIX

The Real World: Helping Your Child Rehearse Life Skills

> Over the years, I have come to
> appreciate the impact my early
> experience has had on how I
> understand and function in the world.
>
> —Nancy Napier, Ph.D.,
> *Sacred Practices for Conscious Living*

Help-Me/Let-Me-Go!

• Ten-month-old Peggy wails in her father's arms. It's her mother's first day back to work, and Peggy, who loves her dad, is nevertheless bereft as Mum walks out the door. She's not sure she'll ever see her again.

• Fifteen-month-old Gary is awed as he watches a waitress pour water into glasses on the table. It's his first time at a restaurant. When he reaches for the glass closest to him, his mother tries to help him, but he balks, "No!"

• Two-year-old Julie stands in the doorway of a large room, peering in at children running about, jumping on mats, throwing huge balls. It is her first day at a kiddie exercise class. She wants to join in but holds her mother's hand tightly instead.

• One-year-old Dirk toddles onto the concrete and looks around for a moment. It is his first trip to the playground. He eyes the swing set, the jungle gym, and the seesaw, but only lets go of his nanny's hand when he spots the sandbox, because it's like the one in his own backyard.

• It's eighteen-month-old Allie's first time at the petting zoo. She can say, "baa-baa" when she sees a picture of a baby lamb and recognizes that this creature is the one in her favorite book. Still, she doesn't quite know whether to cry or to dare and touch it.

Toddlerhood, more than any of life's other passages, is marked by an unprecedented number of firsts, many of which we've already covered—first step, first word, first bite of finger food, first pee in the toilet. But those firsts all happen within the safe, familiar walls of home. The ones described above occur in the real world and require more grown-up behavior. Understandably, toddlers often greet these firsts with ambivalence. It's what I call the "help-me/let-me-go" dilemma: They want to explore, but they also want to know that the familiar is never far behind. They want independence, but they also want to know that a parent is right there, every scary step of the way.

The timing is what makes toddlerhood so challenging. Just as your child develops the intellectual capability to grasp that you—the most indispensable figure in his life—can actually leave him, he develops the physical capacity to venture out on his own. He wants to move away from you . . . then again, maybe he doesn't. When he was a baby, you answered every call quickly and automatically (I hope). But now he has to bear up under your absence at times and soothe himself. He has to make a monumental shift from being the center of the universe to being part of a group and having empathy. The big cruel world out there expects him to have patience and control, to share and take turns. Horrors!

If you can't imagine your little one taking such bold steps away from you and toward more civilized behavior, be assured, ducky, it's not going to happen overnight. Social development (the ability to interact in a variety of new experiences and with people outside the family) and emotional development (the ability to exhibit self-control in the face of these challenges and to self-soothe when things don't go your way) proceed slowly and at your child's unique pace. And while these monumental changes are happening, the help-me/let-me-go struggle can be trying for toddler and parent alike.

Of course, some children are more socially competent than others. Some are better at self-soothing. Researchers suspect that both personality and language development are important factors—obviously, if you have a mellow child who can ask for what she wants and tell you how she feels, she'll have an easier time separating from you, braving new situations, and being part of a group. But no matter what your child's temperament, how well she speaks, or what coping skills she has acquired on her own, emotional and social skills are hard-won by most toddlers. Just as they don't come into the world knowing how to use a spoon or use the potty, they don't come in with a desire to share or knowing how to control their baser instincts and calm themselves when the going gets rough. We have to direct them.

Try This at Home:
Rehearsals for Change

Everything about being a toddler is preparation for a more grown-up life. Every new situation and new relationship is a lesson. If we expect young children to cope in the real world, we have to give them the tools to do it and lots of practice as well. That doesn't mean you rush out and enroll your child in swimming lessons in order to get him ready for his first day at the beach club. Nor do you put him in a kiddie class to teach him social skills. Rather, you start the lessons at home. For each challenge your child will meet, you must plan what I call a *rehearsal for change*.

Rehearsals for Change

A relationship *or* a situation can be a rehearsal for change—a less intimidating, more manageable context that gives your child the practice and skills he needs to handle comparable circumstances in the real world.

Relationship with you → With other adults → With friends
Family dinner → Restaurant
Backyard play → Parks, playgrounds
Bath and water play at home → Pool, beach
Having pet at home → Petting and other zoos
Car rides and quick errands → Shopping
Short trip and sleep at grandparents' → Long trip and hotel
Play date → Play group → Toddler class → Preschool

A rehearsal is a dry run, a time when actors try out the script and perfect their moves. What I define as a rehearsal for change is pretty much the same thing: a way of giving your child practice in the skills she needs to handle various situations in the real world by encouraging her to try them out at home first. A rehearsal for change can prepare your child for relationships, activities—or both. Toddlers who can experiment with more adult behaviors in the safe, familiar, and controlled arms of the family (eating at a table, sharing, being kind to a pet) tend to have an easier time with unfamiliar experiences outside the house, new people, travel, and transitions. In the box on page 168 are several examples; you can probably think of others.

To give your child the practice she needs, see yourself as a director, scheduling and overseeing the various rehearsals. The key to a successful production—her cooperation and willingness to learn—is founded on the bond between the two of you. In other words, if your little one feels a secure attachment to you, she will be willing to show up for rehearsals, learn the script, try out new skills, and develop her talents. It's an interesting paradox: the more she feels you're there for her, the easier it will be for her to try on a new, more independent persona. And if you give her opportunities to practice difficult emotional moments and rehearse *with* you at first, she gets to see that she is competent and can manage herself, initially with you by her side, and finally, on her own.

After all, you are the center of your toddler's universe. It's normal for her to run to you when she's tired, hide her face in your lap when a situation feels too hard, look at you to gauge your reaction, or be upset when you leave. It all goes with the territory of toddlerhood. But each time she sees that you *are* there for her and that you *do* come back when you leave, it promotes her trust not only in you, but in the world. *Oh, Mummy said she'd be back—she came back, so I guess the world is a pretty good place.*

> "A child may not care who cuts his hair or takes his money at the toy store, but he cares a great deal about who is holding her when she is unsure, comforts her when she is hurt, and shares special moments in her life."
>
> —*From Neurons to Neighborhoods*
> (see page 16 for source)

Granted, there will be missed cues and forgotten lines. But each rehearsal will move your child toward greater competence. In the balance of this chapter, I offer concrete examples that will help you schedule and direct rehearsals for change that can help prepare your child for three important types of firsts:

FIRST FEARS: Practicing self-soothing when faced with strong emotions.

FIRST FORAYS: Practicing public behavior in restaurants and other new experiences.

FIRST FRIENDSHIPS: Practicing social skills in relationships with peers.

No Matter What the Situation
Successful rehearsals for change . . .

Involve preparation and forethought
Are realistic, taking into consideration what *the child* can handle
Happen when children are not tired or cranky
Introduce new ideas and skills slowly
Build gradually in duration or intensity
Acknowledge the child's feelings
Show children by adults' example the way they're expected to behave
End the activity or leave the premises, if possible, before a child gets frustrated or
    out of control

First Fears: Identifying Emotions and Practicing Self-Soothing Behaviors

Almost all toddlers have fears of some sort—of separation, of objects or animals, of other adults and children. Because it's impossible to pinpoint exactly what makes a child apprehensive—her temperament, a trauma, the influence of an adult or another child, something she heard or saw—it's hard to tease out the reasons for a particular emotional reaction. The best we can do as parents, therefore, is to help our children acknowledge these feelings, let them know it's okay to talk about them, and encourage them to learn how to soothe themselves. Indeed, one of the benchmarks of a toddler's growing independence is his ability to handle new challenges, and when overwhelmed by them, to manage his emotions.

Encourage your child to rehearse a full range of emotions. If you try to make your kid happy all the time at home, he's in for a shock when he hits the icy reality of the real world. Therefore, you need to allow emotional rehearsals, taking time to help your child identify and address *all* feelings, including those we tend to label "negative," such as sadness and disappointment. How else will he learn to cope with future hurts and the inevitable frustrations that are part of childhood? Equally important, when children don't feel comfortable expressing such feelings, they never learn to be in charge of their emotions—to feel them, withstand them, and let them pass. (See pages 156 and 222 about naming emotions.)

Rule of Emotional Behavior
To learn how to be in charge of their own emotions and to soothe themselves, children need to experience *all* feelings, even those that *you* may find it hard to witness, like sadness, frustration, disappointment, and fear.

Remember that your child looks to you for guidance, even when you're not consciously giving it. To a little one who sees you as the be-all and end-all of her existence, your emotions are her business. Babies of depressed mothers, for instance, often pick up their mother's affect and look sad themselves. And toddlers can "catch" fear and anxiety from their elders as well. In Cheryl's case, for instance, she insisted, "Kevin cries fearfully whenever my mother-in-law tries to hold him."

However, after being in Cheryl's home for a while and observing Kevin, I saw that her little boy was more than willing to allow *me* to hold him, so I suspected that there was more to the story. Cheryl, a successful clothing designer who had tried to get pregnant for several years, had Kevin when she was forty. Now he was her main focus. As he played happily on the floor, I commended her. "Kevin is engaging and curious, and yes, he's a bit shy. But given a few minutes, he seems to warm up to strangers." I finally asked her, "Do you think *you* might feel uncomfortable when your child is happy in someone else's arms? Could he be picking up *your* anxiety?" She cried; obviously I had hit a nerve. Cheryl's mother had died of cancer six months earlier. She was still grieving but didn't want to admit it. She *said* she'd love to get out of the house more, which she could do if Mum-in-law looked after Kevin, but she obviously was ambivalent.

I suggested a series of rehearsals. Cheryl could ask her mother-in-law to come along on play dates so that Kevin could get used to seeing the woman in everyday situations. And the next time her mother-in-law comes to visit, I said, "Sit *with* her on the couch. Put Kevin between the two of you. Don't make a big deal of it, but gradually move to the other side of the room. Then leave the room for increasingly longer periods." A toddler might have a shy nature; he may need to take his time getting used to people. But he also has to know it's okay with Mum.

In all situations, at home or on outings, children take their emotional cues from us, which is why parents are so important *and* influential. A child as young as six or seven months will move toward something and glance back at her mother as if to say, "Is this okay?" and a stern look can deter her. Psychologists call this *social referencing* and have done some fascinating studies to indicate its power. In one, mothers were directed to look into two empty boxes, one red, one green. Looking inside the red one, they said in a monotone, "Oh." Looking into the green box, they exclaimed, "Oh!" in a very upbeat excited voice. Invariably when asked which box he or she would prefer, almost every child chose the green box.

Be there for your child. Although directors don't get onstage with actors, they stand by in the wings in case there's a problem. However, too often scenes are played out like this one. A mother walks into a group and plops her child on the floor. Her little one immediately grabs her leg, and she all but shoos him away: "You're all right, Jonah—now off you tootle." Meanwhile, the child is absolutely freaking out. The mother makes excuses: "Oh, he's tired," "He hasn't had his nap," or "I just got him out of bed."

When he continues to cry, she finally looks at me, embarrassed and confused, desperate for advice. "Get down on the floor *with* your child at first," I urge her. "If you act like you're there for him, you can get up . . . but do it gradually." Even worse are mothers who sneak away from their children. When the little one turns around, he panics because Mum is not where he left her. Can you blame him?

Your style of parenting can also affect your child's willingness to go forth. Heed the power of social referencing and pay attention to the messages you send your child. Are you encouraging him to explore or unwittingly holding him back? Are you letting him know that you believe in him, that you know he's capable of managing his emotions?

Think back to the three mothers you met in Chapter Two (pages 62–64). As they observe their children in a play group, each sends a completely different message to her child. When little Alicia trips over a toy and falls down, she looks at her mum (Dorrie, the Controller) with a somewhat confused expression that says, "Am I hurt?" Dorrie barely looks up. "You're okay," she says sternly. Maybe Dorrie is trying to "toughen her up," a statement she makes frequently to the other mums. But Alicia appears crestfallen; the child thinks she's done something wrong. Exchanges like this negate Alicia's feelings; in time she may not trust her own perceptions, and instead, become dependent on others' opinions.

Clarice (the Enabler) is always leaning in toward Elliott. Even when he is playing contentedly, she wears a slightly anxious look on her face. The nonverbal message she sends to her son is entirely different from Dorrie's: *You'd better stay by my side; I'm not so sure that you're okay.* In time, Clarice's hovering may suppress Elliott's desire to explore. Not trusting his abilities, he might hang back instead.

In stark contrast, Sari (the HELPing parent) is calm and composed around her son. When Damian looks at her, she smiles reassuringly, but goes on talking, letting Damian know that she thinks he's doing fine. When he falls, she quickly assesses his reaction but doesn't rush in. And sure enough, he gets up on his own—he's fine. When he gets into a hassle with either of the other children, she lets him work it out, unless he starts hitting or biting or is the victim of aggression himself.

While a Controller like Dorrie tends to push her toddler too hard, and an Enabler like Clarice tends to overprotect, a HELPer like Sari maintains that delicate balance between supporting her child's growing independence and, at the same time, assuring him that she's there if he needs her. As a result, I suspect that Damian will turn out to be the kind of child who trusts his inner cues and relies on his own judgment, and therefore, can solve problems confidently.

Help your child manage her emotions when she doesn't seem able to. Temperament affects your child's emotional and social functioning, but it's not a life sentence. Even though some children have more trouble with impulse control than others, some are inherently more shy, and some have a naturally gritty disposition that doesn't inspire them to cooperate with others, *parents' intervention makes a difference.* One strategy is to give your toddler reality checks about his behavior without trying to change who he is. Think of it this way: if you were coaching the drama club, you wouldn't question the wisdom of correcting a player's acting or showing him a better way to move across the stage. It's the same with emotional and social coaching. If you have a Touchy child, for instance, and a playmate overwhelms him, you say, "I know it takes some time for you to get used to being at Juan's house, so stay with Mummy until you're ready to play." If you have a Spirited child who hits you to get your attention, you say, "Ouch! That hurts. I know you're excited, Lee, but you may not hit Mummy." If your Grumpy toddler is pulling impatiently on your leg, and you are still eating dinner, say, "I know it's hard for you to be patient, but Mummy hasn't finished her meal yet. When I finish I'll come and play with you." Such corrective exchanges at home will serve your child well in the real world. (I will go into coaching in greater detail in the next chapter.)

Applaud her for self-soothing. When your little one feels scared, tired, overwhelmed, abandoned (for that is what it truly feels like to a one-year-old when you say, "Bye-bye!"), if she naturally turns to an object that signifies comfort or resorts to a behavior that calms her down, heave a sigh of relief. She has taken a giant step toward emotional independence. Maybe it's a ratty old teddy bear or another type of stuffed animal, a tattered, silky piece of cloth, or a cardigan that smells like you. Or perhaps she sucks her thumb, rolls or bangs her head, rocks, or twirls her hair before falling asleep. She might repeat mantra-type songs or babble nonsense syllables, play with her feet, fingers, or eyelashes (my Sophie flicked hers from side to side 'til she had none left!), pick her nose, or even masturbate. All qualify as self-soothing behaviors.

To parents' amazement, children sometimes adopt an idiosyncratic or surprising "cuddle" object, like a plastic block or toy car. Or they adopt an odd calming behavior—one little boy I know gets on all fours and rubs the top of his head on the carpet or mattress. (Curious, I tried it myself once, and it produced a little buzzing sensation in my head.) A child also might employ a dual strategy—suck a thumb *and* twirl hair. In some families, each child finds a different totem. In others, it seems as if even unique self-soothing strategies are genetic. My coauthor's daughter, Jennifer, picked fuzz from a favorite stuffed Snoopy and caressed her top lip with it while sucking her index finger. Her younger brother, Jeremy, who came along three and a half years later, executed exactly the same fuzz maneuver.

What's *Your* Security Blanket?

Before you turn your nose up at that smelly old thing your child adores, think about it. Though we adults don't walk around with anything as obvious as a "binkie" or a stuffed animal, we continue to employ security objects throughout our adult lives. I, for example, always have a tote bag with me containing pictures of my Nan and my children, a few cosmetic items for last-minute freshening up, and tampons . . . just in case. When I leave my bag behind, I feel a bit lost. I don't think it's any coincidence that as a toddler my Nan introduced the idea, giving me a little pink bag to tote about that had my favorite toys and keepsakes in it. I'm sure you have your own transitional object, but you may call it a lucky charm, or a practice such as morning prayer, that makes you more confident to greet the day.

Transitional objects and behaviors are not only normal, they're beneficial. When tired or upset, your child can then retrieve the object or indulge in the behavior, rather than always depending on a source of solace outside herself. Out in the real world, having your "blankie" is like having a best friend. (If your toddler is dependent on a "prop" to calm her down—an object or action supplied and controlled by *someone else*, such as a pacifier, Mum's breast, or Dad's rocking or walking her—you might need to help her develop a *self*-soothing strategy instead; see pages 266–267 for ways of introducing a transitional object when children are eight months or older.)

First Forays:
Practicing Public Behavior

Parents love to take their children on outings. Rehearsals for change increase the odds that these will be pleasant experiences. The trick is to anticipate what will happen in the various settings, analyze what preparation your child will need to handle the situation, and then practice the necessary skills at home first. (Also reread the tips on page 170 as a reminder of what a successful rehearsal for change involves.)

Rule of Public Behavior

Don't bite off more than your child can chew. If a particular setting proves too much, leave.

Following are specific suggestions for the most common types of family outings. You'll notice that Disneyland and other extravagant entertainment venues are excluded. One of the cardinal rules is to choose activities that are appropriate for your child. Even the most stalwart and well-adjusted toddler can be scared by amusement parks. I'm not surprised that half the toddlers I know have been terrified by Mickey Mouse. Can you imagine what it's like to be only a few feet tall and to see that big, black plastic head coming at you?

Family dinner ➔ *Restaurants.* Your family dinner ritual rehearses your child for what she'll encounter in a restaurant. As you know if you read the earlier chapters, I believe toddlers should sit at the table with everyone else in the family at least a few times a week (pages 77–79 and 116–118). Most restaurants have high chairs or booster seats, but you can't expect a child to feel comfortable if she hasn't sat in one at home. After your little one has had at least two months' practice eating at the table with you, take her to her first restaurant outing as a toddler. Even if she dined out with you when she was a baby, she's not necessarily prepared. Indeed, many parents are shocked at their toddler's restaurant behavior: "She used to be so good when we ate out, and now it's a nightmare to take her." Be realistic; look at how your child acts at your own dinner table, and you'll have some indication of what you can expect. How long does she usually sit in her high chair? Does she get upset or distracted easily? Is she a picky eater? Fussy about trying new foods? Is she prone to mealtime tantrums?

Even if your child is a good eater and well-behaved at home, on your first dining-out excursion, don't ask her to sit through a full meal. And don't make a big deal about "going to a restaurant"— your child will pick up on your anxiety and might experience stage fright. Instead, casually stop into a coffee shop that you pass on your Saturday morning walk or after an errand (as long as the stop doesn't coincide with nap time). Bring with you a small toy that your child can take into the restaurant, or give him a single spoon—it's easier than fighting when he wants to grab *all* the silverware. Some restaurants have coloring books, which is great. Have only a bagel and coffee and spend no more than fifteen to twenty minutes. After four or five of these limited restaurant excursions, try breakfast. But be prepared to leave early if that proves too much for your child. Go back to having coffee and bagels for a while.

Remember that no matter how well or how often you rehearse, toddlers have a limited attention span—even the best behaved can't sit for more than forty-five minutes to an hour. Bear in mind, too, that your toddler doesn't yet understand the concept of waiting. When you eat at home, you usually make dinner first and then call everyone to the table. Therefore, he may not be good at just sitting there after you order. Ask your waiter how long it will take for the food to come. If it's going to be more than twenty-five minutes, leave, or elect one parent to take the child outside until the food arrives. If during the meal your child gets restless, instead of trying to cajole him, which usually escalates a child's agitation, use your common sense. Step outside with the child, and let your partner pay the bill.

Stop going to restaurants for a month if the experience repeatedly ends in disaster. In any case, though, avoid fancy restaurants. Most children simply can't handle that kind of setting. Check out a restaurant before you go there, even if it's just to call ahead. Tell the proprietor honestly, "I'm bringing a toddler in. Do you cater to children? Do you have high chairs or booster seats? Can we sit somewhere where we're not likely to disturb other people?" In Britain, almost every pub has a play area, and some even have yards outside. I've noticed that at restaurants that welcome children in the States, there's often a waiting area where toddlers can walk around. Beware of an exclusive diet of family theme restaurants, though. They certainly welcome children, but many of them also tolerate noisy chaos. When you then bring your toddler to a more adult-oriented establishment, you can't blame him for assuming that shouting and running around are appropriate restaurant behaviors.

Backyard play ➜ *Parks, playgrounds.* Being at a park or playground develops gross motor skills, like climbing, throwing, running, sliding, balancing, swinging, and spinning. To gauge your toddler's physical readiness, start by looking in your own backyard, so to speak. If you own a swing set and other paraphernalia, or if you've been taking him to a playground or park since he was a wee lad, his first visit may not be a big deal. If not, the equipment can be overwhelming at first. Don't just plop your child on a swing or a seesaw. Let him explore and examine. He might prefer to just watch other children for a while or he might rush to climb the slide. Either way, wait until *he* makes the first move. In the meantime, have a ball on hand because it's familiar and a blanket if it's a nice day, so you can sit on the lawn and at least have an enjoyable snack and a drink. If, after a few trips, he's still a bit skittish about getting involved, that's okay. He's just not ready. Try again in a month.

Playgrounds and parks give toddlers an opportunity to interact with other children. The experience will help your child learn what it means to share, to wait one's turn, to be considerate of others (say, by not throwing sand). However, keep a close eye on him and on the other kids as well. This setting is different from and more difficult than a play date, where there's only one other child, or even a play group where the children are handpicked. Set firm boundaries. If your child gets overexuberant and becomes aggressive, go home. You need to help him manage his emotions until he can control them on his own. Be prepared for bumps and scrapes, too. Tuck a first-aid kit into your stroller or back pack.

Bath and water play at home ➜ *Pool, beach.* Most children like the water, but even toddlers who love to play in water may not like a pool, a lake, or the ocean. A tub or child-sized backyard basin is a lot tamer than a huge body of water (to a small child, even a pool is gigantic). Particularly if your child is less than enthusiastic about her bath, or is the type who doesn't like to muck around in water (believe me, there *are* fastidious toddlers), don't plan a six-hour water excursion until you find out how she takes to the new setting. Now, I realize that might not be feasible. Perhaps it's a long drive to the nearest water park or beach, and it's not worth it to go for an hour. If that's the case, at least have a Plan B— an alternate place you can visit in the area.

The Dos and Don'ts of Ouch!

Whether the scene is a playground, park, pool, or grassy knoll, at some point or another, your child is going to take a tumble.

Don't rush in—that will probably scare him even more.

Do calmly weigh the situation to assess if he's hurt without showing alarm.

Don't say, "You're okay" or "That didn't hurt." It's not respectful to negate his feelings.

Do say, "Ouch, that must have hurt. Let me hold you for a while."

Safety is paramount. Even if you invest in water wings or other flotation devices—nowadays they even have bathing suits with built-in floaties—never leave your child unattended. Also protect your child's skin. The glare of a pool or sand makes toddlers even more vulnerable to sunburn. Keep at least a hat and a shirt on, so as not to expose too much skin. At the beach, children can also get wind burn. You'll have sand everywhere, and I do mean *everywhere*. Take an umbrella, extra T-shirts, containers for your diapers, sunscreen (one with at least a 60 SPF, if not a total sunblock), and an insulated bag to keep drinks and food cool.

If you know that nap time will occur *while* you're there, plan for the contingency. If your child is used to sleeping in places other than her crib—say, she's willing to lie on a towel or blanket— and she's fairly good about going to sleep when she's tired, just make sure you have an umbrella in case there are no shady areas. If she's a difficult sleeper, try putting her to sleep on your knee with a cuddle.

Having a pet at home ➔ *Petting and other zoos.* Children love pets—a guinea pig, a bunny, a cat or dog. I say this with one important caveat. Never leave a toddler alone with a pet, both for your child's safety and the animal's. That said, pets can be a wonderful way of teaching gentleness ("Be nice"), responsibility ("It's time for Spike to eat—you want to put his bowl down?"), empathy for other living creatures ("It hurts Fluffy when you pull her tail like that"), and caution ("Don't go near Spot when he's eating. He might get angry and snap at you"). If you can't have a pet or don't want to, at least take nature walks with your toddler to help develop her awareness of other creatures, or put a bird

---

Seeing Isn't Doing

When little ones seem interested or good at something, parents sometimes forget what short attention spans they have and jump to wrong conclusions. For example, Gregory, who is almost three, is a phenomenal athlete for a young child. He's out there in the backyard, catching and batting the ball every chance he gets. His dad, Harry, figured his son would enjoy a real game.

As Harry found out, though, *being a spectator is different from playing the game.* Sure, Gregory loves to play ball, but he has no understanding or interest in *the game* of baseball. There he sat, all dressed up in his baseball uniform, his helmet, bat and mitt in hand, upset and wondering why he couldn't actually get on the field and play.

I hear similar stories from other parents. Two-and-a-half-year-old Davy could really whack a golf ball, but when his dad took him to watch a tourney, he was bored silly! Troy loved watching kung fu films, but when his mum then enrolled him in a karate class, he refused to join in. So did my Sophie when I took her to ballet class. Just because she loved to wear a tutu and dance around the house, that didn't mean she was ready for the structure of a class. And there I was, imagining her in Swan Lake!

feeder in your backyard. Once she starts to enjoy and understand stories that feature animals, you can rehearse the idea of petting animals by demonstrating with a stuffed one.

All of the above measures can help prepare your child for the zoo, but remember that zoos *are* different, especially large ones, where the animals are bigger and the setting unfamiliar. Also, toddlers are kneecap height. If the cages are too high, the experience might be more enjoyable for you than for your child. Even at a petting zoo, exercise the same restraint you would in any situation: let your child take the lead. Allie, whom you met at the opening of this chapter, had a typical toddler reaction to a petting zoo: *Mmmm . . . that little lamb looks interesting, but perhaps I'll just stand back a bit.* As a health precaution, bring along a bar of antibacterial soap, and after being with the animals, make sure that you and your child have a good hand washing.

Car rides and quick errands → *Shopping.* Sitting in the car seat is your child's first rehearsal for travel. If you have already done a few quick errands with her, you might attempt a trip to the supermarket or to a department store. Careful planning will help make these pleasant excursions, not torturous trips from hell. So will common sense: if you have to do a large shop, or the department store doesn't provide carts that your child can sit in while you go up and down the aisles, I'd suggest leaving your toddler at home if possible.

Shop when your child is not hungry, tired, or cranky (like the

---

Car Talk

- Use a car seat approved by the U.S. Consumer Product Safety Agency. Place it in the backseat and make sure your child is securely buckled in.

- Look before closing automatic windows.

- Lock doors and windows. If your car has manual locks, place the car seat far enough from windows and doors so your child can't open them, toss objects out, or get a hand caught.

- Don't smoke in the car.

- *Never* leave your toddler alone in a car, even for just a minute.

- Use a window screen or move your toddler to the center of the backseat so she doesn't ride in direct sunlight.

day she's had a booster shot). At home, before you leave, negotiate any treat buying, although my suggestion is to not get her in the habit. If you set it up from the beginning that you don't buy or barter, no matter how much she begs, she'll understand that's the rule. Bring snacks, though, because the sight of so many colorful bags and boxes will make her little mouth water. Supermarkets do to children what bells did to Pavlov's dogs—make them salivate. If she has a meltdown, leave immediately (more on how to do this in the next chapter).

Short trip and sleep at grandparents → *Long trip and hotel.* Even if your child can handle shopping excursions, traveling away from home kicks it up a notch, as they say. It requires planning and no small amount of emotional *and* physical strength. And here's a news flash that might surprise you: There's really no way to prepare toddlers for short *or* long trips. They don't understand place and space. But by excitedly announcing, "We're going to see Grandma Fay," you at least let your child know something special is about to happen.

Moreover, *you* can be prepared. Whether it's a short drive and an overnight at Grandma and Grandpa's or a lengthy airplane trip and a stay at a hotel or motel, call ahead to make sure there's some-

---

When Grandparents Are Far Away

If your own parents live far away and you only get to see them once or twice a year, don't expect your toddler to be immediately comfortable with people she hardly knows. However, the adjustment will be faster if you keep memories alive between visits. Now, in addition to phone calls, you can connect with grandparents via the Internet.

Show your child photographs, too. Most toddlers will look at family albums over and over without ever getting bored. Sit with your child and explain who each person is. "This is Grandma Henrietta, my mummy, and this is Auntie Sandra, who is my sister." It will take a while to sink in, but these conversations will help her keep her long-distance relatives in mind. When she meets them, she may not recognize them at first, but given time, it will all come together.

Have Grandma or Grandpa make a video or read a story on an audiotape and send one weekly. This also keeps them involved.

where for your child to sleep safely and comfortably. Many grand-parents nowadays have cribs of their own (as do hotels). Otherwise, bring your pack-and-play (portable playpen). But if your child associates it only with playing, be sure that you give her an opportunity to nap in it *before* you leave. Three or four days prior to departure, put the pack-and-play in your toddler's bedroom, and let her sleep there as a treat.

Don't forget to pack favorite toys and whatever security object your child uses. If you have a booster seat, bring it, and if necessary, a child-sized toilet seat as well. Also include a few extra outfits and diapers, for unexpected holdovers or mishaps, as well as plastic bags for trash and dirty clothes. For a long trip, pack two meals for your child, too, so you're not caught shorthanded in the event of unexpected delays or if your child is unwilling to eat what's served on the plane. Bring lots of snacks, too—crackers, fruit or melon chunks, bags of cereal, bagels—as well as a bib, spoons, and a pain reliever. If you're going for a week or more, *before* you go, find out the name of a good pediatrician in the area and the location of nearby pharmacies and grocery stores. When traveling abroad, always drink bottled water and be sure to take other health precautions as well. Travel is a dirty business with the masses of people you encounter in airports, poor air circulation, and questionable public rest rooms—a can of disinfectant in your tote bag can't hurt.

TIP: Remember that being a traveling parent doesn't make you a Sherpa. It's one thing to include the above essentials and to factor in delays and mishaps, but don't feel like you have to line your suitcase with a week's worth of diapers and bring every toy in your toddler's room. There are few places on earth where you can't pick up children's necessities. If your child needs special foods or equipment, and you'll be gone for more than a week, consider shipping such items. You and your toddler will travel more comfortably and less stressfully without unnecessary baggage.

Even if the car ride is only a few hours, try to coincide travel with nap time. Some children get into the habit of conking out a few minutes after departure—and still do it as teenagers! Those who don't nap are likely to get the fidgets. Amuse your child with simple games, like "Can you see?" (You spot things and say to the child, "Can you see a doggie? A blue car? An airplane?"). Also, prepare a bag of goodies that includes not only favorite items but also a brand-new toy.

"That worked so amazingly well," Cyndi's mum told me after a two-hour flight with her one-year-old. "She played with some old favorites, and quickly got bored. Then I brought out the new toy, and it was like 'Whoa! Where'd this come from?' She actually sat with it for forty-five minutes."

Once you've reached your destination, don't overdo activities. Be realistic. Give your child time to warm up to strangers, even if the "stranger" is Grandma. (Hopefully, relatives won't take your toddler's initial resistance personally.)

> **TIP:** *If you're visiting friends or relatives, for cripes sake, don't make your child perform. Often, eager and proud parents bombard toddlers with requests: "Show Gramma how you scrunch your nose up. Stand on one leg. Say this. Say that." The child just stands there, and the parent says glumly, "Oh, he's not doing it now." The child senses the parent's disappointment. Please, no performances. I promise, all kids do party tricks . . . if you leave them alone.*

You are the best judge of what your child can handle. Structure outings accordingly. Let's say you're staying at a hotel. If your toddler is a frequent restaurant-goer at home and fairly easygoing, eating out every night might not faze her. If she's not, you might want to figure out ways of doing some, if not all, meals in your room instead. Find a lodging with kitchen facilities, or invest in a travel hot plate. Ask for a small refrigerator, or empty the minibar and use it to store milk, juice, and other perishables. Whatever your arrangements, breakfast in the room is *always* a good idea, because it helps everyone start the day on a relaxed note.

Needless to say, a tired child away from the comforts and familiarity of home can get even crankier and more uncooperative on the road. One solution is to curb your own anxiety—children pick up on parents' stress and are more likely to act up if you curse at another driver or rant at a flight attendant.

Another key is consistency. Even though adults tend to throw away the clock and ignore the rules on vacation, a predictable routine is vital for your toddler; she'll do a lot better if she knows what to expect. As much as possible, maintain your daily R&R—do mealtimes, naps, and bedtimes in the same way and at the same time. If your child doesn't sleep with you at home, don't invite her into your vacation bed. If you have rules about TV and candy, stick to them.

Of course, no matter what precautions you take, when you come home, it will take a few days for your toddler to get on track again. But believe me, if you abandon your routine altogether and relax your rules too much, reentry will take a whole lot longer. (For ideas about how to deal with time changes, see box on pages 186–187.)

Air Travel Dos and Don'ts

Air travel induces a survival-of-the-fittest attitude. Your fellow passengers *won't* be understanding when your mountain of gear holds up the security belt or monopolizes the overhead bins, nor will they take kindly to your toddler's peeking or poking at them or crying during the flight. Below are tips to make your trip smoother and avoid air rage.

Do get a passport for every child—even the baby needs one—and put one adult in charge of carrying everyone's travel documents.

Don't go to the airport without calling ahead to check on the status of your flight.

Do request the bulkhead—the extra room will come in handy.

Don't sit on the aisle—passing food trolleys and passengers are hazards for small (curious) hands and (fidgety) feet.

Do board early—stow your gear before the masses pour into the plane.

Don't sit down while the rest of the plane is filling up—children are calmer on takeoff if they haven't had to sit for the previous half hour. After storing your items overhead and under the seat, go to the back of the plane and stand there until the other passengers have taken their seats.

Do give your toddler a bottle (or breast if you haven't weaned him) on both the ascent and descent—the sucking may help alleviate earaches.

Time Changes and Traveling Tots

It may surprise you to know that infants and toddlers who travel by air usually adapt more easily to time changes; at least for the first three years of life, they go with the flow far more easily than most adults. If you're traveling to a place within a three-hour or less time difference, and you'll be there three days or less, it's not necessary to change your child's routine. If, however, you will be there for more than three days—say, on an extended vacation—you'll need to help her switch gears. It's a good idea to factor in the time change when you make your airline reservations. It's always easier to gain time than lose it.

Daylight savings time changes. In October, almost all of the U.S. "falls" back (gains an hour of sleep). Put your child to bed an hour later, and that will make up the hour. In April, we "spring" ahead (lose an hour of sleep). Shorten the afternoon nap by one hour, so that she'll be ready to go to bed earlier that evening and will be less likely to feel the time change.

Coast-to-coast westbound (gaining three hours). This is the easier coast-to-coast trip, because we're adding more hours to the child's day. It's best to leave at mid-day East Coast time and allow your child to have his afternoon nap on the plane. You will arrive at three in the afternoon West Coast time, and the transition to get him to sleep at his usual bedtime routine will be relatively simple.

Coast-to-coast eastbound (losing three hours). It's best to take an early flight, for instance nine in the morning Pacific time, arriving at six in the evening Eastern time. Keep your child awake for the entire trip, if possible. Distract her with activities; walk up and down the aisles. If you can't keep her up, at least shorten her nap time (wake her three hours before landing), so that she's more likely to get to bed at a reasonable hour.

Traveling for 5–8 hours westbound (gaining time). Going from Europe to the U.S., for example, you would try to allow your child to sleep on the plane for most of the trip. Therefore it's best to leave as late as possible, so that it coincides with his normal bedtime hour.

Traveling for 5–8 hours eastbound (losing time). If you're going to Europe from either coast, it's best to leave on the earliest flight possible, between ten in the morning and noon. Allow your child to sleep for the first half of the journey, but make sure that you wake her three hours before you land.

Traveling for 15 hours or more, westbound (gaining time). The difficulty of this trip (for instance, going from L.A. to Hong Kong) is that, depending on which way you fly, you lose or gain more than a half day—so that day is apt to feel like night to your toddler. It's best to leave around midday, but know that you'll be getting there a whole day later, because of the time changes. Try not to let your toddler take longer than two-hour naps throughout the entire trip, effectively maintaining a typical afternoon routine. By the time you get to your destination, he will be ready for his nighttime routine.

Traveling for 15 hours or more, eastbound (losing time). Coming back from the Far East to the States is harder, because now you are losing so much time *and* spending fifteen hours on a plane. If you can, book an evening flight so that you can get your child to sleep for the first half of the journey. If you have to leave during the day, wake your child around three or four in the morning, so that by the time she's on the plane, she's ready to crash (an unfortunate expression when talking about air travel). No matter how you strategize, it will probably take your child two or three days to get back on track after this trip.

First Friendships: Practicing Social Behavior

It's vitally important to include other children in your toddler's life, because early relationships are rehearsals for valuable social skills. First friendships lay the groundwork for future peer relationships. Besides, it's really good for children to watch their peers— they copy them, learn from them, learn the rules of interaction. Toddlers are easily influenced, too, which can be a good thing. A poor eater is more likely to eat when her friends are eating. Granted, your toddler sees herself at the center of the universe, but through her early socialization experiences, she begins to recognize that others have needs and feelings and that her own actions and behavior have consequences.

Socializing is good for you, too, because it makes parenting less isolating. Seeing other children in action can be reassuring when you hit rough spots or have questions. It's great to share parenting techniques and ideas. For example, I know a group of working mums who meet every Saturday. They love their time together because they have so much in common. Not surprisingly, their discussions center on guilt, nannies, how to divide their time between work and home so that neither is cheated, and whether to let their kids stay up late in order to spend more time with them, as well as garden-variety toddler issues that plague all mums, like discipline, toilet training, picky eaters, and how to get husbands to participate more. This kind of camaraderie among parents of similar-aged children is quite helpful and sustaining. Often, the adults become friends and stay in touch long after their children find other friends.

Rule of Social Behavior

Never push a child into social situations; let him progress at a rate that's comfortable for him, even if it makes *you* uncomfortable.

Social rehearsals for change involve reinforcing people skills at home and structuring play situations that allow your child to practice them. Here are the pieces that need to come together:

Respect your child's style and pace. I've said it countless times in this book and in my first book as well, and I'll say it again: no two children react to the same situation the same way. Certainly, temperament (see sidebar on page 190) affects children's social ease and their ability to grasp the rules of interaction. But so do a number of other factors: focus, attention span, patience, language acquisition, previous social experience, birth order (older siblings provide lots of social experience). Also, a child's basic level of trust and security is critical; the more secure he feels, the more willing he will be to dip his toe into the social stream of life.

If your child is reluctant to join in and wants to sit on the sidelines, let him. Don't keep saying, "Don't you want to play with Juan?" If pushed before he's ready, a child will feel unsafe. Also bear in mind that toddlers are still sensate creatures. They discern their emotions on an unconscious level and sometimes just don't feel secure in certain circumstances.

Keep your own feelings in check. If you feel embarrassed when your toddler sits on the sidelines, you're not alone. Many parents do, but try your best to keep your discomfort to yourself. Don't make excuses for your child's behavior: "Oh, she's just tired," or "She just got up from her nap." Your daughter will sense your disapproval, and it will make her feel bad about herself or think that she has done something "wrong."

Pauline, a very savvy mum, knows her son and accepts his temperament. Even at family gatherings, she knows she has to stick close to him at first, but eventually he'll toddle around on his own. If she rushes him, he can have a major meltdown. Thus, when a relative or another child comes at him, she explains, "Let him get used to you. He'll be fine in a minute."

Don't catastrophize. If your child is reserved and doesn't join in immediately—typically, a Touchy type—it might help you to reframe his behavior:

E-mail: The Benefits of Socializing

Yes, it is exhausting being a parent of a toddler, especially if they are very active and always want to be busy. We attend play group and swimming once a week, which keeps him active. He also sees other children his own age every second day. I find this good for me, too, as we mums get on very well. Tyrone's Grandma comes over once a week, too.

---

he's cautious, a trait that will serve him well in other ways. Likewise, a spirited child might turn out to be a leader, and a Grumpy toddler, a child who becomes inventive and creative. And remember that many adults are cautious in social circumstances: We walk into a party or a strange place and sort of "suss out" the situation. We look around, figure out who looks interesting and whom we want to stay away from. There are always people whom you're attracted to, people you feel more comfortable with, and others who, for whatever reason, turn you off. It's part of human nature. Give your toddler a chance to assess various social settings in the same way . . . no matter how long it takes.

Be persistent. Sometimes after only a session or two, a mother will say, "Oh, no, she doesn't like this group." Then she goes on to another group, and then to a class, and so on and so on. The mother might feel embarrassed herself, or she might find it unbearable to watch her toddler struggle. But by not allowing the child to go through difficult or scary experiences, she prevents her child from practicing control and mood management. She inadvertently teaches her little one that it's okay to abandon anything that's hard or uncomfortable. Such children can become butterflies who flit from one thing to another without ever learning to see things through to the end.

The Five Types

Angel has a very agreeable social nature. She is usually the smiling, happy child in the group, the one who's first willing to share.

Textbook, being the quintessential toddler, takes things from other kids, not because he's mean or aggressive, but because he's curious and interested in whatever another child has.

Touchy holds back or keeps looking back at Mum. She gets very upset if another child takes something, bumps into her, or disrupts her play.

Spirited has a hard time with sharing. He tends to change focus quickly, tear around the room, and flit about, playing with lots of toys.

Grumpy prefers to play on her own. She can stick with a task longer than most kids, but gets upset if another child interrupts her.

Don't give up on socializing your child or quit a particular group because she doesn't jump in immediately. If your child is reluctant to participate and wants to leave, simply say, "We made a promise to come here, and we have to stick with it. You can stay here with me and watch." Lana, the mother of a Touchy toddler, Kendra, recognized that her daughter needed time to warm up to social situations. She didn't make excuses when Kendra came to our Mommy-and-Me group. Instead, she let her daughter sit on her lap. Most sessions, Kendra didn't join in until the last five minutes. But at least she did.

Expect replays of social difficulties in new settings. Attending Mommy-and-Me classes from the age of two months certainly enabled Kendra to get used to other children. But as Lana found out when Kendra was fifteen months old and she enrolled her in Gymboree, each new situation meant going through the warm-up stage all over again. The first day, Kendra had a meltdown at the door. Lana stood with her, outside the room, for fifteen minutes before she'd even walk in. Kendra sat on the sidelines for another five weeks. Lana's fear—indeed, the common apprehension of all parents—was that Kendra would *never* join in. I explained to her, "That's who she is, you have to give her time." Kendra came to love Gymboree; she hated when the class ended. All the same, the sideline scene occurred again at age two, when Kendra joined a swimming class. After weeks of sitting fearfully at the edge, Kendra is now a little fish—and it's hard to get her out of the pool.

Teaching children to manage their emotions is an ongoing process that requires a great deal of patience. You might have to reassure your reticent toddler over and over that it's okay to take her time. You might have to say repeatedly to a naturally aggressive child, "Be nice . . . don't hit." Granted, each rehearsal will help, but it takes a lot of practice. Believe me, it's better to deal with a child's anxiety or aggression now, to put the time in and let her see that you're there to help her, because she'll have to go through it at some point. Indeed, there's often a moment of truth for parents. Those who've made excuses for their children or allowed them to flit from group to group, rather than helping them get through difficult situations, will often say on that first day of preschool, "I wish I had done this earlier."

Look at your own social history. Personal issues sometimes blind parents. If you were a shy child, you might overidentify with what your child is going through. If you had no trouble making friends, you might be inclined to push your child to be more like you. If you were a biter, you might defensively rationalize, "It's just a stage." And you and your partner, unconsciously reflecting your respective childhoods, might disagree about social matters. One says, "push," and the other, "back off." It's important to distinguish your issues from your child's. You can't change what you were like back then or reverse the social difficulties you encountered, but you can become aware of how those dramas left their mark. Don't let your own past affect the way you direct your child in the present.

Structure situations to meet your child's needs. Social situations consist of a setting, the activity taking place in it, and other children and adults. If you know that your child tends to be reticent, you might want to pick an activity that is less stressful—say, music instead of tumbling. If he's affected by bright lights, you'd stay away from brilliantly lit places that might be too overwhelming. If he's rambunctious, a quiet arts and crafts class probably wouldn't be the best choice.

Of course, you might not always have the option. As I said earlier, going to play dates and play groups (which I talk about below) usually means that you've helped create the guest list. Thus, these are easier circumstances to control than playgrounds or other public venues. If there's an aggressive child at the park, there's not much you can do about it once you get there, except to keep a close eye on your child. Likewise, you probably won't know all of the other children at the day care center. You can, however, visit and observe ahead of time; tell the people who run the center all about your child, his past social experiences, what you've learned about him and what he needs. Though you may not have a say in how the place is run, at least you can help pave the way for your child.

Prepare your child for the experience. Dolly followed my suggestions to the letter. She scouted out several day care facilities and found one not far from work in case of emergencies. She made sure there was adequate supervision and that the toys and equipment were appropriate for eighteen-month-olds. And she told the director what kind of food her son liked and gave them a list of numbers to contact her in case they had any questions. All that was excellent, but on Andy's first day, Dolly had a rude awakening. Her normally cooperative and easygoing son allowed her to leave without much fuss but soon fell apart. When the director of the center called to tell her Andy was crying inconsolably, Dolly realized that for all her preparation and groundwork, she had forgotten to prepare Andy for the fact that he was going to be there without her for several hours. Though she couldn't have explained the time to him, she could have taken an hour or so from work for a few days to help get him used to the setting, the staff, and the other children—and left when he was ready.

Arming Your Toddler with Social Skills

Children under the age of two see themselves at the center of their own universe—and everything is about "me," or is quite simply "mine." Sometimes there's just no reasoning with toddlers. Their normal behavior often looks "aggressive" (see sidebar on page 196) to adult eyes. How, then, do we teach them to be considerate and to take others' feelings into account?

Again, think in terms of rehearsing. Children don't come into the world with manners or knowing how to take turns and share. We have to show them both by our own example and by giving them practice. Start by coaching interactions at home. Don't expect much at first—this is hard for toddlers—but be consistent. You can't ask your child to share one day and later ignore her when she tries to snatch a toy away from another child. And when she does share, whether it's because you urged her or because she did it on her own, praise her. "Good sharing, Janet."

Children need us to teach them social skills in order to survive in the real world. Although they don't truly understand social conventions, or what "being nice" means at first, we have to start somewhere, continually reinforcing and stretching toddlers' comprehension and improving their social graces. It's worth the struggle, for there is nothing quite so endearing to other parents, to teachers, even to other children, as a child who minds her manners and is kind and considerate.

Here are the critical skills you'll want to help your child practice, at home and in play situations.

Manners. In the last chapter, I talked about the importance of teaching your child *words* that indicate politeness and gratitude, but you also have to teach her *actions.* Let's say it's afternoon snack time, and Aunt Florrie has come over to visit. First, you say to Aunt Florrie, "I'm so happy you could come. Could I get you some tea?" Then turn to your child, "Let's go get Aunt Florrie a nice cuppa."

She accompanies you while you fix the tea. "Let's have cookies, too," you suggest, putting it all on a tray. Back in the den you hand your child the (plastic) plate and say, "Melanie, would you like to give one to Aunt Florrie? And now, would *you* like one?" This shows the child that you serve others, that guests go first, and that the hostess takes her piece last. It's basic manners. That said, you can probably count on your child grabbing *all* the cookies at first. Correct her gently without shaming: "No, Melanie, we're sharing. This is Aunt Florrie's cookie, and this is Melanie's cookie."

Teaching manners involves modeling appropriate behavior in certain places. You lower your voice to a whisper and explain, "In church, we use our quiet voice and we don't run." It's also a matter of reinforcing the kinds of courtesies that are part of virtually every social exchange: When something is passed at the dinner table, you say, "Thank you." And rather than barge past people, interrupt, or burp in someone's face, you say, "Excuse me." The best way to teach politeness, of course, is to be polite yourself. So when your child brings you a toy, always say, "Thank you." When you want her to cooperate, say, "Please."

Empathy. Researchers have shown that children as young as fourteen months exhibit the ability to care about another person's feelings. You can rehearse empathy by letting your child know that *you* have feelings. If he hits you, say, "Ouch! That hurts." If someone in the family is ill, say, "We have to be quiet, because Mark doesn't feel well." Some children are naturally empathic. One of my aunts who lived with us couldn't walk very well. Our Sara knew Auntie Ruby was sick and she'd run and get her slippers. Even at sixteen months, she demonstrated empathy, and I reinforced it by saying, "That's a good girl, Sara. You're so kind to help Auntie Ruby."

Encourage your child to notice what other children are going through. Even when a ten-month-old acts inconsiderately toward another child, correct the behavior immediately and point out how it feels: "No, no, that hurts Alex . . . be gentle, gentle." When a boy falls down and starts crying, say, "Johnny must have hurt himself. Do you want to see if we can help him?" Walk over to the other child and say, "Johnny are you okay now?" Or when a child has to leave a play group because he's tired or upset, encourage the other children to say, "Bye-bye, Simon. Feel better."

Sharing. Sharing is based on ownership and use—an owner gives something away (sharing candy, for example) or allows another person to use an item with the knowledge that it will be returned. At around fifteen months, children start to grasp the concept of sharing, but they need a lot of help. After all, everything in their world is "mine." "Now" is the only time that exists in little children's minds—"later" sounds much too far away. And no matter how precise you are ("She'll give it back to you in two minutes"), toddlers don't get time. Any delay feels like forever.

In my play groups, when the children are thirteen months old, I rehearse sharing by modeling it: I bring out a plate of biscuits and say, "I want to share my snack with you." On the plate are just enough for each child to have one—five children, five biscuits. As we pass the plate I reinforce the idea that everyone is taking "just one."

We then move on to doing a "share bucket." I ask the mothers to bring five of a particular snack in a plastic bag. I also urge them to talk about sharing at home and to let their children help them prepare for the share bucket: "Let's get our snack bag ready for play group. Can you help me count five [carrot sticks, cookies, Goldfish crackers]?" (It turns into a counting game as well.)

When the children arrive, we put all the snacks into the share bucket. After the play session we have "sharing time." Each week, one little person gets to have a turn handing out the snacks, and his or her mum helps by saying in a polite tone to each of the other children, "Would you like some?" Of course, manners are being taught here, too. The child who takes a snack says, "Thank you," and then we all go, "Good share!"

These lessons help the toddlers understand the idea of sharing toys as well, which, admittedly, is a lot harder. But at least when you say, "Edna and Willy, you can share the truck," instead of fighting over it, they have a rudimentary understanding of what you expect. The goal is to instill in your child a *desire* to share and to reward that, rather than praise a child who is responding to parental instruction ("Give that back"). The best way to do this is to *catch the child when she's being good*—even if it's just an accident!

For example, Marie was busily playing with the garden set in my playroom. She was posting letters in the box, twirling the little plastic birds, just having a rare old time, when along came Juliette. Juliette's mum was ready to jump right in and grab her daughter, but I told her to remember H.E.L.P. "Let's wait and see what happens now," I suggested. Juliette just watched Marie for a moment or two. Then she opened the letter box and handed one of the little plastic letters to Marie. "Good share, Juliette!" I said excitedly. Juliette beamed. She might not have known exactly what I was so happy about, but she surely knew she had done something pleasing.

Of course, sometimes parents *have* to intervene. If your child grabs something from another child, take it away immediately and then:

Curiosity or Aggression?

Although you should *act* in either circumstance, there's a difference between aggression and curiosity—both the intent and what the act looks like. Curiosity looks slow, where aggression is quick and impulsive. So when eleven-month-old Sean sidles up to Lorena, checks her out, reaches over to touch her head, and then pulls Lorena's hair, he is probably just being curious. In contrast, when one-year-old Wesley purposely pushes Terry out of the way, that's aggression.

CORRECT THE BEHAVIOR: "This doesn't belong to you, George. It's Woody's. You can't have it." However, don't lecture or shame your child.

COMFORT HIM: "I know you want to play with Woody's truck. You must be disappointed." This acknowledges the feeling without trying to shield him from experiencing disappointment.

HELP HIM PROBLEM SOLVE: "Maybe Woody will share his toy with you if you ask him." If your child doesn't have verbal language, ask *for* him, "Woody, will you share your truck with George?" Of course, Woody might say no.

ENCOURAGE HIM TO MOVE ON: "Well, George, maybe Woody will let you play with it another time." Try to interest him in another truck.

Taking turns. Children need to learn the basic etiquette of play: you don't grab, you don't push someone out of the way, and you don't ruin another child's construction just because you want to use the blocks *now*. Taking turns is hard for toddlers because it means exercising control and waiting. And yet it is one of life's most important lessons. It's boring to wait—but we all need to learn how to do it.

At home, during your everyday routines, rehearse the script, which gets your child used to the language of taking turns. For example, she's in the tub. Give her a washcloth and keep one for yourself. "Let's take turns. First, I wash this arm, and then you wash the other one." While playing: "Let's take turns. You push a button and let's see which animal noise it makes. Now I push a button."

Children won't voluntarily offer to share or take turns, mind you. But like a good director, you have to coach them. In my toddler groups, I try to head off problems by having more than one of each toy. But it's almost inevitable: one child always wants what another one is playing with.

> **TIP:** *A trick I've recommended to mothers, particularly for play dates, is to set a time limit. However, because children don't understand the concept of time, it's best to use a timer. That way, when two children want the same doll, for instance, you can say, "There's only one doll, so you'll have to take turns. Russell, you go first because you found it. So we'll set a timer. When you hear the buzzer, it's time to give Tina her turn." Tina is more willing to wait because she knows that when she hears "Ding!" she gets the doll.*

Also allow your child to experience whatever feelings come up when he can't get what he wants. Too often, I'll hear a parent say to a crying child, "Oh, don't worry. We'll buy you a gadget just like Barney has." What does *that* teach the child? Certainly, not about sharing; instead, he learns that crying gets his mum or dad to do whatever he wants.

It's important to allow your child to experience disappointment when another child refuses to take turns or share. This, too, is part of life. In one of my play sessions, for example, Eric and Jason were over by the toy box. Jason had the fire truck and was busily engaged with it. Suddenly, Eric glanced over at his little friend. The expression on his face was clear: *Oh, that looks much more interesting to play with. I'll just take it from Jason.* He wasn't being "bad" or even "possessive." In a toddler's mind, everything is his. As Eric reached over to take the truck, I encouraged his mum to intervene as I had shown her in other sessions:

She put her hand out to stop Eric from grabbing the truck: "Eric, Jason was playing with that fire truck."

She turned to Jason. "Jason, do you still want to play with the truck?" Jason understood; he pulled the truck back, clearly indicating he wasn't finished.

"Eric, Jason still wants to play with the truck," she explained, offering him another lorry. "Here's a truck for *you* to play with." Eric pushed it away; he only wanted the fire truck.

"Eric," his mum said again, "Jason is playing with the fire truck right now. You may have a turn when he's finished."

Well, that wasn't quite what Eric wanted to hear, so he pitched the what-do-you-mean-I-can't-have-it fit, at which point his mum said to me, "Now what do I do?"

"Do *not* say, 'I'm sorry you can't have it' or 'Poor baby, I'll buy you your own fire truck.' Nope. Just tell him the truth: 'Eric, Jason is playing with the fire truck right now. You can have a turn later. We have to share. And we have to take turns.' "

When Eric continued to fuss, I said to his mother, "Now, you have to be firm but respectful. Your goal is to avoid, if possible, a further escalation of his feelings: 'I can see that you're disappointed, but you still can't have it. So let's go over here and see what we can find for *you* to play with.' Then, remove him physically." (In Chapter Seven, I talk about what Eric's mom has to do if *that* doesn't distract Eric, and instead, he flies into a fit of rage.)

The Stages of Socialization:
How Your Child Becomes a Social Butterfly

As your toddler matures, his capacity for play naturally grows with him as well. It helps to understand what each stage looks like from your child's perspective.

Notices other children. Babies as young as two months are fascinated by and curious about other babies and their older siblings. Their eyes will follow them around the room at first. Somewhere around six months, when he's able to reach for objects, your child will reach for other children, too. He wonders what it is, probably thinking it's a kind of mysterious toy. *Hey, if I poke this other thing, it cries.*

Copies other children. We look at toddlers and think that they're mean, selfish, or spiteful when they grab a toy from another child. Actually, your child just wants to copy. Seeing another child use it gives your child ideas, and all of a sudden, a toy that a few moments ago held no interest whatsoever has life to it. *Hey, I didn't know that's what that thing does. I want to do it, too.*

Plays next to other children. Toddlers don't actually play with each other, they play side by side, which is why it's called "parallel play." The idea of sharing and taking turns seems irrelevant to your child, who thinks, *Whatever I want to do, I can do, because I'm the only kid in the world.*

Plays with other children. By age two and a half or three, most children master basic social skills, and they can mentally imagine things. Therefore, their pretend play is more elaborate, and they can play games that require them to actually cooperate with one another, such as chasing, rolling, or kicking a ball back and forth. Now when your child sees a playmate he thinks, *If I kick this ball to him, he'll kick it back.*

Setting Up Play Dates and Play Groups

Play dates and play groups help children rehearse social skills, but they present quite different challenges. I suggest that you give your toddler both kinds of experience. I know that some people believe it's not a good idea to have children under the age of two in groups, but I don't agree. As long as the child has a parent by her side, it's good practice even to lie next to another child. Hence, I start my Mommy-and-Me and Daddy-and-Me groups at six weeks.

Play Dates. A play *date* is usually one-on-one, and it's fairly unstructured. One parent calls another, they set up a time and place (usually, one of their houses or a park) where the two children play together for an hour or two.

One of the important issues with play dates is chemistry. Some children just hit it off. Their friendships can last through preschool or even longer. There are also children, usually Angel toddlers, who entertain, instigate, and get along famously with every child, in which case chemistry may never be an issue. But some combinations make for a bad "fit." For example, if you have a Touchy toddler who startles easily and gets rattled when his concentration is disturbed, you might not want his first experience to be with a Spirited toddler who tears around the room and tends to grab toys.

All the same, in the real world, it's the *adults* who make play dates, and they choose other adults whom *they* like. Often, groups are comprised of mothers or fathers who have similar backgrounds and interests and parenting philosophies in common as well. Or a group of nannies get together because they live in the same neighborhood or come from the same country. In either case, the children are thrown together.

Sometimes the chemistry works, such as with Cassy and Amy (see pages 92–93), whose mothers met in a Lamaze class. Fortunately, their two children, one Spirited, the other an Angel, play quite nicely. But sometimes, despite mothers' best intentions and most heartfelt wishes, their children are like chalk and cheese. One always ends up bullied and miserable, and no one, certainly not the parents, has a good time. Another mother, Judy, whose son Sandy is a Touchy child, admitted to me that sometimes she dreads play dates with Abe, Gail's son, because Sandy frequently ends up in tears. Judy finally had to say to Gail, "I don't want to impose my parenting on you, but when you and Abe come over, Sandy is often terrified. And it's infringing on *our* friendship."

TIP: Pairing children boils down to common sense. Even though you might like to be with a particular mother, if every week your child ends up being frustrated, having things taken from him, crying—and you start to dread play dates because you're secretly wondering, what's going to happen next week—make play dates with someone else's child and meet your friend for coffee or a game of tennis instead.

Before a play date, always ask your child, "Which of your toys are you willing to share with Timmy when he gets here and which would you like to put away?" Or you might suggest storing a particular toy that *you* know he treasures or his "blankie" and explain why: "I know this is your favorite thing. Maybe we'd just better put it away." Unfortunately, sometimes a toddler doesn't realize something is his "favorite" until another kid snatches it from him.

Respect must work both ways, of course. Your child

Share Yourself

Let your child know there's enough of you to go around! Especially if you're planning to have more than one child (see Chapter Nine), a play date is a good opportunity to show your toddler that you can hold and hug another child. The day Cassy (see page 200) first noticed her mother picking up Amy, she had a somewhat stunned look on her face: *Hey, my mom is picking up Amy.* She's getting an important message: Mom can be shared, too.

It's important to discourage children from believing that love has to be exclusive. Some children will even push their fathers away when they go to kiss and hug their wives. The father will conclude, "He hates us to cuddle." Instead, he should say to his child, "Come here—we can all hug."

might be the visitor, and there may be playthings the other child refuses to share. Say, "It's okay if Fred doesn't want you to have his toy. It's *his* toy." Then, try to interest him in something else. If he gets upset, say, "I see you're upset, but it's still Fred's toy."

Such difficulties are almost inevitable, but they're not bad. It's how children learn. As a young mother, I would give my child two toys for the play date, and the other mum would bring two as well. If anything got broken, either she or I knew to replace it. You can also cut down on squabbles by asking the visiting mother to encourage her child to bring one or two of his toys as well. I realize that may sound unrealistic, because children have so many toys nowadays, but I believe it's in everyone's best interest—children *and* parents—to at least try to limit playthings.

> **TIP:** *If you're hosting a play date, create a safe space where the children can play. Put your pets away. Limit the time—an hour is usually enough before one or the other gets tired. That's when you get conflict.*

It's great to alternate houses, but if you don't, supply your own snacks so that the burden doesn't rest on only one set of shoulders. If you're the visiting mom, also bring whatever else you'll need—diapers, bottle or sippy cup. Although it's not important to set up "rules" per se for a play date, as I suggest for play groups (see below), it's a good idea to at least know where the other mother stands on certain issues and what her child is like. For instance, if you're the kind of mother who hasn't put her valuable ornaments away and you've taught your child not to touch them, you'd better make sure the other mom is one who's taught her child to respect other people's things! Also discuss whether there are certain foods that shouldn't be served, allergies you should know about, toilet-training issues. What will each of you do if one child is aggressive toward the other?

Play Group. A play *group* involves two or more children and usually has a more structured format than a play date. The benefit of a play group is that the dynamics are more complex, and it gives children many opportunities to practice the kinds of social skills outlined earlier. However, up to the age of three, I suggest limiting play groups to no more than six children—ideally, four. If possible, avoid threesomes, which can be difficult because someone usually feels left out.

To put together a play group yourself (as opposed to enrolling in one where a professional guides you) takes planning. If we think in terms of rehearsals, this one requires lots of stage direction, as well as a more elaborate set and a larger cast than a play date.

1. MEET WITHOUT *THE CHILDREN FIRST TO FIGURE OUT YOUR AGENDA— WHAT KIND OF STRUCTURE AND ACTIVITIES YOUR GROUP WILL FEATURE.* Decide what you want the play group to *be*. What activities will it include—play, music, food? It's also a good idea to plot out the hour. Just as maintaining a predictable routine at home makes life easier for your toddler, a consistent structure in play group helps the children know what to expect and what's expected of them. My Mommy-and-Me sessions have five segments: playtime, share time (snack), music time, and after cleanup, "wind-down time," during which I put on soothing music and the children cuddle in their mothers' laps. It's a format that you can easily replicate on your own turf.

The content naturally changes according to the children's age. Take music. In my six-to-nine-month groups, I play the "Eensy-Weensy Spider" on my tape deck, but only the parents and I sing the song and do the motions. The children sit there rapt but motionless. In the twelve-to-eighteen-month groups, the children are much more animated and try to copy the hand movements. By around fifteen months, most know what to expect and after four or five weeks of hearing the song and watching their mums and me, they can actually do the hand movements. By the time they're two, most will attempt to sing the words as well.

2. DISCUSS GROUND RULES. Talk about your expectations—not only what the children can and cannot do, but what the mothers do when the children don't adhere to the rules (see sidebar on page 204). I get rankled when a child hits or willfully breaks another child's toy and the mother says, "I'm really sorry," but does nothing about it. Such occurrences can lead to very bad feelings among the other mothers.

In one group I visited, the mothers recounted their interactions with a former member. Every time her toddler hauled off and hit another child, the mum made light of it and rationalized, "Oh, she's just going through a stage." (Hitting is behavior, not a stage— more about that in the next chapter.) The other mothers were increasingly miffed by her attitude, and it cast a pall over the group. Finally, one of them spoke up: "We're trying to teach our children self-control. And when our kids don't restrain themselves, we step in. You may not think it necessary to intervene when Beth pushes or hits, and that's your choice. But we don't think that's fair to the other children." Although it was awkward, they asked the mum to find another group.

When you establish rules ahead of time, you are less likely to have such conflicts and tension in a play group. Besides, rules help children learn about boundaries. But let's not be extreme. Even if one of the rules is that children have to ask for things politely, if a child wants a drink of water and he forgets to say "please," give it to him. Encourage him to ask nicely the next time.

3. *PREPARE THE SPACE TO HAVE EVERYTHING YOU'LL NEED.* The area should be safe and able to comfortably accommodate however many children are involved. It's good to have a child-sized table for snacks. I also recommend having at least two of everything. In my groups, I have two (or more) of everything—two dolls, two books, two trucks. Granted, in the real world, there isn't two of everything, but we're training toddlers here, and duplicates help avoid conflicts.

House Rules

Some mothers I knew drew up a set of house rules for their play group. You may not agree with them, but use them as a guide to create rules of your own.

For the children:
No eating in the living room.
No climbing on furniture.
No aggressive behavior (hitting, biting, pushing).

For the mothers:
No older siblings (if one "crashes," he or she is asked politely to leave).
Manners should be encouraged.
If a child is aggressive, he has a time-out until he can behave.
Broken toys are replaced with new ones.

TIP: *If the group is always going to be at one mum's house, everyone should donate playthings. If you rotate from house to house, have a traveling toy box. So if it's at Martha's this week, and Tanya's next, when this week's group ends, Tanya lugs the play*

*box to her house. Next week, the following week's hostess will do
the same thing.*

4. *END AT A PARTICULAR TIME AND HAVE A CLOSING RITUAL.* I've found
that if you don't have a definitive ending to a group, the moms
continue to chat. Before you know it another ten or fifteen minutes have gone by, and the little munchkins start getting tired and
cranky. Instead, at the stroke of the hour, I like to sing a good-bye
song that incorporates each child's name individually: "Good-bye,
Stevie, good-bye, Stevie, good-bye, Stevie, we'll see you again next
week." This not only signifies the end, it also avoids a crush of toddlers rushing for the door.

Roll with the Reality

Despite all your planning, play groups are never seamlessly smooth
happenings. Remember that toddlers first copy and then they play
next to each other, and you can count on the fact that there will be
a lot more imitation than cooperation (see box on page 199 for
the stages of socialization). Children give each other ideas. When
Cassy and Amy play, if Cassy picks up a doll and hugs it, all of a
sudden Amy wants it. Interestingly, Amy has the same doll at
home but never touches it. Because particular toys or activities become part of their routine *in the group*, that's the only place they
play with it. For instance, Barry loved sitting in the toy car in my
playroom but *never* climbed into the one he had at home.

Children shouldn't be expected to share favorite toys at play
groups either. I have a box at my door where we keep special items
"safe" until it's time to leave. If you host a group, encourage your
child to put away things she doesn't want the others to touch, especially comfort items. (If she doesn't, *you* put it away to avoid
trouble; see page 201.)

Even if you structure a particular format, it will take the children four or five weeks to get used to it and to anticipate each segment. Naturally, it will take some children longer than others to
trust the environment. As I explain in the sidebar, some children
tend to be *Interactors*, while others are *Observers*. Even though the

mothers decide to include a music segment or an organized game, some of the children won't participate. That's fine. They will . . . when they feel safe.

I always advise the mums in my groups to hang back and observe, rather than rush in. At the same time, when a child is victimized by a peer, I urge adults to step in: "Protect your child. You're her guardian." Some parents feel too embarrassed to intervene. When Jake hit Marnie, for example, Brenda, Marnie's mother, said to Jake's mum, Susan, "It's okay." Brenda obviously didn't want Susan to feel bad about Jake's behavior. But it's *not* okay. If Susan does nothing about her own son's behavior, at least Brenda needs to take action rather than leave poor Marnie hanging out there defenselessly on her own.

Like the play group where one of the mothers was finally asked to leave (pages 203–204), this instance highlights the importance of ground rules. If a zero tolerance policy toward aggression had been discussed beforehand, Susan would have stepped in immediately when her son hit another child. Had Susan failed to act, Brenda—after comforting her own child—should have said to the little boy, "No, Jake, we have a rule. No hitting." I realize that the idea of disciplining another person's child is a delicate issue, and parents get confused about whether it's their "business" or not.

Observers and Interactors

In my toddler groups, some kids are what I call *Observers*. Often Grumpy or Touchy types, they tend to hold themselves back a bit. They let another child play with a toy before they attempt it. Or they go off in a corner, where there's less stimulation and less interference.

Other children, usually Angel, Textbook, and Spirited types, are *Interactors*. They make eye contact, reach out for other children, kiss them.

Even when children play on their own, these patterns emerge. Give an Observer a new toy, and she'll approach it gingerly, whereas an Interactor will get right down to business. Take an Observer to a new place, and she'll scope it out first, whereas the Interactor will plunge into action almost immediately. Observers often ask for parents' help, whereas Interactors tend to try things out on their own.

Remember:

It's not your business if another child refuses to share with yours. It is your business if another child hits, bites, pushes, or in any other way is aggressive.

In the final analysis, play dates and play groups, as well as other outings, can be fun and exciting for you and your toddler—or a disaster. You won't be able to avoid crises and meltdowns altogether, but in the next chapter, I'll explain how to deal with them.

CHAPTER SEVEN

Conscious Discipline: Teaching Your Child Self-Control

Perhaps the most valuable result of all education is the ability to make yourself do the thing you have to do, when it ought to be done, whether you like it or not.

—Thomas Huxley

Most kids hear what you say; some kids do what you say; but all kids do what you do.

—Kathleen Casey Theisen

Two Moms/Two Different Lessons

In every question parents ask, the word *discipline* seems to crop up repeatedly. If you think about it, discipline is a somewhat militaristic term. The dictionary defines it as both "instruction and exercise designed to train to proper conduct or action" and "punishment inflicted by way of correction and training." Given those meanings, I wish I had another word for it. In any case, let me be clear: *I* don't equate discipline with punishment, nor do I see it as something we impose harshly on children. Rather, I think of discipline as *emotional education*: a way of teaching your toddler to handle her feelings and reminding her how to behave. Because part of this process involves watching your own actions, listening to the way you talk to your child, and being mindful of the less obvious lessons you teach through modeling, I like to think in terms of *conscious discipline*.

The ultimate goal of conscious discipline is to help your child gain *self*-control. To reiterate our theater analogy, young children need lots of rehearsals. You, the director, must hold the cue cards until your little actor memorizes the script, knows the stage directions by heart, and can manage on his own.

Allow me to exemplify this simple idea by telling you how two mothers in the supermarket reacted to a situation that's familiar to all parents. Both have two-year-old boys who ask for candy while their mothers are on a checkout line. (We all know, don't we, dears, that supermarket owners are in cahoots with toddlers; they strategically place racks of candy at cart eye-level and within easy reach!)

Francine and Christopher. As Francine rolls her cart through the checkout lane, Christopher points to the brightly colored candy display. His mum, busy unloading groceries onto the conveyor belt, doesn't notice until he shouts, "Me, want!"

Francine responds gently: "No candy, Chris." She continues to empty her cart.

Christopher, a few decibels louder, now whines, "Candy!"

"I said, no candy, Christopher," Francine repeats, more sternly. "It will ruin your teeth."

Christopher, who by the way has no idea what "ruin your

teeth" means, screws up his little face, starts to whimper, and chants, "Candy, candy, candy . . ."

At this point, other shoppers on line are beginning to stare, some raising eyebrows, or at least that's how it feels to Francine. She is embarrassed and getting increasingly flustered. She tries not to look at Christopher.

Realizing that he's being ignored, Christopher ups the ante, demanding in a screeching voice, "Candy! Candy! Candy! Candy!"

"Young man, if you don't stop that right now," Francine warns with a sharp look, "we're going home." Christopher cries even louder. "I mean it, Chris." He continues to cry and now adds kicking the metal cart to his repertoire.

In the face of her son's symphony of complaint, Francine is mortified. "Okay," she says, handing him a candy bar. "Just this once." Red-faced, she pays the checkout person, explaining to everyone in earshot, "He didn't have much of a nap today. He's just overtired. You know how kids get when they're exhausted."

Though the tears have barely dried on Christopher's face, he's all smiles.

Leah and Nicholas. As Leah rolls her cart through the checkout line, Nicholas eyes the brightly colored candy display and says, "Nicholas want candy!"

Leah answers matter-of-factly, "Not today, Nicholas."

Nicholas starts to whine and in a louder voice demands, "Candy. I want candy."

Leah stops for a moment and looks Nicholas in the eye. "Not today, Nicky," she says without anger but firmly.

That's not the answer Nicholas wants. He begins to cry and kick the cart. Without hesitation, Leah quickly removes her groceries from the conveyor belt and refills her cart. She asks the checkout person, "Could you please watch this until I come back?" The woman nods sympathetically and knowingly. Leah then turns to Nicholas and in an even voice says, "When you behave like this, we have to leave." She lifts him out of the cart and calmly exits the store. Nicholas continues to cry, and Leah allows him his meltdown . . . in the car.

When Nicholas stops crying, Leah says to him, "You can come back to the store with me, but no candy." He nods, still gasping rapid, shallow breaths, the hallmark of having had a good cry. She returns to the market and proceeds through the checkout line without incident. As mother and son exit the store once again, she says to Nicholas, "Good boy, Nicky. Thank you for not asking for candy. You were very patient." Nicholas smiles broadly.

As you can see, discipline is teaching, but parents aren't always aware of what they're teaching. Given identical circumstances, these two boys learned completely different lessons from their mums. Christopher learned that in order to get what he wants, he needs to behave in a certain way—whine, cry, have a tantrum. He also learned that his mum doesn't mean what she says. He can't trust her words because she doesn't follow through. Moreover, his mother will rescue him and make excuses for him. This is potent information, and next time he's at the supermarket with Francine, I assure you, Christopher will replay that same scene. He'll say to himself, *Mmmm . . . we're in the supermarket again . . . candy! Last time I was here, this whine got me a candy bar. I'll try it again.* When Francine attempts to hold her ground, Christopher will dig deeper into his arsenal. *Hey, this isn't working. I guess I'll have to cry louder. Not working yet, eh? Time to try to get out of this cart and throw myself on the floor.* Christopher has learned that he has several tools at his disposal, and it's just a matter of digging around for the right one to get the reward he's after.

Nicholas, on the other hand, has learned that his mother says what she means and means what she says. She follows through. She sets boundaries, and when he crosses them, he suffers the consequences. Also, because Leah didn't yank him out of the store but remained calm herself, she modeled proper behavior for her son, showing him that she was in control of her own emotions. Finally, he learned that when he's good, he earns praise—and to a toddler, Mum's approval is almost as delicious as candy. I venture to say that Nicholas won't have many more meltdowns in the supermarket, because his mum doesn't reward them.

Some toddlers need to be removed from a "hot" situation only once and they grasp the boundary. But let's say Nicholas tries a second time: Mum's at the checkout, and he eyes the candy. *Ooh, candy . . . let's try the whine. Not working? Maybe crying and kicking the cart will do it . . . that's not working either. Hey, where is she taking me now? . . . out of the store? . . . and still no candy. This is what happened last time . . . I don't like this—it's no fun.* At this juncture, Nicholas will realize that there's no reward when he whines, when he cries, not even when he goes over the top and has a full-blown meltdown. His mother rewards only good behavior.

As a parent, you must decide which kind of lesson you want *your child* to learn. You have to take responsibility for your role as director. You are the grown-up. Your toddler needs you to be in charge and to show her the way. Predictability and limits won't cramp her style, as many of today's parents seem to feel. On the contrary, rules make a child feel safe.

In this chapter, I will guide you through the principles of conscious discipline. Your best bet, of course, is to try to *avoid* problem situations. When that's not possible, then at least you can take appropriate actions. If you practice conscious discipline, even after a horrible meltdown, you can heave a sigh of relief, knowing that you've stayed in charge, curbed your own anger, and helped teach your child a valuable lesson in self-control. We're not asking children to be perfect, to be seen but not heard. We're shaping their lives, teaching them values, teaching them respect.

The Twelve Ingredients of Conscious Discipline

Conscious discipline is about making life predictable for your toddler and setting limits that make her feel secure. It's about your child knowing what to expect and what's expected of her. It's about right and wrong and developing good judgment. And it's about teaching a child to obey a certain set of rules. Toddlers don't purposely act "naughty"—their parents just haven't helped them learn the correct way to behave. But when parents create *external structures* to rein children in, it helps their little ones develop *internal control*.

Ultimately, conscious discipline empowers our children to learn how to make good choices, be responsible, think for themselves, and act in a socially acceptable manner. This is a tall order, of course. Although your toddler's brain is developing in ways that enable her to plan, expect consequences, understand your requests and standards, and control her impulses, none of this comes easily. Here are the twelve ingredients of conscious discipline—factors that will help you help her.

1. Know your own boundaries— and set rules. What standards are you comfortable with? Nelly next door might think it's fine for her little Hubert to jump on the living room couch, but what do *you* expect? Only you can make rules for your household. Think about your boundaries and be consistent. *Tell* your child what you expect—she's not a mind reader, for goodness' sake! For example, don't take her into a shop where sweets are sold and suddenly say, "You can't have candy" (unless you enjoy dealing with tantrums). Instead, set the rules *beforehand*: "When we go to the store, you

---

The Twelve Ingredients of Conscious Discipline

1. Know your own boundaries—and set rules.
2. Look at *your* own behavior to see what you're teaching your child.
3. Listen to yourself to make sure *you* are in charge, not your toddler.
4. Whenever possible, plan ahead; avoid difficult settings or circumstances.
5. See the situation through your toddler's eyes.
6. Pick your battles.
7. Offer closed-end choices.
8. Don't be afraid to say "no."
9. Nip undesirable behavior in the bud.
10. Praise good behavior and correct or ignore bad.
11. Don't rely on corporal punishment.
12. Remember that giving in doesn't equal love.

---

can bring a snack. But I will not buy you candy. Would you like me to pack carrots or Goldfish crackers?"

Set a line and keep it firm. Believe me, children ask for every goodie and gadget imaginable—and they will keep asking. If you're ambivalent, they pick up on it. They know if they nag a bit more, they'll get what they want. Unfortunately, what usually happens is that the child's persistence leads to *your* getting angry. You finally lose it and shout, "For God's sake I said no." Taking the seemingly easy route—giving in just to stop a tantrum or because of your own embarrassment—is shortsighted. In years to come, you *and* your child will regret it. Not being clear about expectations is unkind to children. We all have to be respectful citizens, to obey rules, to recognize the value of social protocol. This kind of teaching starts at home and enables a child to fit in and to flourish in the greater world.

2. Look at your own behavior to see what you're teaching your child. Discipline is one area in which environment can play an even greater role than temperament. To be sure, some children have more trouble than others with impulse control or handling new or difficult situations and are therefore harder to discipline. But parental intervention can tip the balance. I've seen Angel toddlers turned into monsters by parents who didn't know how to stay in charge and set limits. And I've seen Spirited and Grumpy toddlers act like sweet little cherubs because their parents are clear, compassionate, and consistent.

Moreover, the way *we* handle situations—set limits without anger, act instead of react, and deal calmly with stressful situations—is the way we *show* children how it looks to be in control of our emotions. For instance, there's a huge difference in yanking a child out of a store and removing him in a calm, nonjudgmental way. The former teaches violence, the latter, self-control. Children are like sponges. Everything we do teaches them. Sometimes, as Francine and Christopher's story illustrates, they also learn things we never intended them to learn. And it's not just during a conflict. Lessons are taught in the mundane moments of life as well. If you're impolite to a store clerk, if you curse at the telephone when you get disconnected, if you and your partner yell at each other, your child will watch such scenes carefully, and in all probability, incorporate your behavior in her own repertoire.

3. Listen to yourself to make sure you are in charge, not your toddler. Often, when mums and dads ask for my advice, they phrase their problems like this:

"Tracy, Aaron won't let me sit on a chair."

"Patti makes me lie on the floor with her and won't let me get up until she's asleep."

"Brad won't let me put him in the high chair."

"Tracy, Gerry makes me stay in his room at bedtime" (at which point I envision Mum or Dad as the hostage of a two-foot-tall kidnapper with a plastic gun).

I ask these parents to listen to their own words so that they become aware of what their child hears. In each of the scenarios represented above, the parent is allowing King Toddler to rule. That won't do. Being a parent means being in charge.

For instance, some toddlers don't like to wear clothes. It might be fine for your child to run around the living room for an hour in the buff, but what do you do when it's time to go out? You say, "We're going to the park. You have to get dressed." If you make rules, your child *will* go along with them or suffer the natural consequence of not going to the park. Problems occur when parents have no boundaries and let their children set the agenda.

That is not to say that we ought to be overbearing or extremely strict, or that we don't offer toddlers a choice ("You can wear your blue shirt or your red one to the park"). It just means that when it comes down to it, after you attempt to get your child to cooperate, after you've tried all the tricks in this (or any) book, *you* must be the one who calls the shots.

4. Whenever possible, plan ahead; avoid difficult settings or circumstances. With very young children who lack the cognitive skills to understand *why* something is off-limits, it's best to steer clear of the more challenging situations. This is usually possible if you think things through. Remember the L in H.E.L.P.: Limit stimulation and limit situations that are too difficult for your child. Whenever possible, avoid "too" situations—anything that's too loud, too frantic (too many kids, too much activity), too demanding (requiring the child to concentrate or sit longer than is reasonable for a toddler), too cognitively advanced, too scary (a movie, TV show), or too physically taxing (long walks). Remember that situation can override temperament. Even if she's an Angel toddler, it would be irresponsible and unkind to take her on a long shopping excursion if she hadn't had her afternoon nap.

Personality is an important factor, however. Decisions about what to do and where to go should be governed by your knowledge of who *your child* is. If she is naturally very active, don't take her to a store where there are delicate items or to a recital where she would be expected to sit still for an hour. If he's shy, don't arrange play dates with aggressive children. If she's sensitive to loud noises and lots of stimulation, an amusement park would be asking for trouble. If he gets tired easily, don't plan outings that tax his physical limits.

When I explained conscious discipline to Bertha, an attorney, she looked at me and shook her head. "Well, those are good ideas *in principle*, Tracy, but they're not always practical," she insisted. She then proceeded to spin out a typical scenario from her own busy life: "I've just finished a long day's work. I pick up my children from the baby-sitter. I have a stinking headache, and I suddenly remember that I need milk and a few things for dinner.

"So, I drag my little ones to the store, shop, and while waiting on the long line (because everyone who left work also has to pick up some last-minute item for tonight's dinner), the kids start whining. They each want to grab a toy hanging from the display near the cash register. I say, 'no,' but their voices grow louder.

"I know I'm *supposed* to respond in a carefully modulated voice, 'No toys, children. When you behave like that we have to leave the store,' but this isn't the right moment to teach a lesson. I don't have the time nor the patience to sit in the car until they calm down. I've got to get dinner ready and if I lose even fifteen minutes, I'll hit traffic and then all hell will break loose in the car. My children will get hungry, cranky, and bored and will end up fighting with each other or screaming at me. I'll start yelling, and at that point, I'll want to check out and head for Mars.

"What happens then, Tracy?" Bertha asks skeptically. "How do I *avoid* that kind of difficult situation?"

"I'm no magician," I respond. "If things have gotten that far, you're in for it. Nothing in my baby whisperer's bag of tricks will help," I admit, "except to learn from the experience."

And what do you learn? *Planning,* my dears. Check the cupboard the night before to make sure you don't have to shop with your child (or children) at the worst possible time. If at the last minute you realize you've forgotten to check and now need to pick up a few items, shop *before* you fetch your children from day care. If you don't have the time, you'll be in better shape if you've at least anticipated such an impromptu excursion by keeping a supply of Goldfish crackers or other healthy, nonperishable snacks in your glove compartment or trunk. Also, have on hand one or two travel toys that are reserved exclusively for the car. Bring these items into the store if you don't want your child to get bored, beg for sweets, or throw a tantrum when you refuse to cave in. Planning may not solve every problem, but it certainly can alleviate the ones that crop up repeatedly . . . as long as we learn from them.

5. See the situation through your toddler's eyes. Behavior that seems "bad" or "wrong" to an adult may mean something quite different from a toddler's point of view. When sixteen-month-old Denzel grabs his friend Rudy's toy, it doesn't mean he's "aggressive." When he steps on his older brother's jigsaw puzzle on the way across the room, it doesn't mean he's "thoughtless." When he bites his mother's arm, it doesn't mean he wants to hurt her. And when six or seven books and a basketful of toys come crashing down from a shelf in the playroom, it doesn't mean Denzel is "destructive."

What's really going on in each of those instances? Denzel is a toddler who is attempting to be independent and to get his needs met, but he still has a way to go. In the first instance, he doesn't have the verbal capability to say, "I want to do what Rudy is doing." In the second, he doesn't have the physical coordination to step over his older brother's puzzle (and probably doesn't even notice it as he makes a beeline for a toy truck on the other side of the room). In the third instance, his teeth hurt, but he has neither the awareness nor the physical control to choose a more appropriate object to teethe on. In the fourth, he wants Mum to read him a story, but not understanding cause and effect, he doesn't realize that if he pulls out his favorite book everything on top of it will come tumbling down as well.

As I pointed out in Chapter Six, sometimes what appears to be aggression in a toddler is simple curiosity. It is, for example, no accident that toddlers favor poking their baby siblings' eyes. Eyeballs move; they're squishy. Who wouldn't want to experiment? And some misbehavior is a matter of your toddler being at the wrong place at the wrong time. Or your child may be overtired, a physical state that tends to make toddlers more impulsive, and sometimes, aggressive. Also, if you've been inconsistent about setting boundaries, you can't expect your toddler to *guess* your standards. If you let him jump on the couch yesterday, how could anyone blame him for thinking that it's okay to jump on it today?

> **TIP:** *Help your child obey the rules you set. A common rule, for example, is "no ball throwing in the house." We adults know that balls are meant for playing outside. So why do we keep them in toy boxes? And when a child then throws a ball in the house, why are we surprised?*

6. *Pick your battles.* Monitoring a toddler can be exhausting: "No, Ben, you may not have that." "Be gentle." "Ben, don't stand so close to the ironing board." On some days the constant teaching can get on your nerves. Still, discipline is part and parcel of parenting a toddler. It's important, though, to know when it's absolutely necessary to enforce your boundaries and when it's okay to relax them a bit. Clearly, when you're stuck in a no-win situation, you have to make a decision—do I hold the line or give in gracefully? Be creative.

Let's say it's cleanup time and your child is a bit overtired. When you say, "Time to clean up," she responds with a loud "No!" If she's the type of child who is usually good about putting away her toys, why ask for trouble? Help her. Suggest, "I will put your blocks away while you put dolly to bed in the toy chest." If she continues to balk, then say again, "I will help you," and proceed to put everything except one item away. Hand that to her and say, "Here, you can drop this into the toy box." Praise her (but not excessively) when she's done it: "Good job."

Suppose you're trying to get your child dressed. If you're already late and you know that he's usually a dawdler, you haven't planned this very well. You don't have the time to put on one article of clothing every fifteen minutes, as you usually do, so what's the alternative? You allow your child to show up at day care, or wherever he's going, wearing his pajamas. He'll realize soon enough that he's dressed inappropriately for public viewing and probably won't put you through the same scene again. (He'll just figure out some other way to be obstinate!)

The point is sometimes you need a quick solution. Time is a factor and something has to give. Use your judgment and ingenuity, but don't make excuses or go into long explanations. For instance, you're at the mall, your child refuses to walk another step, and you're already late. Don't launch into a lecture ("We have to hurry—Mommy has a doctor's appointment in fifteen minutes"). Not only is your narrative above her head, it might make her go even slower. (Children instinctively know just where a parent is most vulnerable.) Cut to the chase; pick her up and get where you're going without a hassle.

7. Offer closed-end choices. Toddlers are often more cooperative when offered a choice, because it gives them a sense of control. Instead of threatening or squaring off *against* your toddler, then, try to involve her and make her part of the solution. But be sure you propose closed-end choices—questions or statements that force a concrete response, not a "yes" or "no" answer: "Do you want Cheerios or Cocoa Puffs?" "Do you want to put your blocks away first or your dollies?" (see the box on page 220 for other examples). These have to be real choices, not fake ones. Real choices are alternatives you've narrowed down in your own mind which leave no room for interpretation. For example, if you're undressing her and you say, "Are you ready for your bath now?" you're not really asking for her input. You're indirectly telling her what's going to happen. And by making it a question, you also risk her answering "no." A more appropriate choice question would be: "When you take your bath, do you want to use the red washcloth or the blue one?"

Offering Choices

Demands/Threats	Choice Statements/Questions
If you don't eat, we're not going to the playground.	When you're finished eating, then we can go to the playground.
Get over here . . . now.	Do you want to come over here by yourself or should I get you?
You have to have your diaper changed.	Do you want me to change your diaper now, or after we read this book?
Let go of Sally's toy.	If you can't let go of Sally's toy, I can help you.
No, Paul—you cannot play with my lipstick.	Do you want to give me that lipstick or should I help you let go of it? Thank you— what good cooperation. Now would you like to hold my comb or my mirror?
Don't slam that door again.	Please close the door gently.
Stop talking with food in your mouth.	Finish chewing and then you can talk to me.
No! We are not going to stop for ice cream on the way home. You'll ruin your appetite.	Yes, I know that you're hungry. You can have a [mention a delicious snack] as soon as we get home.

8. *Don't be afraid to say "no."* No matter how much forethought you give to a situation, there will be times when you'll have to deny your toddler's request. Ask yourself: *Am I one of those parents who thinks it's necessary to make my child happy all the time?* If so, it might be hard for you to see your little one crumble in the face of a stern "no." Recently, for example, I spent the day with a mum and her two- and four-year-old sons. Whenever they wanted something, they whined—and she gave in each time. She could never say "no" because she desperately wanted her boys to be chipper all

the time. Not only is that unrealistic, it's also important for children to understand that there's a range of human emotions, including sadness and anger and exasperation. In the long run, she'll make them and herself miserable, because life is about frustration and disappointment, and they won't be prepared for it. As that classic Rolling Stones song reminds us, we can't always get what we want. We set children up for a rude awakening if we never teach them to accept "no" for an answer. (That doesn't necessarily mean *saying* "no" repeatedly; see the Tip on page 158.)

> **TIP:** *When your child is upset, rather than cajoling, which ignores his feelings, or trying to convince him that he doesn't "really" feel bad, which encourages him to "stuff" his feelings, allow him to fully express* all *his emotions. Say things like, "I know you're disappointed," or "It looks like you're really angry about that" to let him know it's normal to have emotional reactions and even to be unhappy.*

9. Nip undesirable behavior in the bud. Catch your child *before* he acts out, or at least in the act. Watching a group of nineteen-month-olds at play, I observed that one of the boys, Oliver, who had a history of getting a bit too excited with his playmates, was starting to lose control. His mum, Dorothy, had noticed, too. Instead of saying to herself, *This is a phase he'll grow out of,* Dorothy kept a watchful eye on her son. At one point, Oliver picked up his Radio Flyer truck, and Dorothy, realizing that he was winding up to throw it, said in an even but cautioning tone, "Oliver, we do not throw toys." Oliver put the truck down.

You might not always be able to catch your child *before*, but you can usually step in *while* something is happening. For example, Rebecca called me to complain about her family's mealtime drama. Usually, after fifteen minutes in his high chair, fifteen-month-old Raymond began to throw his food. "That means he's not interested in eating, luv," I explained. "Take him away from the table immediately. If you make him sit there, you're asking for trouble. While you attempt to feed him, he'll try to squirm out of his chair, arch his back, or scream."

"Yes! That's exactly what happens," Rebecca exclaimed, as if she had just gotten a reading from someone on the Psychic Friends network. (Little did she realize that I'd seen hundreds of toddlers do the same thing.) My suggestion was simple: a half hour after she had removed Raymond from the table, she should try to put him in his high chair again to see if he was hungry. She stuck with the plan for two days. Picking him up and taking him down so often was really hard work, but Raymond is now eating his food instead of throwing it.

It's also important to help your child understand *what* he's feeling when he misbehaves. Look at the context. If he missed his nap, he's probably tired. If he didn't get his way, he's probably frustrated or angry. If someone hit him, he's obviously hurt. Name the emotion straightaway: "I know that you're [insert emotion]." Needless to say, you should never shame your child or accuse him of being "naughty" for having an emotion. At the same time, let your child know that emotions are not an excuse. Inappropriate behavior, whether it's hitting, biting, or having a tantrum, must stop regardless of how he feels. The goal is to teach your child to identify and *manage* his emotions.

10. Praise good behavior and correct or ignore bad. Sadly, some parents are so focused on "no," they forget to notice when their child does things right. In actual fact, though, it's even more important to notice children's *good* behavior than to reprimand bad. Consider, if you will, a lovely couple, Maura and Gil, who came into my office one day with their adorable child, Heidi. They claimed that their eighteen-month-old "whined constantly." As Mum and Dad related their tale of woe, each accusing the other of "spoiling" the child, Heidi stood contentedly in the play garden, busily shoving plastic envelopes into the mail slot, opening and closing the various doors and latches.

Meanwhile, Maura and Gil barely noticed Heidi, until she, sensing that their attention was elsewhere and not on her wonderful accomplishments in the garden, started whining. Suddenly, they were all over her, making a big fuss about her alleged distress: "Oh, poor baby, what's the matter?" Gil said sympathetically. "Come here, honey," said Maura. You could almost feel their pity. Heidi, in turn, climbed into Gil's lap for a few minutes and then scooted back to explore other toys. The same pattern was repeated at least five times during the hour-long consultation. When Heidi was good, playing independently and *not* whining, no one said a word. When Heidi was bored, whimpered a bit, and then turned to Mum and Dad for soothing, she was instantly rewarded.

Maura and Gil were surprised when I told them that they had *taught* Heidi to whine and to depend on them for solace. Their behavior was also compromising their child's attention span. They looked at me, puzzled. "Instead of waiting until she whines," I suggested, "praise Heidi while she is amusing herself. Simply say, 'Good playing, Heidi. That's wonderful!' Secure in the knowledge that you're paying attention to her, she'll be encouraged to stay at tasks longer than when she senses—accurately—that you're not. Whenever she whines," I added, "either ignore her or correct the behavior by saying, 'I can't answer you unless you talk in your best voice.' " The first time they corrected Heidi, I explained, they were to model what a "best voice" sounds like: "Don't whine at me, Heidi. Say it like this: 'Help me, Mommy.' "

> **TIP:** *Be aware of what you "reward" with your attention—whining, crying, nagging, yelling, running in church. Instead, praise your child when she cooperates and acts kindly, when she's quiet, when she plays independently, and when she lies down to soothe herself. In short, make the good moments last by acknowledging them.*

11. Don't rely on corporal punishment. I was once in a mall and saw a mum give her child a swift smack on the legs followed by a yank. "You bully!" I exclaimed. The woman was aghast.

"I beg your pardon?" she asked.

Undaunted, I repeated myself: "I said, 'You bully. How dare you hit someone so small!' "

She responded to me with a string of curse words and off she went.

I'm often asked, "Is it okay to spank my child?" From the look on my face, most parents know my answer. I then ask a question instead: "When you see your child strike another child, what do you do?"

Why You Shouldn't Spank

Despite recent claims to the contrary from so-called parenting experts, I believe that *any* type of hitting is bad. When people rationalize ("A little swat here or there never did *me* any harm") or minimize ("It was just a tap"), in my mind it's like someone with a drinking problem saying, "I only drink beer."

It's a momentary solution. Spanking doesn't teach a child anything about misbehavior. It only teaches them that it hurts to get hit. He may behave better for a while, because he naturally wants to avoid pain. But then the child doesn't learn any skills, and he's certainly not developing inner control.

It's unfair. When a big person loses control and hits a little person, he or she is being a bully.

It's a double standard. How can you hit a child when you're angry or frustrated and not expect her to turn around and do the same thing?

It encourages aggression. As my Nan says, "You beat the devil in," meaning that you make children *more* defiant by hitting them. Research backs her up: children who are spanked tend to hit peers, especially those who are younger or smaller, and try to solve problems with violence.

Most reply, "I stop them."

"Well, if it's not all right for your child to strike another child," I point out, "then what gives *you* permission to hit? Children are not our property. Only a bully would strike someone who is unable to strike back or defend himself."

That goes for light swats on the behind or a tap on the hand as well. My feeling is that if you hit a child or demonstrate violence in *any* shape or form, you have lost control and it's you, not your child, who requires help.

Sometimes, a parent will argue, "Well, my dad hit me and it never did me any harm."

"Well," I answer, "that's not true. It *did* do you harm. It taught you that hitting is okay—and in my book it's not."

Physical punishment is a short-term solution that *teaches nothing positive.* Instead, it teaches children that we hit when we are frustrated; we hit when we don't know what else to do; we hit when we lose control.

Short Fuse Alert!

Even parents who are against spanking can spontaneously strike a child. It sometimes happens out of fear, a knee-jerk reaction when a child runs into the road or courts danger in some other way. Or it's the result of parental frustration. You lose control and hit because your child repeatedly does something annoying—for example, tugging at your sleeve or pulling on a magazine you're reading. Even if you only deliver a tap on the tush, take responsibility:

Apologize. Say, "I'm sorry. It was wrong for Mummy to hit you."

Look in the mirror. In what ways are you not taking care of yourself? Are you eating properly, getting enough rest, having marital problems? If so, your fuse could be shorter than usual.

Assess the circumstances. Was there something about this particular situation that hit a personal hot spot? Once you know what your triggers are, try to avoid similar situations or at least remove yourself before your blood starts to boil. We all have our breaking points. Here are the most common answers when parents are asked, "What sets you off?"

- Noise
- Whining
- Sleeping problems
- Crying, especially inconsolable or excessive crying
- Testing behavior (you ask the child not to do something and he keeps at it)

Don't feel guilty. Every parent makes mistakes; don't beat yourself up. Laying yourself at your child's feet gives him too much control. Guilt also can make it hard for you to discipline him properly in the future.

---

12. Remember that giving in doesn't equal love. Many parents, particularly those who work out of the house, find it hard to discipline their children. Their thinking goes like this: *I'm out all day. My child hasn't seen me, and I don't want to be the heavy all the time. I don't want my son to think, "Oh darn, every time Dad comes home, he tells me off."* Well, my dears, remind yourself that conscious discipline is about *teaching,* not punishing. Don't see yourself as a drill sergeant.

Quite the contrary, you are helping your child see that cooperation is fun and that it feels good to behave nicely.

If you don't help your child learn about boundaries, you're not doing her any favors. You may give in to your own guilt ("Poor baby—he doesn't see me all day"), fear ("She'll hate me if I discipline her"), or denial ("He'll grow out of it"); or you may abdicate responsibility ("I'll let the baby-sitter handle it"). In any case, you're not teaching her what every child needs to learn: *how to control herself.* Each time you give in, each time you settle for a quick fix to "buy" your child's love or make yourself feel better, I assure you that *next time*, your child will up the ante. Even worse, at some point, you will become frustrated with your child's behavior— behavior that you inadvertently encouraged. You'll wake up one day and feel you have lost control. You'll be right; you *have* lost control. And it isn't your child's fault.

At the same time, I urge you to give yourself permission to make mistakes. Conscious discipline takes lots of practice. From the time my daughters were young, I have had firm and clear boundaries, just the way my mum and my Nan had with me. I wasn't perfect by any means; I exploded more than once. And I feared that when I lost my temper, I'd leave indelible marks. However, a few mistakes, a few inconsistencies, don't mar an entire childhood. Now that I have teenagers, memories of toddler discipline are like a walk in the park. My daughters test me all the time. I have to be creative and lighthearted about it all, but at the same time, in control. Baby whispering experience notwithstanding, I'm still far from perfect.

What I've found, and I've seen in other parents as well, is that when you are consistent and clear about your rules, not only do you feel better about yourself and the kind of parent you are, your child also feels secure. He knows your boundaries and respects you for your word. He loves you for your honesty, knowing that when you say something, you follow through.

The Rule of One/Two/Three

As my Nan always admonished, "Start as you mean to go on." In other words, pay attention to the messages that you send your child. Especially in highly impressionable young children, bad habits can develop quickly. Christopher, the little boy you met at the beginning of this chapter, has already figured out how to get candy in the supermarket, and every time his mum gives in, he will keep adding ammunition to his arsenal—tools that will come in handy as he becomes more demanding and realizes he can keep pushing his mother. In the same vein, a child who tonight asks for—and gets—another two stories, a drink of water, an extra cuddle, will tomorrow night ask for even more (more about such chronic difficulties in the next chapter).

Are Others Better at Disciplining Your Child?

Does your child respect the boundaries of an alternative caretaker—a nanny, a grandparent, an aunt—more than your own? Many parents feel jealous when that happens, fearing that the child doesn't love them as much, but it's not about love, it's about setting boundaries. It might be time to *learn* from the other caretaker rather than resenting him or her.

Conscious discipline is a matter of getting your thinking cap on, preventing bad habits rather than waiting until you require a cure. When you see a certain type of undesirable behavior, you say to yourself, *This could be a potential problem if I let it get out of hand.* It may be something that's "cute" now, like running naked around the dining room table daring you to catch him for his bath, but when your child gets older his defiance won't be so adorable.

To every situation, whether it's whining or a full-blown tantrum, hitting you or hitting another child, bedtime reluctance or waking in the night, mealtime misbehavior or meltdowns in public, refusal to take a bath or reluctance to get out of the tub, apply this simple *One/Two/Three* rule:

One. The first time your child does something that crosses a line you've set—climbs on a couch that's off-limits, hits another child in play group, tugs on your shirt to breastfeed in public after you've weaned him—you *take notice*. You also let the child know that she's crossed the line. (At the end of this chapter, on pages 240–241, you'll find suggestions and "scripts" for many common behavioral issues.) For example, if you're holding your child and she hits you, the first time it happens, restrain her hand and say, "Ouch, that hurts. You can't hit mummy." Some children stop at one, and that's all it takes. But don't count on it.

Two. The first time a child bites or throws food at the table might be an isolated incident, but the second time it happens, suspect that you're witnessing the onset of a pattern and that the behavior could become habitual. Hence, if your child hits you again, put her down and remind her of the rule: "I told you, you can't hit Mummy." If she cries, tell her: "I'll pick you up again as long as you don't hit me." Remember that the *kind* of attention you give a particular behavior determines whether your child will continue it. Cajoling, compromising, and caving in, as well as extreme negative reactions, like yelling, tend to reinforce undesirable behavior. In other words, *over*reactions usually encourage a child to misbehave again, either because she perceives the interaction as a game or because she's not getting enough atten-

Going Too Far

Following are common mistakes parents make when trying to discipline their children that involve saying too much or saying things beyond a young child's grasp:

Overexplaining: A classic real-life example occurs when a toddler is about to climb onto a chair and the parent launches into an elaborate explanation: "If you climb up there you might fall and hurt yourself." Instead of talking, the parent should *take action* and physically restrain the child.

Being vague/obtuse: Certain statements, such as "No, that's dangerous," have a number of meanings. Instead, saying "Don't climb on the steps" is specific and clear. Likewise, statements such as "Would you like it if I hit you?" (commonly uttered when a child hits) don't mean anything to a toddler either. Better to say, "Ouch, that hurts. You may not hit."

Taking it personally: I cringe when a parent says, "It makes me sad when you misbehave." Telling children that their behavior causes you to feel unhappy gives them too much control and power. It also implies that *they* are responsible for your moods. It's better to say, "When you behave like that, you can't be around us."

tion for her good behavior and this new strategy is an effective way to get you to notice her.

Three. The definition of insanity is to do the same thing over and over and expect different results. If a negative behavior pattern continues, you have to ask yourself, *What am I doing to perpetuate it?* Try not to get to "three."

Let's say your toddler hits another child: The first time it happens, look your child square in the eye and say, "No. You may not hit Manuel. That hurts him." The second time it happens, remove your child from the room. Don't do it with anger; simply take him out and explain, "You cannot play with the other children if you hit." If you're firm to begin with, your child will probably stop. If not, and two becomes three—then it's time to take him home. (Constantly allowing a child to get to "three" tends to set up the kinds of chronic behavior problems covered in Chapter Eight.)

Pleading/apologizing: Discipline has to be delivered without ambivalence and with a sense that you're in control of your emotions. A parent who pleads ("Please don't hit Mummy") and then goes on to apologize ("It makes Mummy sad when she has to give you a time-out") doesn't seem to be in charge.

Not managing your own anger: Discipline should come from a compassionate place inside you, not from anger (also see the sidebar on page 239). Never threaten your child. Moreover, it's best not to hold on to your feelings. Your toddler will quickly forget about it, and so should you.

Remember the story in Chapter Six (pages 203–204), about the mother who was asked to leave a play group because her child hit and pushed other children? Mum not only let Beth go past the One/Two/Three limit, she kept making excuses: "It's a phase. She'll grow out of it." Not true. The only thing toddlers grow out of, luv, is their shoes!

Meanwhile, I felt sorry for Beth. She suffered because the adults in the group resented her mother's attitude. In allowing her daughter to misbehave, the mother was teaching her to use force rather than cooperate. Understandably, neither children nor adults wanted her around. I don't believe that Beth, or any child for that matter, was inherently "naughty." Sure, some toddlers test constantly; they see how far they can go, what reaction they get, what's responded to. Some lose control more often than others. But through it all, they're looking to their parents to set limits. When a mother or father doesn't acknowledge a child's behavior problems or take steps to help her through it, sadly, it's the child who eventually gets a bad name.

Respectful Intervention

When your child misbehaves in any way, it's always best to take action calmly and quickly. However, it's also important to *intervene respectfully*. That is, remain composed and compassionate. Never embarrass, shame, or humiliate your child. And always be mindful of teaching rather than punishing your child.

For example, at one of my play groups, Marcos, a Spirited child by nature, was becoming increasingly excited. This is quite normal for toddlers, especially Spirited toddlers with exuberant personalities. When they are in a group, especially four children or more, there's a lot going on. They copy other kids, want to play with the same toys, and this sometimes leads to conflict. Unfortunately, what often happens is that a parent tries to dominate or appease the overstimulated toddler. Feeling a bit desperate and embarrassed, a mother or father might try to calm the child down or shut him up by offering this toy or that. Or the parent takes the other tack, yelling or yanking the boy into submission. Either strategy tends to have the reverse effect. The more energy the parent exerts, the more agitated and/or obstinate the child

---

**Respectful Intervention
at a Glance**

State the rule: "No you may not. . . ."

Explain the effect of the behavior: "That . . . hurts/made Sara cry/isn't nice."

Make the child apologize and give the other child a hug: "Say, I'm sorry." (But don't let your toddler use "sorry" to gloss over the bad behavior.)

Explain the consequence: "When you [restate the behavior], you may not stay; we'll have to leave until you calm down." (This may also be a good opportunity for a time-out; see page 256.)

---

becomes. In his toddler mind, he says to himself: *Hey, this is a great way to get Mummy's (or Daddy's) attention. She's not even talking to the other mothers now.* The mum's so-called intervention is actually a reward for bad behavior.

Fortunately, at this particular play group the mothers had agreed to take action immediately whenever a child became aggressive. Therefore, when Marcos, wild-eyed and clearly overtired as well, suddenly went at Sammy and shoved him, Marcos's mum, Serena, wasted no time. She first gave her attention to the injured, wailing child who was on the floor: "Sammy, are you okay?" When Sammy's mother went to comfort her child, Serena then initiated the following respectful intervention with her own son:

SHE STATED THE RULE: "No, Marcos, you may not shove."

SHE EXPLAINED THE EFFECT OF HIS BEHAVIOR: "That hurt Sammy."

SHE MADE HIM APOLOGIZE AND HUG THE OTHER CHILD: "Say, I'm sorry. Now give Sammy a hug."

Marcos, like many toddlers, said "sorry" and gave a hug, but in his mind the words and action were magic, negating and excusing what he had just done. When Serena realized this and noticed that her son was continuing to be rambunctious, she knew she had reached "two" and had to follow through.

SHE EXPLAINED THE CONSEQUENCE: "It's good that you said sorry to Sammy, but now we have to stand

---

Know Yourself

Parenting style (see pages 62–64) is strongly linked to attitudes about discipline and to the actions parents take.

The **Controller** is apt to discipline in anger. She often yells at or yanks her child, or even worse, punishes physically.

The **Enabler** is likely to apologize for her child, make excuses for his behavior. She doesn't do much to discipline her child until a situation gets so out of hand she's forced to take action.

The **HELPer** strikes a happy medium. She hangs back long enough to let her child work out difficulties on his own and to evaluate the situation, but intervenes immediately and respectfully when necessary. She knows it's important for her child to have his feelings, so she doesn't try to talk him out of them or cajole him into a good mood. She is able to make rules and levy consequences when her child oversteps the boundaries she's set.

---

outside until you calm down. You may not play with other children when you push or shove."

Although some children get so keyed up that going home may be the best option, it is often enough to remove your toddler from the setting for ten or fifteen minutes. This is the form of "time-out" I prefer for young children, rather than leaving them alone (see box on page 237). In someone else's home, ask if you can use a spare bedroom; in a public venue, stand in the hallway or even a bathroom. The goal is to help your child regain control. If you know that holding him will make him balk even more and perhaps start hitting you, then put him on the floor. Encourage him to express whatever emotion the incident has brought up by saying the words *for* him, "You look angry." When your child has calmed down, say, "You're calm now, so we can go back to the other children."

Given this kind of break from the action, most children will settle back into the group without incident. If not, say your good-byes immediately and head home. Don't make your child feel guilty for leaving, though. Remember that this is hard for him, too. He needs to know that you're his ally in helping him learn self-control. (By the way, if your child has been hit or witnesses such a scene, don't explain *why* Marcos was taken out *unless your child asks*. Remember that children imitate other children. You don't want to plant any ideas in your child's head, reinforce the bad behavior by giving it too much attention, or label the other child as a "naughty" boy.)

Knowing Your Child's Tricks

Many children are natural-born actors; they can turn the charm on and off at will. Parents think they're "cute" and suddenly all bets are off—discipline falls by the wayside. I saw this at a friend's home recently. As I was busy talking to his mum, Henry began to swat at Fluffy, the cat. His mother jumped right in. "No, Henry, you may not hit Fluffy like that. It hurts her." Restraining his hand, she added, "Be gentle." Henry looked up at her and with the sweetest, most angelic smile said, "Hi," as if nothing had happened. I sensed that mother and son had been here before. At only nineteen months, Henry knew that his "hi," and the broad endearing smile that accompanied it, would make his mother melt. And sure enough, Mum smiled proudly. "Isn't he cute, Tracy?" she asked rhetorically. "Don't you just love that face?" A few minutes later, Henry clunked Fluffy on the head with his truck and was now chasing the poor cat around the living room. (I couldn't help worrying that if his mother didn't discipline Henry, Fluffy soon would do it *for* her . . . with claws.)

Then there's the "feel-sorry-for-me" face. The same toddlers who can pretend-cry during play can fake emotions at other times as well. Gretchen, seventeen months, "put on her pout face," as her mother described it, whenever she wanted attention. Mum thought the expression—eyes downcast, bottom lip projecting—was adorable and utterly beguiling. The only problem was that "the face" had become a tool in Gretchen's arsenal. Besides the fact that Gretchen could now manipulate her mother with her bogus look of distress, Mum now had no way of knowing whether her daughter was really sad or whether she was manipulating her.

I'm sure *your* toddler has a few tricks up his sleeve, too. And though he may be the cutest, most clever child this side of China, if he's using charm or sadness or some other ploy to sidestep discipline, it's best not to admire his acting skills. Remember that each time you ignore misbehavior, you're not helping your child learn self-control. Cajoling or caving in is like putting a Band-Aid on a cut without treating the infection underneath. You might have momentary relief, but bad usually becomes worse. Next thing you know, your child throws a wobbly, or as you Yanks put it, has a tantrum.

The Tantrum Two-Step

Tantrums, unfortunately, go with the territory of early childhood. Granted, the chances of an out-and-out meltdown are greatly reduced if you religiously heed my One/Two/Three ground rules and intervene respectfully. Nevertheless, if you're the parent of a toddler (and I presume you are, or why else would you be reading this book?), you'll probably have to deal with a tantrum or two along the way. They often occur in the most embarrassing (for parents) settings, like friends' houses, church or synagogue, or public places such as a restaurant or supermarket. Your child collapses on the floor, screaming, legs kicking and arms flailing about, or he might just stand there stamping his feet, yelling at you at the top of his lungs. Either way, you want to crawl into a dark hole somewhere.

Tantrums are essentially attention-seeking behavior and loss of control. While you may not be able to escape tantrums altogether, you can discourage your child from using tantrums to subvert your rules or overstep your boundaries. My suggestion is actually a simple two-step process, whereby you *analyze* (understand what caused the tantrum) and *act*.

1. Analyze. Understanding the cause of a particular tantrum gives you clues about how to stop it. There are many reasons for tantrums. After all, that "help-me/let-me-go" struggle can be exhausting to a toddler. Fatigue, confusion, frustration, and overstimulation are all common causes.

A lot of temper tantrums also happen because toddlers can't express themselves, and if you observe carefully, you'll see that your child may be trying to tell you something. Our Sophie never liked going to children's parties. When she pitched a fit at her first party, I had hoped it was a fluke. But on a second go at a birthday gathering, when she got so upset that she went screaming for the door, I realized that socializing with lots of people was a troublesome area—obviously, a party was too frantic an experience for her. On one hand, I didn't see any point in not going to parties at all. Sophie was quiet and shy enough and needed practice in various types of settings. But I also wanted to respect what her tantrums were telling me. Hence, I either went to a party for only a few minutes at the beginning, or arrived just in time for the singing of "Happy Birthday" and cake. I'd ask the parents if it was okay, explaining, "She's just not able to handle the whole event."

Worst of all, though, are the "I-want-what-I-want" tantrums, which are designed to manipulate and control the environment—in other words, *you*. Though such tantrums are calculated to break a parent's will (and often succeed, thereby ensuring repeat performances), children who act them out aren't actually being willful or spiteful. They're just doing what their parents inadvertently have taught them to do.

One way to tell the difference between tantrums designed to manipulate and those that result from frustration or a physical cause, such as fatigue or overstimulation, is to apply the simple *ABC technique* I introduced in my first book.

A STANDS FOR THE ANTECEDENT—*WHAT CAME FIRST.* What were you doing at the time? What was your toddler doing? Were you interacting with him or busy with something or someone else? Who else was around? Daddy? Grandma? Another child? What else was going on in his environment? Was your child defending himself? Was he denied something he wanted?

B STANDS FOR THE BEHAVIOR—*WHAT YOUR TODDLER DID.* Did she cry? Did she look and sound angry? Frustrated? Is she tired, scared, or hungry? Did she bite, push, or hit? Is what she did something that she never does? Often does? If she picked on another child, is this something new, or a habitual pattern?

C STANDS FOR THE CONSEQUENCE—*THE USUAL RESULT OF A AND B.* Here it's important to take responsibility for how *your* actions shape your child. I don't think one ever "spoils" a child. What happens is that parents unintentionally reinforce bad habits and don't have the awareness or skills to change them. I call this accidental parenting (see page 247; also, each of the problems laid out in Chapter Eight is due to accidental parenting)—a process by which mothers and fathers, unaware of how they may be reinforcing a pattern, keep doing what they always did. For example, they continually cajole a child out of a "bad mood," are inconsistent about rules, often placate to avoid embarrassment or further conflict, or all of the above. The parents may succeed in stopping the undesirable behavior in the moment, but they inadvertently strengthen the bad habit in the long run. *They reinforce the behavior by giving in.*

The key to changing the consequence, therefore, is to *do something different*—allow the child to have his feelings but not try to appease or cave in to his demands. Let's revisit the examples of

Francine and Christopher, Leah and Nicholas, the mothers and sons you met at the beginning of this chapter. If you look at the ABC in both cases, the *antecedent* was Mum's diverted attention at the checkout line, coupled with the intriguing display of candy.

Christopher's *behavior*—whining and then kicking the cart—resulted in the *consequence* of Francine caving in to his demands. Although giving in to Christopher's demand for candy temporarily alleviated the stress of that embarrassing moment in the supermarket, Francine unwittingly taught Christopher that his arsenal of tantrum behaviors was quite effective—and he will use them again.

Thoughts on Embarrassment

Yes, it's embarrassing when your child has a meltdown, but it's not as embarrassing as if he keeps doing it. Therefore, before you try to amuse your child or give him something to appease his anger, consider this: if you don't change the pattern, you're in for countless repeat performances.

With Nicholas, the *behavior* was the same as Christopher's but the *consequence* was not, because Leah *did something different* so as not to reinforce the inappropriate behavior: she didn't give in. Nicholas probably won't drag out his tantrum arsenal the next time he and his mum are in the market. If he does, though, and she maintains her stance, he *will* learn that there's no reward in pitching a fit. I'm not saying that Nicholas will be "cured" of tantrums, or that his behavior will be exemplary forevermore. But because his mother refuses to give this particular kind of unpleasant interaction her attention, it won't become entrenched.

Naturally, not all tantrums are the result of accidental parenting. Your child might be frustrated because he can't express himself, tired, or coming down with a cold, all of which can exaggerate his neediness and heighten his emotions. A tantrum can also be the result of a combination of factors that snowball out of control: a tired child doesn't get his way or is shoved by a playmate. But when you apply the ABC method and realize that a string of tantrums—usually, replays of a similar situation—are the result of your reinforcing negative behavior, you need to take steps to change the pattern.

Time-Out!

What It Is: The use of a "time-out" period is sorely misunderstood. It's not about taking a child to her room as punishment. It's a method of avoiding a full-scale battle, a time *away from the heat of the moment*. A proper time-out helps a child regain control over his emotions and prevents parents from accidentally reinforcing the bad behavior. With toddlers, I advise parents to do time-outs with their children, not even to leave them alone in a crib or playpen.

How It's Done: If you're at home, take your child away from the scene of the crime. Say he has a tantrum in the kitchen; bring him into the living room and sit with him until he calms down. If your child acts up in public or at another person's house, take him into another room. In either instance, tell him what you expect of him. "No, we may not go back until you're quiet." He understands more than you realize. Verbal reinforcement, accompanied by being taken away from the situation, will get your message across. Return when he's calm and quiet, but if he starts misbehaving, leave again.

What You Say: Name the emotion ("I can see you're angry . . .") and tell him the consequence (". . . but you may not throw your food"). End with a single, simple sentence: "When you behave like this you can't be around [us/other children]." Do *not* say, "We don't want you around."

What *Not* to Do: Never apologize: "I don't like to do this to you" or "It makes me feel sad that you're in time-out." A child should never be yanked or yelled at; rather, calmly lead him away from the center of the action. Never lock your toddler in a room alone.

2. Act. No matter what causes a tantrum, when a toddler is out of control, *you* need to be the child's conscience. He doesn't have the cognitive skills to reason, or to think through the cause or effect. The best way to stop a tantrum is to remain calm yourself and to allow the child to ride out the emotions *without an audience*. In other words, take away the attention that the tantrum was meant to elicit. To that end, I prescribe the *Three Ds*:

DISTRACT. Your toddler's short attention span can be a gift when he's on the verge of a meltdown. Show him another toy. Pick him up and let him look out the window. Distracting rarely works when a child has launched into a tantrum, because at that point he's caught up in an emotional cyclone. And don't confuse distraction with cajoling, whereby you keep at it, trying different objects or activities even as the undesirable behavior escalates.

DETACH. As long as your child is not endangering herself, someone else, or property, it's best to ignore a full-blown tantrum. If she's on the floor, screaming and kicking, walk away or at least turn your back. If you're holding your child and she is yelling and hitting you (or in any other way being aggressive), put her down. Say calmly but emphatically, "You may not hit Mummy."

DISARM. When children have tantrums, they are not in control of their emotions. An adult has to help them calm down. Some respond well to a parent's arms encircling them, while others become even more agitated when restrained. You also can disarm by removing a child from the setting that upset her in the first place. If her anger is escalating rapidly, give her a time-out (see box on page 237). This not only removes her from the situation, averting further conflict and danger, it also allows her to save face. However, disarming a child should never be done with anger or physical brutality.

Use the *D* that feels most appropriate, or use all three. You need to assess the situation and also gauge what might be most effective with your child. One thing is for sure: idle threats *don't* work—following through does (see advice about *chronic* tantrums in the next chapter, pages 271–274).

There is no doubt that tantrums, especially in public, can be humiliating and frustrating to a parent. No matter which of the *D*s you employ, it's also important to check into your *own* emotional state as well. If you're not already aware of them, become familiar with your "anger cues"—physical signs that tell you you're about to lose it (see sidebar on page 239). I've said repeatedly throughout this chapter, and I'll say it again, conscious discipline is not meted out in anger. One should never humiliate, scream, insult, threaten, yank, spank, slap, or use any kind of violence when disciplining a child, especially an impressionable and helpless toddler. If you have trouble with your own anger, there's no way you can help your child control her impulses.

When you feel your blood starting to boil, leave the room. Give *yourself* a time-out. Even if your child is wailing, put her into a crib or playpen to keep her safe and remove yourself for a few minutes. I often tell parents, "No child ever died of crying, but many have been scarred for life by chronically angry parents." Talk to friends; ask what *they* do when their child's behavior is over the top. Or seek the help of a professional who can give you strategies that will help you manage your anger.

To stay in charge in a very compassionate and caring way is a gift to your child. To say what you mean and mean what you say gives you credibility that will see you not only through the toddler years but serve you both well when your child reaches his teens (that's not as far away as you think, ducky). He will respect you for teaching him boundaries and for reining him in. And he will love you all the more. In short, conscious discipline doesn't break the bond between you and your child; it strengthens it. I know it is difficult at times to hold the line—toddler-testing can try even the most stalwart souls. But as you will see in the next chapter, if you let your limits slide, long-term bad habits are a lot harder to break.

Anger Cues: What's Happening to Me?

Just as important as tuning in to your child's moods is the knowledge of how *you* change when your child stamps her feet, says "no," or has an out-and-out meltdown in public. I asked mothers how their bodies tell them *they* are about to lose it. If you don't recognize yourself in any of the following, figure out what your physical anger cues are.

"I get hot all over."

"I get hives."

"I start to take it personally."

"My heart beats faster."

"It's almost as if I stop breathing."

"My chest starts heaving, and I breathe faster."

"My palms sweat."

"I start grinding my teeth."

Conscious Discipline
Simple Guide

Challenge	What to Do	What to Say
Overstimulation	Remove him from the activity.	I can see that you're getting frustrated, so let's take a little walk outside.
Tantrum in public place because he wants something	Ignore it. If that fails, remove him.	Wow, that's impressive, but you still can't have it. You can't behave like this in [wherever you are].
Refusing to cooperate when dressing	Stop, wait a few minutes.	When you're ready we'll start again.
He continues to run around	Stop him; pick him up.	We can leave when you have your shoes and socks on.
Shouting	Lower your own voice.	Can we use our quiet voice, please?
Whining	Look her in the eye and imitate a "best" (nonwhining) voice.	I can't listen unless you use your best voice.
Running where it's not appropriate	Restrain him by putting two hands on his shoulders.	You may not run here. If you continue, we'll have to leave.
Kicking or hitting when you pick her up	Put her down immediately.	You may not hit/kick me. That hurts.
Grabbing toy from another child	Stand up, go near children, and encourage her to give it back.	William was playing with that. We need to give it back to him.
Throwing food	Take them down from high chair.	We don't throw food at the table.

Challenge	What to Do	What to Say
Pulling another child's hair	Put your hand over whichever hand is wrapped around the other child's hair; stroke your child's hand.	Be gentle, no pulling.
Hitting another child	Restrain him; if he is agitated, take him outside or to another room until he calms down.	You may not hit. That hurts Jim.
Hitting repeatedly	Go home.	We have to leave now.

CHAPTER EIGHT

Time-Busters: Sleep Deprivation, Separation Difficulties, and Other Problems That Steal Hours from Your Day

My concept of a spoiled child is that of an anxious child, searching for limits. If no one provides them, she must keep searching.

—T. Berry Brazelton

To Catch a Thief: Neil's Story

I can always tell when parents are dealing with a "time-buster," a frustrating, seemingly endless and prolonged behavioral difficulty that robs hours from their days—and nights. They usually begin their tale of woe by saying, "Tracy, I've begun to dread . . ." and they fill in the blank with "leaving the house," "naps and bedtime," "baths," "meals," or some other everyday occurrence that has turned into a nightmare. They have no idea how many other parents are victims of similarly exasperating situations.

To exemplify, I will relate the true tale of two-year-old Neil and his parents, Mallory and Ivan. The saga is a bit long, a play-by-play description of how one family generally spends their evenings. Bear with me—it is all too typical of the kinds of time-busting stories I hear. You might even recognize snippets of your own life. Mallory, who tells the story, explains that in their home, Neil's bedtime ritual begins at 7:30, with bath time, which he loves. "The problem," Mallory begins, "is that it's always a battle to get him out of the tub. I warn him two or three times by saying, 'Okay, Neil, bath time is nearly over.'

"But when he starts to whine, I relent: 'Okay . . . then five more minutes.' Five minutes pass. I remind him, 'Neil, now let's get out.' He continues to fuss and whine, and I back off a little, saying, 'Okay, but this is the last time. Finish squirting your bottles and playing with your duck, so you can get out of the tub and ready for bed.'

"After a few minutes, I finally put my foot down: 'Okay, that's it,' I say somewhat sternly. 'Out of the tub, *now*.' At that point he decides to pull away from me and I find myself struggling to grab his slippery little body. 'Come here, Neil,' I insist. I get him in a vise-like lock and he's kicking, fussing, and protesting, 'No! no! no!'

"He scoots out of my arms, dripping wet, and runs to his room. I follow the trail of damp footsteps in the carpet, puffing to catch him, dry him, and wrestle his jammies on. I start pleading, 'Come here. . . . Please put your jammy top on. . . . Let me finish dressing you.'

"At last, I've got the pajama top over his head, and he starts yelling, 'Ouch! ouch!'

"I feel terrible. 'Oh poor, Neil,' I murmur. 'Mummy didn't mean to hurt you. Are you okay?'

"At this point, he's giggling, so I get back to business, 'Okay, time to get into bed. Because it took you so long to get out of the bath, we have time for only one story tonight. Why don't you choose a book you'd like?' Neil goes to the book shelf. 'You want that one?' I ask as he begins pulling several books off the shelf and throwing them to the floor. 'No? That one? Oh, *that* one.' I figure it's best to ignore the mess he's made, although it galls me, because it took me half an hour to get him to clean up his room, which admittedly I did more of than he.

"But at least now we're moving toward the end of the day. Book in hand, I say to him, 'Okay, scoot into your big-boy bed.' He gets under the covers. I snuggle him a bit and start to read to him, but he is still very agitated and uncooperative, turning pages even before I finish reading them. Suddenly, he bolts upright and then stands up on the bed, trying to grab the book out of my hands. 'Lie down, Neil,' I say. 'It's bedtime.'

"He finally lies down, seems to be mellowing out, and I heave a sigh of relief. I say to myself, *Maybe it'll be easier tonight,* but a moment later, his eyes pop open, and he exclaims, 'I want a drink.' *It was too good to be true,* scoffs a voice inside me.

" 'Okay, I'll get you water,' I offer, but just as I'm about to leave the room, he screams. I know that cry: *Don't leave me.* 'Okay, you can come with me,' I say, resigned to the fact that if I don't let him come with me, it will lead to World War III. I carry him downstairs. He has a few sips—he wasn't really thirsty (he never is), and up we go again. As I put him into bed, something catches his eye, and he sits up and attempts to climb out of bed.

"At that point I've had it. I put my hands on his shoulders and raise my voice, 'Back into bed *now,* young man. Don't make me tell you again. It's nighttime and you *have* to go to sleep.' I start to turn off the light, but he's crying and clinging on to me for dear life.

"I can't take it. 'Okay,' I say grudgingly, 'I'll put the light back on. Do you want another story? But this is the last one. Lie down and then I'll read.' At this point, nothing I say seems to matter. He stands there, stiff as a board, tears still glistening on his cheeks. He doesn't move. 'Lie down, Neil,' I repeat. 'Please. I won't tell you again.' I insist.

"He won't move. I then try to distract him: 'Here,' I say, shoving the book at him. 'Help me turn the pages.' Nothing. Now I threaten, 'Okay, Neil, lie down or I'll leave. I mean it—I will go out. If you don't lie down, Mommy won't read you the book.' At last, he lies down.

"I read for a few moments and I notice that he's falling off to sleep, so I move ever so carefully, so as not to disturb him. But his eyes spring open. 'It's okay,' I reassure him, 'I'm here.'

"When he finally closes his eyes again, I wait a few minutes and then gingerly put one leg on the floor. I hold my breath. He tightens his grip around my hand. So I lie there, perfectly still, waiting a few minutes more. I then attempt to slither off the bed. I almost make it, but all of a sudden, Neil opens his eyes. There I am, half hanging off the bed. I say to myself, *One false move and I'll fall on the floor and then I'm done for.* But he settles in again. I wait. By now, my foot is numb, and I have a cramp in my arm.

"Finally, I roll onto the floor, and on all fours, creep toward the door. *Made it!* I slowly open the door . . . and to my horror, it creaks. *Oh, no!* Sure enough, I hear a little voice from the other side of the room: 'No, mummy—no go sleep!'

"I cringe. 'I'm right here, honey. I didn't go anywhere.' But my comforting words fall on deaf ears. Neil starts crying. So I get back onto his bed *again* and try to console him. He wants me to read him another story. I'm ready to slit my wrists or choke him, but I read the story again. . . ."

Mallory's voice trails off. She's embarrassed to admit that the process then starts all over. Neil doesn't fall asleep until eleven, at which point Mallory once more steals out of his bedroom on all fours. "I roll into bed, exhausted every night," she says, "and I turn to Ivan, who has been watching TV or reading, apparently unaware that I've been held captive for the past three hours by our child. When I say, 'Another night from hell,' he looks puzzled. He tells me, 'I thought you were in the office paying bills or something.' I inform him, with more than a hint of resentment in my voice, 'Well, tomorrow night, it's *your* turn.' "

The Roots of All Time-Busters

Other parents' time-busters and the details of how they play out may be different, but the root causes can be traced to one, several, or even all, of the following:

- Parents don't stick to a structured routine.

- Parents allow the child to be in charge.

- Parents don't start as they mean to go on.

- Parents don't set limits.

- Parents have no boundaries—they respect the child but don't demand respect in return.

- Instead of accepting their child's temperament, parents keep hoping it will change.

- Parents haven't helped the child develop self-soothing skills.

- A crisis occurs, such as illness or an accident; parents relax their rules but never reestablish them, even after the child is better.

- Parents are arguing with each other, not paying enough attention to their child—and in time no one knows what the problem is.

- Parents are dealing with their own "ghosts" of the past, which makes it hard for them to see their child clearly.

Mallory is at the end of her rope. "It's always an ordeal, Tracy. I feel like I'm Neil's hostage. Is it a phase? Will he grow out of it? Is it because I work out of the house and he doesn't see me enough? Does he have a sleep disorder? Or maybe A.D.D.?"

"No to all of the above," I reply. "But you're right about one thing: you *are* his hostage."

Time-busters are exhausting; they cut into our own time and couple time. They not only put stress on the parent/child relationship, they can drive a wedge between the adults as well. One parent blames or resents the other. They often argue about the best way to handle the situation (more on this in the next chapter, pages 311–313). While they're at it, though, no one is attending to why the problem developed in the first place or how to alleviate it.

Our toddlers don't mean to be thieves, stealing valuable hours from us. And we parents don't mean to be accomplices, but we often are (see sidebar). The good news is that it is possible to *change* such chronic problems. In this chapter, I'll walk you through some of the most common time-busters I encounter—sleep difficulties, separation anxiety, pacifier addiction (which can contribute to or cause sleep disturbances), chronic tantrums, and mealtime misbehavior. In each case, I help parents follow a sensible course of action (explained in greater detail below):

- Figure out what *you* have done to encourage or reinforce the problem.
- Make sure *you* are ready to change.
- Use the ABCs to analyze the problem.
- Have a plan and stay with it.
- Take small steps; each change could take two or three weeks.
- Be respectful; your child needs to have some control.
- Set limits and stick to them.
- Pay attention to small bits of progress.

Taking Responsibility

When mothers and fathers consult me about a time-buster dilemma, it's not my goal to make them feel guilty or feel bad about their parenting skills. At the same time, in order for them to help their child, they have to take responsibility for the ways *their behavior* shaped him or her in the first place. This brings us back to the concept of accidental parenting (pages 235–236), whereby mothers and fathers unwittingly reinforce undesirable behaviors. Because habits develop so quickly in young children, one can't avoid accidental parenting altogether. Every parent has, at some time or another, given in to a child's unreasonable demands, responded too attentively to whining, ignored bad behavior when a toddler flashes that winning smile. However, when negative behavior patterns persist over many months, even years, they're harder to change. And they turn into time-busters.

To transform almost any kind of long-standing problem that plagues a household, I generally recommend the following course of action:

Figure out what you have done to encourage or reinforce the problem. Don't think of your child as "spoiled." Look in the mirror instead. (Answer honestly the questions in the "Look at Yourself" sidebar on page 249.) Mallory's inability to set limits and the fact that she was letting her son be in charge actually reinforced Neil's dawdling in the tub and his obstinacy at bedtime. Until *she* changed, he certainly wouldn't.

Make sure you are ready to change. When a parent consults me and then greets every suggestion I make with, "Well, we already tried that," I suspect that he or she isn't ready to change the situation. Parents are often unaware of their own reluctance—indeed, they are genuinely upset about the problem. All the same, there may be an unconscious agenda at work. It may be that Mum feels needed when her child is clingy or wants to nurse long after he has been weaned. Or she craves the closeness of cuddling with her "baby," who is now two and a half, even though she realizes that Junior's climbing into her bed every night isn't doing much for her marital relationship. Sometimes former career women invest all their energy in parenting, and dealing with "a problem" sparks the old challenge and makes them feel successful. Certain fathers secretly enjoy their child's aggression. Others are reluctant to discipline because they themselves grew up in very strict homes and are therefore determined to "be different." When I sense any kind of reservation on a parent's part, I say straightaway, "Your toddler hasn't got a problem—it's *you* who needs help."

Use the ABCs to analyze the problem. Use the ABC technique (pages 235–236) to figure out the *antecedent* (what came first), the *behavior* (what your child does), and the *consequence* (what pattern has been established as the result of *A* and *B*). When sleep, eating, or behavioral difficulties persist over the long term, multiple issues are usually involved. Still, if you look closely and thoughtfully, you can figure out what's going on and how to change it.

In Neil's case, the antecedent was that during transitional times, such as bath and bedtime, Mallory kept relaxing her rules. *Just one more . . . just five more minutes . . . just a drink.* Neil's behavior was that he tested constantly and didn't respect limits. In addition, he was fearful of Mallory's leaving him. The consequence was that Mum, feeling "sorry" for him, kept giving in, inadvertently prolonging her son's difficulties and teaching him how to manipulate her. I explained to Mallory, "Neil has learned that you don't follow through. What's more, you've broken his trust by sneaking out on him, so he doesn't feel like it's safe to relax. He knows that if he falls asleep, you'll leave. To change the situation, you have to change what *you* do."

Have a plan and stay with it. Consistency is critical when changing a time-buster. If for the past eight or twelve months a woman has been habitually nursing her child several times during the night, the child naturally *expects* to dine at 3:00 A.M. Now, in order to change the pattern, Mum needs to be just as consistent in refusing to allow it (on pages 254–262, I share an actual case of this sort). Likewise, if Mallory tried one approach to Neil's dawdling and something else tomorrow, it wouldn't work. She'd be back to square one. I'm not one to insist on rigid schedules or clock-watching, but if bath time is from 7:30 to 8, she can't let it run until 9. She has to review her daily routine and stick to it.

Look at Yourself

If you answer "yes" to any of these questions, you might have more to do with your child's time-busting problem than you realize.

- Do you feel guilty about setting limits?

- Do you tend to be inconsistent with rules?

- If you work outside the house, do you let standards slide when you're home?

- When you say "no," do you feel sorry for your child?

- Does your child tend to have tantrums only when *you* are around?

- Do you tend to placate or cajole?

- Are you afraid your child won't love you if you discipline her?

- Do you get upset when your child doesn't seem happy?

- Do your child's tears make *you* feel sad?

- Do you often feel that other parents are "too strict"?

Take small steps; each change could take two or three weeks. There are no quick fixes. With infants, it's relatively easy to change habits; with toddlers, long-standing patterns are more entrenched, and you can't make sudden or severe changes. For example, Roberto and Maria, parents of nineteen-month-old Luis, came to me about his difficulties with daytime naps. "To get him to sleep, we have to take a ride in the car, several times around the block," Roberto explained. "When he's asleep, we pull into the garage and leave him in his car seat." The parents had rigged up an intercom so that they could hear Luis wake up. This had been going on since Luis was around eight months old. His parents couldn't suddenly pull the rug out from under him; they had to fade away their son's dependence on the sensation of movement.

The first week, they made the ride progressively shorter. The next week, they started the car but didn't drive anywhere. The third week, they put Luis in the car seat but didn't start the car. He still wasn't sleeping in his crib for naps, so now they had to work on that. They relocated to his bedroom, using a rocking chair to make the transition easier. The first few times, it took Luis forty minutes to fall asleep—after all, this wasn't the car. Roberto and Maria gradually reduced the rocking time, setting new goals every four or five days to move Luis along. Ultimately, they didn't have to rock him at all and were able to get him to sleep in his crib. The whole process took three months and a lot of patience on the parents' part.

Every time-busting situation requires a similar series of steps, each one tackling a particular part of the problem. Tim and Stacy, who allowed Kara to share their bed, had to first take turns sleeping in Kara's room on a blow-up bed placed next to her crib. They couldn't carelessly abandon their daughter; they had to respect her fear and let her know they were there for her. The second week, they began to move the blow-up bed farther from her crib. By these gradual increments, they were eventually able to get their daughter to feel safe enough on her own to sleep in her crib.

Be respectful; your child needs to have some control. Offer choices. When Neil was in his bath, I suggested to Mallory that instead of saying, "It's time to end your bath," to which he could respond, "No!" she ought to give him a choice: "Would you like to pull the plug out or should I?" Choices give a child a sense of control and therefore encourage cooperation. (See pages 219–220 for more about structuring choice sentences and questions.)

Set limits and stick to them. When Neil opted not to pull the plug and said, "No go out of bath," Mallory had to maintain her boundaries or she'd lapse into the old pattern. "Okay, Neil," she said without emotion. "I will pull the plug out *for* you." When the water was gone, she put the towel around him (while he was still in the tub), lifted him out, carried him to the bedroom, and closed the door, thereby eliminating his escape route.

Pay attention to small bits of progress. Time-busters don't disappear overnight, but don't lose hope. Keep your goal in mind, even though you may only inch toward reaching it. Some parents, looking for instant solutions, get stuck and can't see beyond the problem. Or when I help them conceive a plan, they exclaim in horror, "Two months? That's how long this is going to take?"

"Take it easy," I reply. "Think of all the time you've already lost dealing with this issue. Two months is nothing! The trick is to hold on to tiny victories. Otherwise, you'll feel as if you're going to deal with this dilemma for the rest of your life!"

Mallory, for instance, was trying to reverse the effect of many months of inadvertent conditioning. Neil *would* keep testing her, and she would have to rise to the occasion every time. We worked on possible "scripts" she could draw from and talked through various other parts of the bedtime ritual as well. Instead of letting him defy her, she offered Neil choices about dressing: "Would you like to put your jammy top on first or the bottoms?"

When Neil answered, "No!" rather than chasing him and turning it into a game (in his mind) or a battle (in hers), she *did something different*, which taught him the consequences of his behavior. "Okay. Let's get a book instead. If you get cold, tell me. Then we can put on your jammies. Would you like this book or this one?" When he chose a book, she told him, "Good choice. I'll read it when you get into bed." A few minutes into the book, Neil said, "Want jammies on." Mallory asked him, "Are you cold, honey?" In this way, she helped him identify what it feels like to go without pajamas after a bath. "Okay, let's put your jammies on now so you won't feel cold." And miracle of miracles, Neil was cooperative! Without his mother yelling or humiliating him, he had learned the natural consequences of refusing to get dressed.

Now, mind you, this was no magical conversion. Mallory (with a little help) stuck to her guns throughout the entire bedtime ritual. She told Neil, "I will read to you when you get into bed. When the ringer goes off, we turn out the light. Do you want to set the ringer? No? Okay, then mummy will." Neil then complained, "No, I do it." When he turned the timer on, Mallory said, "Good job." To avoid the trip downstairs for water, Mallory already had a glass at the side of the bed. "Would you like your water now? No? Okay. It's here when you want it. Now lie down and I'll read you the story."

When Neil started to fuss and protest, "No go bed," Mallory was firm: "Neil, I will lie here with you while I read, but you have to lie down, too." At that point, she didn't say another word—no cajoling, convincing, or threatening. He then launched into his usual song-and-dance, started to cry, and refused to get into bed, but Mum simply repeated, "It's bedtime, Neil. I will read you a story when you get under the covers." Her little boy continued to protest, but she paid no attention to his antics. When the timer rang, and he was still not in bed, Mallory got up and gently lifted him into her arms. When he started kicking and screaming, she told him, "No hitting Mummy" and then laid him down. She said nothing else.

After a while, because *Mallory* had changed and was not responding to Neil's shenanigans, he stopped. He wasn't being rewarded with his mother's attention, so what was the point? He got in bed. Mallory said quietly, "Good boy, Neil. I'll stay here until you fall asleep." When he asked for a drink, she handed it to him without saying anything. She didn't try to sneak out. Several times, he looked up from his pillow to check on her. She said nothing, but he saw that she was still there. He finally fell sound asleep. It was ten o'clock, a good hour earlier than usual.

To their credit, Mallory and Ivan stuck with the plan for the next several weeks. They took turns, which gave Mallory a much-needed break. After about two or three weeks of establishing this new bedtime routine and taking care to set firm boundaries, Mallory and Ivan became *parents* once again. They then were able to make another important change: instead of lying with Neil every night as they had been, they sat at the side of the bed until he fell asleep. Two months later, they were able to leave the room *before* Neil fell asleep, which on most nights, was well before nine.

Admittedly, this situation had gotten completely out of control. Neil was running the show, and because the parents weren't working as a team, the burden fell on Mum's shoulders (a common problem; see "Chore Wars," pages 308–310). The tug-of-war had existed for over a year. Needless to say, Mallory would have had far less of a problem if she had taken action once she realized that the evening ritual was forever running into overtime.

To be sure, all parents have lapses. And one or two nights of a child being more revved up than usual doesn't always turn into a serious problem. But when a particular pattern leads to endless frustration, exasperation, and arguments, something has to change. It's best not to "wait and see." Time-busters don't undo themselves. As habits are reinforced over the long term, they become more deeply ingrained.

Important Reminder
Problems don't magically disappear.

If a time-buster is causing conflict in your relationship, you need to do something different with your child.

If conflict in your adult relationship is causing a time-buster, you need to do something different in your relationship (pages 308–317).

Leanne: A Chronic Sleep Problem

The most common time-buster is sleep deprivation, and the worst scenarios involve a toddler who wakes up repeatedly and needs to be nursed back to sleep. One of two things typically happens in these cases. Mum keeps getting up throughout the night, trying to appease the child by thrusting a pacifier or a boob into his mouth every time he cries. Or parents try the delayed-response approach (better known as "Ferberizing"), whereby the child "cries it out" for increasingly longer periods. The first approach robs the parents of sleep—and doesn't teach the toddler a thing. And the second can be traumatic, breaking a child's trust in his environment. Either way, the parents are beyond exhaustion themselves.

Victoria was one such parent. Her daughter, fourteen-month-old Leanne, was in the habit of getting up every hour and a half and would not go back to sleep without being nursed. A few days earlier, bleary-eyed from the months of sleepless nights, Vicki had crashed her S.U.V. into a station wagon. Luckily, no one was hurt, but the incident underscored how off-kilter her life had become. This was one mother I didn't have to ask whether she was ready to make changes.

Victoria admitted that until her accident, she thought her daughter would grow out of her incessant need to nurse. The other mothers in Vicki's breastfeeding support group nourished that illusion.

"She just isn't ready," Beverly insisted. "When she is, she'll sleep like a baby all through the night." Vicki said to herself, *Leanne's not exactly a baby,* but pushed the thought out of her mind.

"It took Joel two years," Eunice offered.

"My daughter feeds five times during the night," Doris chimed in, "and *I* don't have a problem getting up. It's just one of the sacrifices you make when you're a mother."

"We sleep with our child," said Yvette, adding that it was no big deal to turn over and pop a boob into her son's mouth.

Relating the women's comments to me, Victoria asked, "Am I expecting too much from Leanne?" Without waiting for an answer, she went on, nervously. "She is so adorable. I hate to see her upset.

I know she's not hungry every time I nurse her, but why does she wake so often? We've tried the sleep-in-the-bed routine, but then *no one* gets any sleep, and it makes her even worse. When I slept with her, she had my breast in her mouth practically all night. When I moved, she would cry out and reach for my breast. I'm at my wit's end."

I took Victoria through a time-busting game plan.

Look at what you've done to contribute to the problem. I explained that between six and nine months of age, a baby's sleeping pattern begins to resemble an adult's—every hour and a half to two hours, she goes through a cycle of sleep. If you watch babies or adults on videotape, you see constant motion as they go from light sleep, or REM sleep as it is known, into deep sleep, on and off throughout the night. They toss, turn, throw a leg out of bed, pull at the sheet, murmur, even cry out. Babies and toddlers often wake throughout the night, some for as long as an hour or more, talking, babbling, cooing. If no one disturbs them, they go back to sleep on their own.

However, independent sleep is a *learned* practice. Starting from day one, parents have to *teach* their infant how to get to sleep on her own and to feel safe in her crib. If not, by the time the child reaches the toddler years, you often see signs of this difficulty at naps or at bedtime, or both. It was clear to me that Leanne had never been taught how to go to sleep on her own. Instead, she was trained (accidentally, of course) to associate the act of going to sleep with having Mum's breast in her mouth. At the end of a sleep cycle, when she went into REM, she had no skills to send herself back into a deep sleep. Her mum's breast had become what I call a *prop*—any device, be it a human breast or pacifier, or an intervention, such as rocking or the motion of a car, that causes an infant distress when withdrawn.

"Oh, I've ruined her," Victoria lamented.

"I wouldn't go as far as that," I reassured her. "And we'll have none of this 'Oh, poor Leanne' sentiment. Pitying her won't help her or solve your problem. You've done your best so far, and in fact, have done a great job in being consistent. Now we have to show you how to be consistent with the right practices! Your ability to stick with a plan will help you transform Leanne's habit of nursing throughout the night into a more positive pattern."

Use the ABCs to analyze the problem. It was obvious (to me at least) that the *antecedent* here was the fact that Leanne had never been taught to sleep on her own; her *behavior* was extreme crankiness and a demand for mum's breast whenever it was time for naps or bedtime. The *consequence*, a firmly entrenched pattern of excessive suckling, was repeatedly reinforced because Vicki always gave in. Listening to Vicki recount a typical day, I became even more certain: Leanne generally wakes up at around 5:30 A.M. Her mum nurses her and then goes downstairs. Leanne plays for about forty-five minutes. When she starts yawning, her mum takes her back upstairs, sits in the rocking chair, and nurses her until she falls asleep. "Some days if I'm lucky," Vicki added, "she lets me lay her back in her crib. Other days, she won't let me move."

A lightbulb flashed in my head. "Wait a minute: You said, she won't *let* you move. What do you mean?"

"Well, even though she seems to be asleep, the moment I attempt to get up out of the rocking chair, she screams. So I put her back on the breast and she falls asleep again. If I try again in a few minutes, she gets hysterical. So after two attempts, I usually just sit in the rocking chair for an hour."

"Wow," I exclaimed, "that must be uncomfortable."

"Not really," Victoria said, "not anymore. My husband bought an ottoman that we keep by the rocking chair. I gently slide my legs onto it when Leanne is asleep. He got it for me because one morning I was so tired that I dozed off and Leanne almost slipped out of my arms."

When Leanne wakes up again, usually around 7:30, Victoria gets her dressed and ready for the day. Leanne eats solid foods for breakfast, and then at around 10:30 when she gets tired, Victoria takes her upstairs and nurses her. "Usually, she's so good she falls asleep in five or ten minutes for about a twenty-minute nap. If I catch her, I can send her back to sleep in five minutes by nursing her again. But if I miss her first cry, then it can take me up to an hour to get her down again. By then, though, she's hungry, so I feed her and she usually goes back to sleep for another twenty minutes."

Dear parent, if you're tired just reading this saga, believe you me, I was exhausted listening to it. And so far we've only gotten to 11:30! When Leanne wakes up, Victoria manages to squeeze in a walk. Mum never puts her daughter into the crib during the day to play, because she's so afraid it will cause her to scream. She sometimes takes her on an errand, but only if she nurses her in the car to send her to sleep first, because, as Victoria explains, Leanne "won't let" her put her into the car seat. She arches her back and screams bloody murder. "I swear some days the neighbors probably think I'm torturing her," Victoria confides.

"Well, it seems to me," I say at this point, "that she is torturing *you.*"

The remainder of the day goes pretty much the same way until Doug, a plumber, gets home from work at five. After Mum feeds her, Dad gives Leanne her bath, and Victoria gushes, "He is *so* good. He reads her a story and he then hands her to me. I nurse her again and she goes down for an hour."

I ask why she doesn't let Dad have a go at putting Leanne down. "Doug has tried several times," she responds, "but she won't let him. She screams and I can't bear it. So I go in and nurse her. She sleeps again, gets up at eight, plays with Dad, and at around 11:30 P.M., I nurse her. She sleeps until around 12:30, I nurse her, and she goes back to sleep. If I'm lucky, she'll make it to around three, but that's not very often. She usually wakes again at 4 and at 5:30, when the day starts again." Victoria pauses and then recalls wistfully, "One night I wrote on my calender that she slept a straight five hours . . . but that was just once."

Obviously, this was a deeply ingrained, long-term problem that wouldn't be solved overnight. Victoria and Doug would need a plan, a series of steps that would gradually fade out Leanne's time-busting behaviors and replace them with the skills of self-reliance.

Have a plan and stay with it. "Twice a day, when Leanne is happy," I told Vicki, "put her into her crib. The first time you do it, she may cling to you and cry. Try to take the focus off her mood by distracting her. Put a blanket over your head and play peekaboo. Amuse her. Jump up and down, playing 'silly mummy.' If you keep at it, she'll be entranced. It may last only four or five minutes at first.

A Conspiracy of Silence

Although the most common time-busters are sleep-related, there tends to be a conspiracy of silence around bedtime problems, as Rebecca's experience illustrates:

"I was on jury duty and talking with a group of women in the waiting room about how it took me hours to get Jon to sleep last night," she recalls. "An older woman took my hand reassuringly and confided that when her daughter was a baby, she or her husband had to sleep with her every night. Only now that the girl was a teenager could her mother discuss it. 'I had so much shame,' she admitted. With that, another woman piped in, embarrassed to say that she was *now* doing the same thing.

"It made me feel a whole lot better to realize I wasn't alone, but I was also puzzled. 'That's odd,' I said to both of them. 'I was at a birthday party recently and all of the mothers said *their* kids go right to sleep and make it through the night.'

" 'They're lying!' both women responded in unison and laughed."

Reassure her that she's safe by saying, 'You're okay, honey. Mummy is right here.'

"Now this is important: don't wait for her to cry. Take her out of the crib when she is happy, even if she's just been in there for two minutes. Each day, build the time up—try to get to fifteen minutes over the course of two weeks. Give her playthings in the crib and encourage her to begin to see this as a great place to be. During this time, though, don't change anything else. She'll spend more and more time amusing herself if you don't hover over her. After two weeks, when she's busy with a toy, start to move away from the side of the crib. Don't try to sneak away. Casually tell her, 'Mummy is right here.' You want to strengthen her trust in you. Stay in the room, but fold laundry or tidy her closet."

In the past, Leanne had panicked whenever Vicki tried to put her down because she knew her mum was going to leave. She hadn't yet learned to be on her own, not even to sleep, and she wasn't able to relax because of this fear. Giving in each time by nursing her certainly didn't improve the situation. In fact, it sent Leanne a message: "You *do* need me." Now, Vicky had to build Leanne's confidence in herself and help her withstand time alone in the crib, so that she would feel safe when she woke up and her mum wasn't around. But I warned Victoria that she had to go slowly. Reinforcing Leanne's trust and encouraging her independence would take time—and lots of adult patience.

Take small steps and be respectful of your child's need for control. "You were right, Tracy," Victoria reported two weeks later. "The first time, she cried. But she loves this little hand puppet, so I jumped up with it and she laughed. The second and third time, though, that game didn't work so well. She lasted maybe two minutes in the crib. But I always took her out while she was still happy. Then it got surprisingly better.

"By the end of the second week, I was nervous about moving away from the crib. So I played a game of 'Silly Mummy' first. Then I walked toward her dresser, which is on the other

Taking Care of Yourself

Changing your toddlers' sleep habits can be hard on you. Here's how to alleviate your own stress:

- Wear headphones or earplugs to reduce the earsplitting sound of your child crying.

- If you're losing patience, hand your child off to your partner. If you have no partner, or he or she isn't at home, put her down in a safe place and step outside the room.

- Keep a long-term perspective. You will feel proud of yourself after you've succeeded in teaching your child how to sleep.

side of the room, and started tidying up her drawers. To my amazement, she was okay but a little unsure, so I just talked to her, casually and calmly, letting her know I thought she was fine. By the end of the third week, I became more adventurous and actually went out of view for a second. I told her, 'I'll be right back. I have to take these dirty clothes to the hamper.' I held my breath but she was content playing on her own. I'm not even sure she noticed my absence!"

I congratulated Victoria. In the wake of such success, I knew she

Tracy's Top Ten Pet Peeves: Things you should never do or say to your child

Invariably when parents relate a time-buster, one of these top ten is part of these story:

1. Spank (see pages 223–225)

2. Slap

3. Shame: "You're such a crybaby."

4. Yell: (Ask yourself, "If I have to scream at my child, is it because I let him get away with so much that eventually I crack?")

5. Degrade: Saying, "Ugh! You wet yourself," instead of, "I see you need to get changed."

6. Blame: "You've made me mad," or "You've made me late."

7. Threaten: "If you do that again, I'm leaving you here," or "I'm warning you, you're going to get it." (Worst of all is, "Wait 'til your father gets home.")

8. Talk about a child over her head: Most comments can wait, but if you must say something, spell or change the name and gender.

9. Label: "You're a bad boy," instead of, "When you shove, you can't play with Ralph."

10. Ask a question the child can't answer: "Why did you hit Priscilla?" or "Why can't you behave in the market?

was eager to move on to the next phase of the plan, which focused on the excessive nursing. We had to start with Leanne's naps. Vicki couldn't very well expect her little one to go cold turkey, but I told her to break the latch the moment Leanne started to drift off to sleep. She was sure her daughter would cry. "You're probably right," I said. "That's to be expected. Put her back on, and again, as she starts to doze off, break the latch. Do this for fifteen minutes. If she is still crying, change the scene. Go downstairs. Twenty minutes later go back up and start the process again."

Leanne did *not* like the change. The first time, she became enraged and started screaming. "I felt sorry for her," Victoria admitted in a phone call the next week, "so I caved. But the second day, I was determined, so I took her off my breast as soon as she started dozing off. When she got upset, I took her out of the room for a few minutes, as you suggested. After five attempts, she finally went to sleep on my lap without the breast. By the seventh day, I could sit with her in the rocker, and she twiddled with my shirt but went to sleep without nursing."

Pay attention to small bits of progress. Three weeks later, Leanne was able to fall asleep at nap time without a breast in her mouth, but she was still waking up during the night wanting to suckle. Doug and Victoria would have to work as a team, I explained. I asked Victoria point-blank: "Are you willing to let your hubby pitch in?" Here Victoria had a personal stumbling block: she was enjoying being *the* parent and wasn't all that eager to share her authority.

"Right now you keep taking Leanne from Doug," I pointed out. "In doing so, you inadvertently send *her* the message that Dad is the bad guy and you are her savior. When Leanne wakes up in the middle of the night, you have to allow Doug to go to her, too."

I explained the idea of *sensible sleep*—a balanced method by which you encourage a child to sleep in her own bed, but at the same time, you comfort her rather than leaving her alone to figure it out by herself. Children who are accustomed to receiving an oral reward every time they cry naturally have a difficult time falling asleep without it, so this wasn't going to be easy. But we knew that Leanne could put herself to sleep during the day. With her parents' help, I had no doubt that she could learn to do the same thing at night.

I instructed both of them, "When she cries, stay with her. Use your physical presence, not Vicki's breast, to let her know you're there. When she cries really hard, pick her up and hold her. Expect that she'll be pretty upset the first few nights and may cry hard even though you're holding her. She may even arch her back and try to push you away with her feet. You'll probably have to hold her for around forty minutes or more to get her to calm down. As soon as she stops crying, lay her down again. Chances are she'll start to cry again. Pick her up straightaway. Do this as many times as you have to. You may have to pick her up and put her down as many as fifty times, even a hundred!" I told them to actually count so that they could see their progress, to keep a log, and report back in two weeks.

The first night, Leanne cried on and off for almost two hours. Her parents stayed with her and comforted her. "It was so hard to hear her cry," Victoria later recounted, "but we never left her. We picked her up and put her down, forty-six times the first night, twenty-nine the second, and twelve, the third. By the fourth night, she slept from nine to 4:30 A.M. I wasn't sure if it was because she was so exhausted or that we were too tired to hear her. But then, on the seventh night, she slept a straight nine hours. On the ninth night, she got up twice, but we stuck with the plan—we didn't cave in. I think she was probably testing us. Now it has been eleven nights of her sleeping through. The most amazing thing is that when she wakes in the morning, we hear her talking to her animals. She actually plays independently. As soon as she whimpers a bit, we get her out, though, so as not to break her trust again." Although Vicki and Doug insisted that getting Leanne to sleep through the night was "a miracle," to me the success was a testament to their determination and strength.

Cody: "Mommy . . . Don't Leave Me!"

Separation anxiety is a component of many time-busters. Both Neil and Leanne had the same fear: if I let Mum out of my sight, I might never see her again. If that sounds overly dramatic, bear in mind that to most toddlers, their mother is their lifeline. The two greatest challenges for young children to conquer are learning that when Mum leaves the room she isn't gone forever—and developing the self-soothing skills that will see them through her absences.

Although separation anxiety goes with the territory at this age, when I see a toddler who is unusually clingy or has difficulties at nap and bedtime, I wonder whether the parents have given in too much or if somehow, somewhere, the child's trust has been broken. His parents may not always be truthful, sneaking out or saying that they'll be "right back" only to reappear hours later. When they try to leave, can we blame the toddler for pitching a fit at the door? Actually, the parents are pretty miserable, too. They end up leaving the house late, angry, and most likely feeling guilty because their bereft child is screaming as if there's no tomorrow.

Certainly, if a child isn't getting enough attention, or if his parents aren't tuned in to his needs (or, the reverse, they hover), or if they are less than honest with him, any and all of these issues must be addressed. At the same time, when a child relies solely on external soothing, we also need to start teaching him how to draw from his own *inner* resources. In such cases, if the child has not already adopted some sort of security item on his own, I'm inclined to suggest that the parents try to introduce one. The older the child, the longer it will take, because he has already become dependent on "other" and now he needs to learn how to rely on "self."

As I said earlier (pages 174–176), many children automatically zero in on a transitional object by the time they're eight or ten months old, and such children tend to be more independent and better at self-soothing by their toddler years than children who haven't adopted one. Cody, whose mum, Daryl, called when her son was fourteen months old, fell into the latter category. Behind his back, many adults called him "Clingy Cody." Or they labeled him "spoiled." But what had happened in his household was certainly not Cody's fault. He was just doing what everyone had taught him—a classic case of accidental parenting that evolved into a time-buster—so I helped Daryl develop a course of action.

Figure out what you have done to encourage or reinforce the problem. From the time he was a baby, Cody was never given the opportunity to spend time on his own. When Daryl wasn't holding him, a babysitter was. He was never left in the crib or playpen. Indeed, if his eyes were open, someone was at his side, or holding him, or in some other way engaging him. Even when Cody started sitting on his own and was able to play with toys in a more interactive manner, there was Daryl by his side, showing, explaining, teaching—but never letting him make his own discoveries. As a result, Cody barely could play for five minutes without gesturing for his mother or crying. Talk about a time-buster! Daryl literally couldn't go anywhere without him.

Use the ABCs to analyze the problem. Hearing all this, I asked, "What does Cody do when he's tired of playing, or when you leave the room?"

"He cries as if the world were coming to an end," Daryl answered.

Of course, that's what he did. Analyzing this situation using the ABCs, the *antecedent* was that Cody was never left alone and therefore had never learned to self-soothe. His *behavior* was predictable; he cried when he was alone. Since the *consequence* was always the same—someone, usually his mum, came running—the pattern was set.

Make sure you're willing to change. I saw that this family's problem had two components. First of all, Daryl had to be willing to change. She had to learn how to recite the H.E.L.P. mantra (see pages 43–45), which would remind her to hold back and encourage her son's exploration, rather than always rushing in to rescue him. Second, when Cody was upset, scared, or needy, we had to find a way to transfer his dependence from his mother to an inanimate object that he could access *on his own* even when she wasn't around. Both changes would take time. At the outset, I advised Daryl, "You'll have to monitor your own behavior as carefully as your son's."

Make a plan. We broke the plan down into small steps, starting with Cody's playtime. I taught Daryl about H.E.L.P., and urged her to restrain *herself* whenever Cody grabbed a toy or initiated an activity. This was as hard for her as it was for Cody. She was accustomed to playing with her son and constantly interacting, rather than observing and letting him take the lead. But I stressed, "You only have to make small, incremental changes. And start during the day, when Cody is less likely to be cranky."

Take gradual steps. At first, Daryl positioned herself on the floor. When Cody brought one of his toys over to her, she was careful about letting him make the first move. Of course, because Cody was so accustomed to her intervention, he'd usually plop a toy, like his little xylophone, into Mum's lap and ask her to play it while he watched. Now, to nudge him toward independence, Daryl took the xylophone from her lap and placed it on the coffee table instead. She handed her son the mallet. "Cody, *you* play it for Mummy," she said cheerily. Cody tried to grab her arm, a clear message that said, "No, *you* do it," but rather than reinforce his neediness, Daryl stuck to her guns. "No, Cody, *you* play it, not Mummy," she repeated.

Some days, Cody played on his own. Some days, he pitched a fit. In a matter of weeks, though, he became more comfortable amusing himself without Daryl's intervention. Mum was so excited that at first she tended to go overboard with her praise. However, she discovered that saying, "Good job, Cody," tended to break her little boy's concentration and deter him from carrying on. Her voice served as a reminder of her presence, and he immediately wanted to revert to their old pattern of interaction. I suggested that instead she wait ten or fifteen minutes before applauding his independent play. And she should compliment him in a more casual way, rather than making a big deal of it.

Set limits and stick to them. At this point, Cody could play on his own only when his mother was in the room, but he was more independent than he'd ever been. It's important to note progress but not to get stuck. Keep moving the child toward the goal, which in this case was to get Cody to withstand his mother's absence. Little by little, Daryl began to inch farther away from him, and finally, was able to raise herself up onto the couch, so that he was playing a good six or seven feet away. As difficult as it was for her, she also made sure that she busied herself by reading or doing the household bills. Whenever Cody came over to her to check in, she would say, "I'm right here. I didn't go anywhere." She'd then resume whatever *she* was doing, giving him the message that it was time for him to go back to *his* activity.

It was one thing for Daryl to move from the floor to the couch, quite another to move out of the room. When she first attempted this, saying (and meaning), "I'll be right back, Cody. I have to get something in the kitchen," he immediately cried, stopped what he was doing, and ran after her. Daryl stopped and returned to the den. "Cody, I said I'd be right back. I can see you from the kitchen and you can see me."

Give your child some control. This was an ideal time to introduce Cody to a transitional object that he could cling to in his mum's absence, something *he* could control (see also pages 174–176. Since he didn't seem to favor a stuffed animal or adopt any kind of "blankie" on his own, Daryl gave him a soft, well-worn sweatshirt and suggested that he "hold this for Mummy until I get back." She continued to talk to him as she left the room and while she was in the kitchen. Over the weeks, she made the times away slightly longer, but only by one-minute increments per day.

Once Daryl could leave the room and stay out for a good fifteen minutes, she began to tackle nap time—a classically difficult transition for a clingy toddler who frets that his mom won't be there when he wakes up; therefore, he reasons, it's best not to sleep at all. Now when she put Cody down for his nap, Daryl also gave him her sweatshirt. At first, Cody threw it over the side of his crib. But Daryl calmly picked it up and held it, together with Cody's hand. She stayed with him, talked in soft, comforting tones. Here, too, she worked *gradually*, each day staying a minute less.

Don't give up too easily if your child initially rejects a security item. Instead of assuming that he doesn't want it, keep offering it. Be patient. Present the item when he needs soothing—and when you're comforting him—so that he begins to make the association. Keep in mind that your goal is to help him develop his emotional independence and a longer attention span as well. Once he's not so concerned about your being there, he'll be able to focus better and stick with his own endeavors for increasingly longer periods.

Rejoice in small victories. Daryl knew she was in the homestretch when Cody suddenly became so attached to her sweatshirt that he wanted it by his side or in his hands almost all the time. Daryl started calling it his "lovey" (a term coined by pediatrician T. Berry Brazelton) and soon Cody did, too. One day, Daryl wisely asked Cody, "Where could we put your lovey so that you'll always be able to find it?" He tucked it behind a cushion in the den.

The ultimate test came when Daryl decided to leave the house. The first time, Daryl said to Cody, "I'm going to the store, honey, and Freda will be here with you while I'm gone. Do you want to get your lovey to keep you company while I'm out?" Cody wasn't happy, but by now he was using his lovey to sleep. Reluctantly, he stuffed it under his arm.

As it turned out, the entire process took six weeks. It might have been longer if Cody was any older (or if Daryl had not stuck with the plan). It might have taken less time if his mum had called me before Cody's habits became so entrenched. This is not an isolated or unusual case. In many families today, parents tend to be *over*focused on children. They do it out of love and a desire to be attentive. When the balance tips this way, and parents unwittingly thwart their child's emotional independence, they must take a few steps back.

Parting with Those Pesky Pacifiers

While we're on the subject of separation, I would be remiss if I didn't cover the use of pacifiers. You may have noticed that they are not listed among the self-soothing objects mentioned on pages 174–176. I would rather see a toddler sucking his thumb or a bottle (of water) than munching on an object that he can't put back into his own mouth.

Make no mistake: I'm not totally against pacifiers. I actually recommend them for infants under the age of three months, when the sucking reflex is most intense. At that point an infant doesn't yet have the physical capability to find her hands, and a pacifier provides the oral stimulation she needs. But after she's gained control of her limbs, if a grown-up continues to shove the pacifier into her mouth, it becomes a prop (see page 255). The child didn't choose it; she can't put it into her mouth without help, so it's not a method of *self*-soothing. Nevertheless, she becomes dependent on the feeling of the pacifier in her mouth. And if she hasn't gotten rid of her passy by the age of six months, it's a hard habit to break.

Indeed, analyzing the many sleep-related time-busters that parents consult me about, I often find that the toddler is addicted to his pacifier. Tons of letters on my Web site are from anxious parents who get up four or five times a night to reinsert pacifiers. One of the stories from a mum who e-mailed was an example that mirrors other parents' plight: Fourteen-month-old Kimmy was falling asleep every night with a pacifier in her mouth. Once she was in a deep sleep, her mouth would open and the pacifier would slip out. Because Kimmy was so accustomed to the sensation of the pacifier, its absence invariably woke her—her security was gone. On her good nights, Kimmy searched for her passy and popped it back into her mouth on her own. More often, though, her pacifier got tangled in the covers or fell to the floor. Poor Kimmy, awakened from a deep sleep and in a panic, screamed her head off until her mother came into her room and helped her find it. Only then could Kimmy (and the rest of the household) get back to sleep.

I find too that parents sometimes prolong a child's dependency. They use pacifiers all day long, like a gob-stopper—to calm children, or worse, to shut them up (which is why in England we call them "dummies"), which of course does nothing to help the child learn how to self-

---

"Blankie" Tips

- **Leave it!** Unless your child is using a self-soothing item in an obsessive manner—all day long and to the exclusion of other activities—let him be. (This doesn't apply to pacifiers; see the "Pesky Pacifiers" section, pages 267–271.) Besides, the best way to break children of bad habits is to ignore them. By trying to coax, or worse, by engaging in a struggle, you will probably only increase your child's devotion to his beloved object or activity. I promise that if you leave him alone, he will eventually find more internal (and acceptable) ways of shutting off the world.

- **Wash it!** Cloth or plush security items should be laundered often (and when your child is in bed). If you wait too long, the smell as well as the item itself will comfort him. Therefore, washing it will be almost as traumatic as taking it away.

- **Duplicate it!** If your child favors a particular kind of stuffed animal or toy, buy at least three of them. She probably won't be lugging her security blanket off to college, but expect several years of wear and tear.

- **Take it!** If you're traveling, make sure you take whatever item makes your child feel safe. One family missed a plane when Dad remembered that teddy was left behind.

soothe. When a parent tells me, as Josie did, "Scooter won't let me take his pacifier away," I urge her to look at *her* needs. After all, she's the one who gives Scooter the pacifier; she is in control.

"I always take the pacifier with me, even when he doesn't ask for it," Josie confessed. In short, the pacifier was *her* crutch, not Scooter's. Josie had somehow imbued the pacifier with magical qualities: *It would keep her son quiet. With pacifier in tow, she could get him to nap anywhere. She would never be embarrassed in public.* Not only was this so-called magic an illusion, but by whipping out the pacifier the moment her little boy started to fuss, Josie wasn't allowing him to express himself—she wasn't listening.

If you're reading this book, and your child still has her passy, I assume she is eight months or older. Of course, whether or not you take it away from her is up to you. I realize it can be scary to a parent. Indeed, the aunt of four- and five-year-old children recently summed up her reluctance: "It's the only thing I have." Still, bear in mind that whenever your child can't find her pacifier, you'll be called upon to search for it. And the longer you wait to help her develop self-soothing strategies, which in turn will foster her independence, the harder it will be to get rid of that pesky pacifier—and the more sleepless nights you will suffer. In the box on pages 270–271 are the methods I suggest to break the habit. Only you can figure out which one will work best for your child.

Big Boy/Big Bed?

Many parents wonder when it's time for their toddler to make the transition to a big bed. I say, ducky, wait as long as you can! Many toddlers are still a wee bit top heavy; they need to grow into their heads. Also, wait until he's comfortable in his own crib. Otherwise, you're just giving him another out. In the meantime:

Keep a big bed in his room. Rather than invest in a novelty bed he'll get tired of in a year or two, buy a standard twin and add safety sides.

Wait for your child to show an interest in sleeping in his big bed. Start him off without the box spring, so he's low to the ground, and at nap times only, as a treat.

Be aware of risks—lamps and other things he might pull over. If you're not sure, spend time in the room, watching your child to see what dangers he is drawn to.

Cutting Out the Pacifier: Two Methods

The older your child is, the more difficult it will be to break the pacifier habit, no matter which method you use. In any case, before you attempt to eliminate the pacifier, introduce a comfort item if your child doesn't already have one (reread Cody's story, pages 262–67). Once he becomes attached to a silky or a stuffed animal, he might automatically become less dependent on his pacifier.

Gradual Elimination. Start by cutting down during the day. For three days, allow your child to start naps with his pacifier, but as soon as he's sleeping, take it out of his mouth. For the next three days, eliminate the pacifier at nap time. (I assume you will have already acclimated him to a comfort item.) Simply say, "No more pacifier for nap time." If he cries, comfort him, rather than sticking an inanimate object into his mouth. Give him his security item, hug him or pat him, making your physical presence known, and say, "You're okay, honey. You can sleep now."

Once your little one is accustomed to napping without a pacifier—if he's under eight months, it usually takes about a week, longer if he's older—then do the same thing at night. First, allow him to fall asleep with the pacifier in his mouth and then take it away. He may wake up in the middle of the night, crying for his pacifier, which he's probably been doing all along. The difference now, though, is that you withhold it. Comfort him with gestures, not conversation, and make sure that he has his security object in hand. Don't give in or act like you feel sorry for him. After all, you're doing a good deed here: you're teaching him the skill of going to sleep on his own.

Cold Turkey. I don't recommend cold turkey—sudden withdrawal—for children under a year, because they have trouble understanding what "all gone" means. However, older children sometimes have no trouble giving up their pacifier, especially when they realize it's simply not there for them. As one mum in England told her little one, "Oh, dear, dummy's gone."

"Where'd it go?" her daughter asked.

"Dust bin," said Mum cheerily.

Now, that little one probably didn't even know what a dust bin was (for you grown-up Americans, it's a garbage container outside the house), but she accepted her dummy's demise and went on with her life. Some children will cry for an hour, but then seem to forget about it. Others will keep asking and continue to be upset, but this rarely lasts for more than a few days. Twenty-two-month-old Ricky, for instance, went absolutely nuts when his dad told him one day, "Your pacifier is gone. It was making your teeth bad." Ricky could have cared less about his teeth. He cried and cried, but Dad, to his credit, didn't show any emotion in response to his son's tears. He didn't say, "Oh, poor Ricky. His passy's gone." Three nights later, Ricky got over it.

A Combined Approach. Some parents do a combination of gradual elimination and cold turkey. To break eleven-month-old Ian of his passy habit, Marissa made his relinquishing it part of their wake-up ritual. Every morning, she'd greet him, give him a big hug, extend her hand, and say, "Now it's time to give Mommy your pacifier." Without a fuss, Ian would turn over his passy. For the next month, though, he continued to sleep with his pacifier. Observing him at night, Marissa realized that Ian's pacifier was not a habit that disturbed his sleep, because he didn't wake up once it slipped out of his mouth. So one night Marissa finally sprung it on him: "No more pacifier. You're a big boy." And that was that.

Whatever method you use, be realistic. After all, this is a kind of "withdrawal" experience for your child, but hang in there. Expect a few nights of crying. Eventually, it will get better. And in years to come, the getting-rid-of-the-pacifier story will work its way into your family folklore.

Phillip: Chronic Tantrums

Although I covered tantrum strategies in the last chapter (pages 233–239), I want to point out here that when parents repeatedly placate tantrums, a child's demanding, out-of-control behavior can become a devastating time-buster. Also, tantrums usually indicate that there are other issues, not the least of which is that the parents have lost their authority.

I spent an hour on the phone with Carmen and Walter, parents in St. Louis who called about their twenty-two-month-old son. Phillip, to use their words, "transformed into a horribly aggressive, mean-spirited child" when Bonita, now six months old, was born. Phillip, it seems, can't bear it when his parents' attention is diverted from him, especially if they focus on his baby sister. When Carmen changes Bonita, for instance, Phillip often throws a tantrum. To appease him, Carmen tries to give her boy a cuddle, at which point he kicks and bites her. When that doesn't work, Dad intervenes, saying, "That's not nice, Phillip," and the adults end up rolling on the floor in an attempt to calm him.

At night, Phillip sleeps between his parents and won't go to sleep unless he's holding his mother or father's ear. If he pinches or pulls, they allow it. No one has ever said to Phillip, "That hurts," or "No, you may hold my hand but not my ear." Needless to report, both parents are utterly exhausted. Grandma Rosa, who lives several hundred miles away, tries to come at least once a week to give Carmen a break, but no one spends separate one-on-one time with Phillip.

Carmen and Walter try to head off trouble before it starts, or at least that's what they think they're doing. For instance, they told me that when they recently took Phillip and Bonita for a ride, they allowed him to take a huge bag of toys in the car. No matter—he quickly tired of them. And when he got bored, Phillip tried to get out of his safety seat. "You unbuckle that belt, and I will stop this car," Walter screamed at him, threatening. "Sit there 'til we get home—or else you'll be in trouble, young man!" Phillip finally stopped, but Walter had to raise his voice several decibels to get his son to listen.

It was very clear to me that everyone was letting this little boy run the show. He was barely two, yet Carmen and Walter kept trying to reason with him. By refusing to set limits—in effect, abdicating their responsibility as parents—Phillip's mum and dad were unwittingly teaching him to be manipulative. His "aggressive" and "mean-spirited" behavior was really his begging for limits.

"Love isn't about letting your child hold on to your ear, allowing him to inflict pain without saying a word," I said to Carmen and Walter as tactfully as I could, "nor is it about giving him a barrel of toys to amuse him. And it's certainly not about letting him run roughshod over you and his little sister. Your son is screaming out for boundaries—screaming. I fear that it's a matter of time before he hurts his little sister. *That* would certainly get you to pay attention, wouldn't it?"

"But we're such a loving family," Walter kept saying. And indeed they were. Carmen was calm and soft-spoken, and Dad clearly had his heart in the right place, too. "And Phillip used to be such a sweet little boy," Carmen added. I didn't doubt that, but at some point the two of them had to start being parents. Phillip needed more than love—he needed them to rein him in.

"Let's start with the tantrums," I suggested, because that was the most pressing issue. "Whenever he loses control, you have to keep doing one thing that you're both comfortable with," I explained. "For example, when he pitches a fit, say, 'That's unacceptable.' Take him to his room, sit with him, but don't talk to him."

To their credit, Carmen and Walter complied. But instead of rejoicing after their first attempt—which worked, by the way—they started feeling sorry for Phillip. "We don't want to be harsh parents, or to upset him," Walter admitted. "When we told him his behavior was unacceptable, he put his head down and walked out of the room."

I explained that in all likelihood, Phillip initially threw temper tantrums spontaneously—out of frustration, fatigue, mixed in with a bit of jealousy toward Bonita, the little pink-faced intruder who was taking time away from him. Instead of nipping his behavior in the bud, the parents reinforced it by trying to cajole or placate him each time he was out of control. And now, Phillip knows just how to get their attention.

I also tried to get these parents to see the forest beyond the trees. "Rules, limits, and disappointment are part of life. Phillip has to be prepared for the reality that his teachers will tell him 'no.' And when he doesn't make the baseball team, or when his first girlfriend dumps him for another guy, those defeats are going to break his heart. All the same, he has to be able to cope with such painful moments, and *you* need to give him the skills to do it. Besides, don't you think it's better for him to learn those lessons now, at the hands of compassionate parents, rather than have the cruel world teach him?"

Based on the incidents Walter and Carmen had related, we worked out a simple plan:

First, *they* had to become accountable: "Listen to your words: 'Phillip won't let me,' " I echoed. "Now it's one thing when my fifteen-year-old insists, 'My mum won't let me,' but when you say '*My toddler* won't let me,' what's going on? How out of control is your household when a two-year-old boy won't 'let' his parents do something? You want to make him happy all the time. But if you don't step in *now*, this child is going to grow up manipulating his environment . . . because you're allowing him to."

Second, they must begin to assert themselves as parents. I suggested limiting Phillip's choices throughout the day—at meals, one of two cereals; in the car, one of two toys. Contemplating this part of the plan, Carmen asked, "But what if he whines and says, 'I want to take these, too' and he trots out the usual bagful?"

I told her she had to be *the parent*. "You say, 'No, Phillip. You can take your robot *or* your truck.' You can't let him control you," I stressed.

Finally, if Phillip had a tantrum while either of the parents was playing with or changing Bonita, they would say, "Phillip, that's unacceptable." If he continued, they would take him upstairs, kicking and screaming if necessary. I warned that behavior at this age always gets worse before it gets better.

Shannon: Mealtime Madness

Although parents don't necessarily lose sleep over it, mealtime misdemeanors can be embarrassing, annoying, and a colossal waste of time. Worse, bad eating habits can last for years. The problem starts innocently enough—parents may be sticklers for manners or worry that Junior isn't eating enough. They might force or cajole their toddler into submission. Either way, this is not only a losing battle, the mealtime dramas then spill over into other parts of the day.

Carol had asked me to visit because her one-year-old daughter, Shannon, was becoming "extremely obstinate." She said "no" to everything. In and of itself, that didn't sound like much of a "problem," as most toddlers go through a negative stage. But what often happens is that the parents give too much attention to the negativity and accidentally reinforce behaviors that later come back to haunt them.

I happened to arrive at lunchtime. Shannon was in her high chair. Mum kept trying to give her a piece of bagel, even though the little girl kept throwing her head back and turning away from her. Both mother and child were getting increasingly distressed.

"Take her down now," I suggested.

"But she hasn't eaten all the bagel."

I told Carol to look carefully. Her child was kicking her legs, grimacing—her face was scrunched up, her lips closed tight. No matter, Mum kept pleading, "Just one more piece, honey, please . . . open wide."

At this point, Carol decided that the problem was the bagel. "What do you want instead, honey? Do you want cereal? Want a banana? How about some yogurt? I have some melon, too. See?" Shannon refused to look. Instead, she just sat there, shaking her head from side to side, more vehemently it seemed with each offering.

"Okay, okay," Carol finally said. "I'll put you down." She took her daughter out of the high chair, washed her little hands, and Shannon toddled off. Carol proceeded to follow her into the playroom with a bowl of applesauce in one hand and the uneaten piece of bagel in the other. "Mmmm," she crooned after Shannon, who kept moving. "Delicious! Have a bite . . . just one piece, sweetie." Talk about not respecting the child!

"You just told her that mealtime is over," I said, reciting the obvious. "Now she's in play mode and you're still chasing her. Just look at her: she's all over the floor, pulling toys out, and you're sneaking up from behind, trying to cram bits of food into her mouth."

Carol looked at me, finally understanding. We talked some more, and I asked about other parts of Shannon's day. As it turned out, Shannon was "uncooperative" at bath and bedtime, too. "Do you always give her so many choices, the way you did at lunch?" I asked at one point.

Carol thought for a moment. "Well, yes," she said proudly. "I don't want to impose *my* will on her. I want her to learn to think for herself."

I asked her to give me examples. "Well, when it's bath time, I'll say to her, 'Do you want to go for your bath?' and when she says 'No,' I say, 'Okay, do you want a few more minutes?' "

Knowing full well that Shannon had no idea what "a few more minutes" meant, and having heard this scenario more times than I can count, I interrupted. "Let me venture a guess at what happens next. When a few minutes are up, you give her a few more, and maybe even another few minutes after that. Finally, you get so exasperated, you pick her up and whisk her upstairs. At that point, she's probably kicking and screaming, right?"

Carol looked at me, stunned. I went on, "And I'll bet once you get her into her nightclothes, you *ask* her if she's ready for bed, right?"

"Yes," Carol answered meekly, "and she always says, 'no.' " I could tell that Mum was starting to see where this conversation was going.

"Carol, she's *one*. And you're the parent!" I remarked. I explained that Shannon's mealtime behavior was symptomatic of a larger problem: Carol was giving her too much control and too many choices—and they were fake choices, to boot. A real choice is when the parent chooses two acceptable alternatives and says to the child, "You can have a bagel or yogurt," rather than spinning out a verbal smorgasbord. "Do you want your bath now?" isn't a real choice, because the parent knows the child *has* to have a bath. What's more, it calls for a "yes" or "no" answer, which gives the child an easy out. (See pages 219–220 for more about giving choices.)

Ironically, although she was giving Shannon too much control, she wasn't giving her enough respect. "When she's not hungry, don't make her sit there," I admonished. "Listen to her. Act according to her physical needs, not your own desire to have a 'good eater.' And for goodness' sake, don't sneak up on her. That just makes matters worse. You need to *prepare* her for whatever you expect her to do, not take her by surprise."

I warned Carol, "You don't have to have too many more rounds of that mealtime drama before Shannon doesn't want to get into her high chair at all. She'll associate eating with a stressful situation. And it certainly won't improve her appetite. These are power struggles you won't win, Carol."

Here was a growing time-buster, a situation that would probably worsen in months to come: Shannon was already well on her way to becoming Queen Toddler, ruler of the house. Her stubbornness would increase. And if her parents didn't give her limits and teach her restraint at home, they couldn't very well expect her to act appropriately *outside* their home, could they?

"Don't even try to take this child to a restaurant until you've backed off and let her see that you respect her and that mealtimes don't have to be a struggle," I advised. "If you don't, I assure you that in a public place she'll do whatever she can to disrupt your meal. And when you visit family for Thanksgiving dinner, Shannon won't sit at the table there, either. Grandma will have a fit because Shannon is running around, spilling stuff all over the sofa, and you'll want to crawl underneath it!"

Over the next two months, Carol and I had weekly phone consultations. The first part of the plan was to work on mealtimes. Carol was to make it clear that if Shannon wanted to eat, it would be at the table (in her high chair), but she would also end the meal when Shannon no longer wanted to eat.

Within two weeks, Shannon "got" the rule—no table, no food. She came to trust that when she was finished eating, she didn't have to arch her back or kick to get her message across. She knew that when she lifted up her arms, rather than force her to sit in the high chair, Carol would help her get down. Just as important, Carol improved, too. Instead of offering fake choices, and allowing Shannon to call the shots, she became better at phrasing real choices ("Would you like to read in bed with Mom or Dad?" and "Would you like the book about fairies or the Barney book?"). Not surprisingly, other parts of the daily ritual went more smoothly as well. Of course, little Shannon still has her moments of negativity, but Carol is now in charge and no longer wastes hours of every day waging battles she can't win.

To be sure, undoing a chronic problem is at first as exhausting as dealing with the time-buster itself. But it's important to look down the road a bit. I'm sure you don't want your child to continue having sleep difficulties, excessive tantrums, or any of these other problems when he or she is three or four. Therefore, it's best to handle these challenges *now*. A few more weeks or even months of difficult days and sleepless nights are worth it to change any situation that has gotten so off course.

Keep in mind the larger picture as well. Parenting is a hard job and the most important work you'll ever do. To raise children alone or as part of a team requires you to be creative, patient, smart, and to stretch your limits beyond anything you've ever done, especially when it comes to discipline. And as you'll see in the last chapter of this book, this thoughtfulness and farsighted vision will become even more important if and when you decide to expand your family.

CHAPTER NINE

When Baby Makes Four: Growing Your Family

Nothing endures but change.

—Heraclitus

There is little less trouble in governing
a private family than a whole kingdom.

—Montaigne

The Big Question

Asking the parents of a toddler, "When are you going to have another one?" or "Are you trying yet?" is enough to make their brave souls tremble. To be sure, some couples are methodical planners. Even before their first child is conceived, the partners seem to know what kind of spacing between children is optimal (at least for them), and if they are lucky as well as decisive, their bodies cooperate. Not everyone has such peace of mind or good fortune, though. Indeed, from my experience, the question of whether to have another child—and, if so, when—is more often fraught with indecision and worry. Can we handle it? Will we have enough money? If the first child was an easy baby, will our good fortune last? If she was a handful, do we have the fortitude to do it again?

During the first pregnancy, the couple might have had vague concerns, but now they *know* what parenting is really like—how rewarding and also how exhausting, how thrilling and also how complex. The parents of a toddler have "a family" already. Do they really want to make it bigger?

In this chapter, we'll look at the issue of future children and family size, how to prepare and help your toddler deal with a sibling, and just as important, how to keep yourself and your relationship on an even keel. Goodness knows, as you add new members to your family, there are more personalities to contend with. You have to be prepared not only for the joys of a growing brood, but also the potential problems that can arise.

To Be or Not to Be (Pregnant Again)

Make no mistake: this *is* an important decision. Certainly, both parents have to weigh whether there's enough money in the bank, room in the house, and of course, love in their hearts to give a second child the kind of care and attention she'll need. Usually, it's Mum who has to consider her career: If she left it for the first baby, is she willing to stay home even longer to care for another baby? If she is now back at work, and it has been hard for her to split time between her first child and the office, can she do it with two? Or the reverse might be the case: With her firstborn, the woman discovered ministering to an infant was all she needed—she enjoyed breastfeeding, cuddling, and caring for the baby far more than she ever imagined she would. When the baby started to walk, stopped nursing, or started talking, she knew the honeymoon was over and longed to hold an infant. All the same, she has to ask herself if she's really ready to go through it again.

Often, partners don't agree about whether or when to have a second child, and the subsequent debate can be a difficult storm for a relationship to weather (see pages 308–317 for more about couples). There is no such thing as a little bit pregnant, luv—these are differences partners *must* resolve. Each has to honestly look at *why* he or she wants a second baby. Is it because family or friends are pressuring her? Is it because of his own childhood? Is it because one or both have a bias against only children and they think they *have* to give their child a sibling? Is it because the biological clock is running out? Or all of the above?

Following are stories of three couples who found themselves in the throes of doubt about having a second child. Two agonized over the decision; one had a little help from Mother Nature.

John and Talia. John and Talia's long-awaited first child, Kristen, now three, arrived after five years of infertility treatments and two miscarriages. Talia, who was close to forty, knew that her chances of getting pregnant again by using her frozen embryos grew slimmer the longer she waited. But John, thirteen years older than his wife and with two children from a previous marriage, wasn't so sure about having another child. He certainly adored "his midlife gift," as he referred to his precious little girl, but he would be in his seventies when Kristen reached adolescence. Talia used John's argument to bolster her own. "That's precisely *why* it's important for us to try to have another one," she insisted. "Kristy will need company—other than her aging parents." After a few months of their going back and forth, John finally agreed with Talia. He didn't want Kristy to grow up alone. To everyone's surprise, Talia got pregnant almost immediately. Kristen now has a brother.

Should We . . . or Shouldn't We?

Although every should-we-have-a-second-baby story has its unique twists and turns, to make this decision, parents need to consider many factors:

- **Physical readiness.** How old are you, what kind of shape are you in? Do you have the energy for another child?
- **Emotional readiness.** Consider your temperament and your willingness to put in more time and energy. And are you ready to give up that intense closeness with your firstborn?
- **Your first child.** What is his temperament, what was his infancy and toddlerhood like, and how well does he adapt to change?
- **Finances.** If one partner has to quit work, can you stay afloat? Afford paid help? Do you have sufficient savings for emergencies?
- **Career.** Are you willing to put it on hold? Will it be there for you when the children are a bit older—and do you care?
- **Logistics.** Do you have enough space for two children? Where will the new baby sleep? Can he or she share a room with your first child?
- **Motive.** Do you really want this child, or are others pressuring you? Are you concerned about being the parents of an only child? Is your own childhood, with lots of sibs or none at all, influencing your decision?
- **Support.** Especially if you're a single parent, who will help out?

Kate and Bob. Kate, who ran a small clothing boutique, wanted to "give my son a sibling," but there were many other factors to consider as well. At 35, she enjoyed working in her own business. She had been more than willing to take time off when she had Louis, but she had always planned to go back to work and did so when Lou was six months old. It hadn't been easy, though, even with a part-time nanny, because her little boy was truly a Spirited child who had a mind of his own and very erratic sleep patterns as well. Many mornings Kate had to drag herself into the store. Bob, who had come from a family of five children, wanted at least two, and Lou was already two and a half. To complicate matters, Kate's father was dying. "I hope he lives long enough to see Lou's sister or brother," her mother would say, adding, "And I'm not getting any younger myself."

Kate felt tortured and guilty. She had always wanted two children herself, but memories of sleepless nights were still fresh in her mind, and the thought of going back to breast pumps and diapers sent her careening into a panic. In the end,

Kate relented and was happy that she did. Malcolm, an Angel baby, arrived a few days short of Lou's fourth birthday.

Fanny and Stan. Sometimes, even though a husband and wife discuss or argue about the prospect of a second child, the decision is made *for* them by forces beyond their control. Fanny and Stan, both 40, had adopted their first child after losing a long, long bout with infertility. Little Chan, who came to them from Cambodia when he was only two months old, was their dream come true. He immediately bonded with the two of them, adapted quickly to their home, and was a very easy, agreeable Angel baby to boot. One morning, when Chan was five months old, Fanny woke up retching. She figured she had come down with the same stomach flu that Stan had had a week earlier. Imagine her shock when the doctor told her she was pregnant. As joyful as the news was, though, she worried whether she'd have the energy for two children under the age of two, not to mention the financial resources. By then, though, it was a moot point. Baby #2 was already on the way.

If we lived in a perfect world, everything would fit neatly into place. Pondering the decision about a second baby, you would run down the list of considerations and happily note that you were ready on all fronts. You would decide what age difference you'd like between your children (see box on page 284). And you'd get pregnant right on schedule.

More often, though, parents have to grapple with the fact that not everything goes as planned. You would like to have more money in the bank, more space, more time with your first child. Or you may not be thrilled about putting a particular project on hold. Still, you are torn. Your biological clock is ticking, your first one was just so much fun, and your partner is pushing for a second child. Even though not everything is perfect, you take the plunge (or you don't; see the box on page 285).

Different Ages/Different Stages

There is no "ideal" time to have a second child. Ultimately, you have to figure out what's best for you and hope that Mother Nature cooperates.

11–18 months "Irish twins" are born within a year of one another, but any small age difference is difficult. Two are in diapers and you need to double the baby equipment. Disciplining the older child may be harder, too, because daily life is so physically exhausting. The good part is that you get through the difficult years earlier than when children are more widely spaced.

18–30 months This is smack in the middle of the first child's negativity and a time when he is most ambivalent about independence. The older child won't get as much of you as he needs and wants. Attentiveness and separate time for the older one can mediate many problems. And depending on the first one's temperament, there either will be lots of fighting or a strong, enduring bond between the two.

2½ to 4 years The older child is less likely to feel jealous because she is more independent, has her own friends and a steady routine. Because of the wider spacing, children are not compatible playmates and might not grow up being close, although their relationship can change as they get older.

Over 4 years At baby's birth, the older child is often disappointed in "the blob," because he had imagined an instant playmate. He can participate more in care of younger one, but parents have to be careful not to make him *overly* responsible. There is less sibling rivalry and often less interaction as well.

The Waiting Game

Your hormones are raging, there's a new life growing inside you, and your toddler is scurrying about. Some days, you're in heaven, imagining an idyllic scene with your happy family—at the dinner table, opening presents on Christmas morning, or perhaps enjoying a vacation at Disney World. Other days, you're in hell. *How will I tell my toddler?* you ask yourself. *What can I do to prepare him? What if he's not happy about it? What if my partner is having second thoughts?* As your mind spins round and round, you always light on the scariest question of all: *What have I gotten myself into?*

What about *One*?

For the first time in history, there are more single-child families in the U.S. than families with two or more. Ironically, although parents these days are increasingly opting for onlies, there is still a strong bias *against* having one child. The obvious prejudices are usually trotted out: An only child is spoiled and demanding. She never learns how to share. She expects the world to be as accommodating and accepting as her doting parents. Without a baby brother or sister, the naysayers insist, she is bound to be lonely. G. Stanley Hall, a psychologist in the 1900s, put it even more harshly: "Being an only child is a disease in itself."

Give me a break! The most recent research indicates that only children tend to have a slight advantage when it comes to self-esteem—and higher intelligence than peers with one sibling. Granted, their parents may have to work a bit harder to make lots of social plans for the child and to include friends on family outings so that he or she isn't the sole focus of their attention. They have to be careful to maintain their boundaries and not make the child "a pal" with whom they share adult information and emotions. But a good parent is a good parent. If there's one child at home or five, the parents' skills, physical and emotional well-being, and the love and limits they provide mean far more than how many places are set at the dinner table.

A little ambivalence about growing your family is normal and understandable, but if after careful consideration the idea of getting pregnant again goes against the grain, stand up for your right to have an only child. It's fine to have a family of three. As your child grows up, stress that this was your *choice*. Guilt, disappointment, and regret are more likely to make a child feel deprived of a sibling than the fact that he's your one and only. (Besides, some siblings grow up and never talk to each other!)

Nine months can seem like a long time when you're on an emotional roller coaster. You need to take care of yourself, stay connected to your partner, and at the same time, help your little one prepare. Let's start with the adults.

Know that what you're feeling is normal. There isn't a parent out there who doesn't say, "I hope we're doing the right thing" in the midst of a second pregnancy. The panic hits at different times and for different reasons. The beginning months may be bearable, but as you begin to gain weight and it gets harder to lift your toddler, the impending birth starts to feel like an impending disaster. Or life might be merrily rolling along and suddenly your child passes through a difficult stage. You can't imagine handling *two* children or having to go through this a second time. Feelings of dread can also wash over you at an unexpected moment: You're walking down the street with your partner, perhaps coming out of a movie or a great restaurant. It reminds you of what life was like *before* your first child. As it is, with so little time for romance, you think to yourself, *We must be crazy to do this again.*

When panic hits, recite the serenity prayer: "God grant me the serenity to accept the things I cannot change, the courage to change the things I can, and the wisdom to know the difference." Pregnancy, ducky, is something you *can't* change, but your attitude is another matter. So take a deep breath, call a sitter or a friend, and do something nice for yourself (consider the suggestions on pages 317–320).

Talk about your fears. Recently, Lena, an interior decorator seven months into her second pregnancy, and Carter, an accountant, asked me to visit them because they were awash in second thoughts. I'd known them since Van was born two and a half years ago.

"I'm wondering mostly about Van," Lena began, "whether I give him enough attention as it is. Can I really share myself with a second child?"

Help! Mum Needs Help! (A Checklist for Dads)

Mum will get even more tired during her second pregnancy than she was during the first. She's not only carrying around excess weight, she also has to run after a toddler. Dad (or anyone else who can help out—Nan, Gramps, Aunt Irene, a best friend, other mothers, a paid caregiver) must come to the rescue. Dad and other helpers should do any or all of the following:

- Take Junior off Mom's hands, whenever possible, and have a standing date with him as well.

- Run errands.

- Cook or bring food in.

- Give Junior a bath—it's hard and uncomfortable for Mum to bend over.

- Don't complain about the extra work—that will make Mum feel worse.

"I don't think we've had enough time with Van," Carter agreed. "And now, to have another child coming along. . ."

"When would be the *right* time?" I asked, knowing full well that there was no such thing. "And how will you know when Van has had *enough* time with the two of you? When he's four? Five?"

They both shrugged, getting my point. I suggested that they recall *why* they had decided to get pregnant seven months ago. "We never intended for Van to be only child," Lena said. "We had always planned on having two or more. When Van was born, I quit working for a few months, but my career has blossomed ever since. Work has been going well for both of us, so we're in great financial shape. And we figured that Van would be three when the baby arrived. He'd be in a play group with friends and have a life of his own."

It was sound reasoning. Lena and Carter had also renovated part of their home, opting to expand their present quarters rather than chance a disruptive move to a new home. They had obviously done their homework. What's more, the two of them did seem gloriously happy. Van was a wonderful little boy, they had a terrific live-in nanny, and Lena had just won an award for her interior design.

But there was more to the story. First of all, Lena was beset by raging hormones and a good fifty pounds of extra weight. Van often got upset because she couldn't carry him and had trouble explaining why. Lena also shared with me an unexpected wrinkle in her and Carter's carefully plotted plan. Impressed by her recent success, a very wealthy man asked her to help him renovate his newly acquired mansion in Malibu. As much as the job would translate into gobs of money, prestige, and visibility, and in all probability lead to a great deal more work as well, it also meant time—time that a woman about to give birth to a second baby wouldn't have.

As we talked, I knew that both Lena's body and the specter of a missed opportunity, not the coming of a second child, were the causes of her distress. "You must feel like an old lop horse," I told her, using a Yorkshire expression for a horse that lugs the trolley in a coal pit. "That alone can make life seem bleak." Just as important, though, the client's call felt like a once-in-a-lifetime opportunity, and Lena knew in her heart she'd have to turn it down.

"You've got to air your disappointment," I said. "If you try to sweep it under the rug, there's a good chance that it will creep up on you later and bite you in the rear. Even worse, you'll resent the baby when she finally arrives."

Remember that life isn't Burger King: you can't always have it "your way." We all have wishes in life, things we want to do, but we can't have or do them all. When you have misgivings, aside from reviewing your reasons for getting pregnant in the first place and *feeling* your disappointment over missed opportunities, you must accept life on life's terms. As I told Lena, "You could try to negotiate with the man about this job, ask him to work around the demands of your family, but is that what you really want to do? Even though it doesn't feel like it now, you will have other fabulous offers, but you'll never again have a chance to spend time with your baby."

A few days later, Lena called to tell me that she felt much better. "I kept thinking about why we had decided to have this baby—it *is* the right time for us. I also made peace with my decision not to take the job, and now I'm even a bit relieved." Lena's plight is a common one among women these days. With careers and children, something always has to "give." Just remember that jobs come and go, but babies are forever.

Small Children/Great Expectations

It's one thing to deal with your own issues, quite another to handle a toddler who may not be old enough to understand why your belly is swelling or why you can no longer whisk her up into your arms. Here are some stop-gap measures that can make the transition a little smoother.

Remember that your child doesn't get it. When you say, "There's a baby in Mummy's tummy," your toddler doesn't have a clue what that means. (Hey, it's hard enough for us grown-ups to fathom the miracle of life!) Your child might proudly point to your bulging belly and parrot the right words, but he has no idea what the new arrival will mean *to him*. I'm not saying that you shouldn't prepare your child, just that when you do, don't expect too much.

Don't tell too soon. Nine months is an eternity in a toddler's life. If you tell your toddler, "You're going to have a baby [sister/brother]," he'll think it's going to happen tomorrow. Although many parents break the news months ahead of time, in my opinion, four or five weeks before the baby is due is time enough to start (in the meantime, prepare him in other ways, as I explain below). You know your child, however; base your decision on his personality. Obviously, if your child notices that your waistline is expanding, and asks about it, make that your starting point.

Whenever you tell him, keep it simple: "Mummy has a baby in her tummy. You're going to have a [brother/sister, assuming you know the gender]." Answer truthfully any questions that your child asks, like "Where is the baby going to stay?" or "Is it going to sleep in my bed?" Also, try to get across the point that this baby isn't going to come out walking and talking. So many parents tell toddlers excitedly, "You're going to have a new playmate." Then they bring home a little critter that does nothing but sleep, cry, and suck on Mummy's breast. Who wouldn't be disappointed?

> ### E-mail: A Mother Who Broke the News Early
>
> During our second pregnancy, we talked to our son as openly as appropriate about the baby, where it came from, what life would be like when it got here, and so on. We tried to help him mentally adjust and get used to the idea long before the baby came. When our daughter arrived, we got our son a present which we told him was from his baby sister (an idea we got from a magazine). That helped him feel like his baby sister loved him and wasn't imposing on his life to be mean.

Six months before the baby is due, get your toddler into a play group. Sharing and cooperation are lessons best taught with peers. Even if the age difference will be small, your toddler will have little in common with the baby. Only twins learn from each other about sharing. Being with other children will at least give her some understanding of what it's like to share. But don't expect her to automatically make the leap once the baby is born. She'll have trouble enough grasping the concept of sharing toys, so don't have too high expectations when it comes to sharing *you*.

Display affection for other children. Let your toddler observe you interacting with other little ones (a good idea even if you're not expecting; see sidebar, page 201). Some children could care less when their mums hold or kiss another child. Some become indignant—it never occurred to them that their mother could be interested in anyone else. And some are amazed. The look on fourteen-month-old Audrey's face when her mother, Peri, picked up one of the other children in the play group was that of utter shock. Her little eyes popped open, and the expression on her face said, *Hey, Ma. What are you doing? That's not me.* It was good for Peri to show Audrey that Mummy could be shared.

At home, too, when your toddler pushes Dad away because he's hugging or kissing you, let her know that there's love enough for *both* of you. A mother recently told me that her two-year-old "hates it when we cuddle." Instead of resigning herself to the situation, I urged the mother to correct the child's behavior by saying, "Come here—we can all hug."

E-mail: Turning a Minus into a Plus

One of the ways in which I prepared my older son for the baby's arrival is this: As I got further along in my pregnancy, I found it extremely difficult to pick up my three-year-old son due to my growing belly. I would say to him, "I can't wait for the baby to come so that Mommy can pick you up again!" or ask, "What's the first thing Mommy's going to do when the baby comes?" to which my son would reply, "Pick me up!"

When my husband brought my son to the hospital after our new baby was born, I put the baby in his bassinet and picked up my son and held him close to me, just as I had promised!

Expose your toddler to babies. Read him books about baby brothers and sisters; show him pictures in magazines, as well as pictures of himself as a baby. Best of all, let him see real babies and talk about them. Say, "This baby is bigger than the one in Mummy's tummy," or "Our baby won't be this big when she's born." Also make him aware of how fragile babies are: "This is a new baby. Look how tiny her fingers are. We have to be very careful with her—she's fragile." Believe me, it will be much easier for him to be gentle with someone else's baby than the one you bring home from the hospital.

TIP: Many expectant parents customarily take hospital tours and bring their toddler along, thinking that it will give them a sense of where Mummy will go to have the baby. I disagree. Hospitals can be a scary place for a young child. It can also be confusing to think that "the baby" is going to come from the place where people go when they're sick.

Be sensitive to your toddler's point of view. Even though she doesn't fully understand what's happening on an intellectual level, I can assure you that your child knows things are changing. She hears conversations (even when you don't think she's listening) that invariably include the phrase "when the baby comes," and she knows that something *big* is about to happen. She notices that you lie down more often and probably wonders why everyone keeps saying, "Be careful of Mummy's tummy." She watches as a formerly unused room is painted "for the baby." And perhaps you've started moving her to a "big girl bed" (see sidebar on page 269). Though she doesn't necessarily connect it with your pregnancy, it's another significant deviation from the norm.

Be concious of your words. Don't go through her old things and tell her, "This used to be yours and now the baby is going to wear it." Bring her on shopping excursions for the layette, but don't make a big deal of how "cute" the little clothes are. When she goes to touch a baby toy, let her examine it, but don't say, "That's for the baby—you're a big girl now." It wasn't that long ago that she loved pastel-colored stuffed animals. Why *wouldn't* she assume they're for her? Most important, *don't* tell her how much she's going to love her new sibling, because she might not!

Plan to stay out overnight without your toddler. That way, when you go to the hospital, it won't be his first time without you. Grandma and Grandpa, a favorite aunt, or a good friend can come over, or have the toddler stay at their house. Or pay someone to sleep in for a night at your house. Three days in advance is time enough to prepare a child under two for the overnight: "Joey, you're going to stay at Nana's house in three days [or, 'Nana's going to come here and stay with you']. Shall we mark it down on the calender? Let's tick off the days." Also, let him help you pack his bag—put in his jammies and toys. If he'll be staying at home with Nana, let him help get her bed or room ready.

A month or two later, when your due date arrives, both you and your toddler should have a bag ready. When it's time to leave, make sure you make more of a fuss about his going to Grandma's again (or about her coming to visit) than about your leaving to have the baby. Simply say, "Mummy is going to have the baby today. You will be [run through the plans]." Since he will have had some overnight experience without you, remind him of the fun he had, and that just like last time, you'll see him soon.

Weaning Reminders

Go slowly. Figure that it will take you at least three months.

Don't mention the baby. You're weaning *for* the toddler's sake, not because you've got another one on the way.

Do it as if you weren't pregnant. See the suggestions on pages 118–124.

Use your common sense and trust your instinct. You'll get a lot of advice about preparing your child for the baby. Some family centers even offer sibling preparation classes, but don't take everything you hear as gospel. At one of these classes, parents were told to "overindulge" their older child. Maya, who knew better, told me, "This child is coming into our life to enrich it, not to be isolated and not to have an older brother who rules the household. I knew that would cause problems." Maya is correct: in a family, *everyone's* needs are important.

Wean your toddler, if possible. As I discussed in Chapter Four, weaning occurs in all animal species as a natural consequence of growing up. Whether it will be a traumatic experience for your child or a gentle transition depends on how you handle it. In some societies, when babies are spaced closely, women routinely "tandem nurse," but this is an exhausting proposition. Granted, if you have Irish twins (born within a year of each other), or the first baby still requires the nutrition that only breast milk can provide, you might have to nurse both children, but I always advise mums to carefully consider whether there might be an alternative solution.

Certainly, if your toddler is two or older and is still nursing to soothe himself, rather than because he needs breast milk, weaning him prior to the baby's arrival is kinder *to him*. If he is suckling only for comfort, you need to figure out ways of reassuring and comforting him without the use of your breast. It's also a good idea to introduce a security object now, before the baby is born, and to help him find ways to self-soothe (reread Leanne's story, pages 254–262, and Cody's, pages 262–267). Otherwise, there's a good chance that he is going to resent the new baby bitterly, and it will be a lot harder to deal with his anger when baby makes four.

Enter the Intruder

You can't blame *any* toddler for feeling displaced when a new baby joins the family. Imagine how *you* would feel if your husband brought home another woman to live with you *and* told you to love her and take care of her. Essentially, that's what we ask young children to do. Mum disappears overnight, and a day or two later returns from the hospital with a squirmy little blob that cries continually, is the first thing that visitors ask to see, and seems to capture both parents' attention and concern. Adding insult to injury, everyone talks about how the toddler has to be a "big boy" and watch out for the new baby. *Hey, wait a minute!* says a little voice in his head. *What about me? I never asked for this intruder.* This is a normal response. Everyone has jealousy and feels it, but adults know enough to hide it. Children, however, are the most truthful creatures on God's planet—they show their feelings.

Should My Toddler Visit the Hospital?

Often, parents bring the older child to the hospital after the baby is born. That might be your choice, too, but remember to take your toddler's temperament into consideration. She might get upset when she realizes that you're not going home with her. Also, don't be disappointed if she doesn't gush with heartfelt pride when she sees the baby. Give her time, and allow her to be curious and to express her feelings—even if they're not what you hoped for.

There's no way to predict exactly how a child will react to a new baby. His personality, how you prepare him, and the events swirling around him when the baby comes home all have an impact. Some children are fine from the beginning and stay that way. My coauthor's firstborn, Jennifer, three and a half when Jeremy came home from the hospital, was a little mother from the moment she laid eyes on her brother. In part, this was because of her temperament—she was an easygoing, caring Angel child—and probably because of the age difference as well. She'd had a lot of one-on-one time with her mother and father, which undoubtedly made her more willing to embrace this little creature without fearing that he would encroach on her territory.

At the opposite end of the spectrum is the child who immediately resents the baby and becomes very demanding. Daniel's anger was overt. And the moment he first clopped his baby brother on the head, this clever twenty-three-month-old immediately grasped an important reality: *Oh, so this is how I get the attention away from that stupid baby.* Olivia, too, let her anger show loud and clear. A few days after the baby came home from the hospital, when Aunt Mildred suggested that the four of them pose for a family portrait, she kept trying to shove newborn Curt off Mummy's lap.

Most often, a toddler's disdain for the baby comes out in more subtle ways. She might become aggressive toward other children, rebelling physically because she hasn't got the words or has been discouraged from expressing her anger about the baby. She might refuse to do simple tasks that she's never balked at before, like putting away her toys. She might start throwing food at the table

---

E-mail: In Love with Baby Sister

I recently had a second baby. We prepared our son, who is nearly three, by constantly talking about the baby, explaining that Mummy would have to go to hospital to have a baby. I also got Tyler to help me decorate Jessica's room, which he was very excited about doing. He even packed up his old baby toys and arranged them for her in her new room. While I was in the hospital, he went shopping with my husband and bought Jessica a new soft toy, which he was proud to do. He absolutely adores her and can't stop kissing and talking to her. Sometimes it's too much, though!

---

or refuse to take a bath. Or she might regress: start crawling again even though she's been walking for months; wake up during the night, after months of sleeping soundly through. Some children also go on a hunger strike, or they try to grab Mum's breast even though they haven't nursed for months.

Is it possible, as they say in Westerns, to head trouble off at the pass? Not always. Sometimes you just have to deal with whatever comes up. But the following bits of advice might help minimize this momentous transition.

Schedule one-on-one time with your toddler. When the baby first comes and sleeps a lot, steal little bits of time to be with your firstborn. Squeeze in an extra cuddle; play a bit longer than you normally would; let your toddler have quiet time with you while you rest. But don't simply leave one-on-one time to chance. Pencil your toddler in the way you would a steady lunch date with a friend. Weather permitting, try to be away from home for a short time during the day—go to the park, feed the ducks, go to a coffee shop, or just take a walk downtown. Bedtimes should also be reserved for one-on-one time.

A Doll Won't Do It

I don't agree with the idea of giving your toddler a doll on the day the baby is born, so that she has her own "baby." A doll is *not* like a baby—it's a toy. You can't expect a young child to treat it like a living thing. Instead, she'll drag the doll around by its hair, pummel it, and abandon it in back of the settee. A few days later, you'll discover the doll, with sticky red goo smeared around its face, because your little one tried to feed it a jam butty (what we Brits call a jelly sandwich). That's no way to treat a real baby!

Regardless of your planning, though, the baby will require your attention at some point when you don't expect it. It's best to be honest about such possibilities and to prepare your toddler. If, for instance, you're about to dive into your toddler's favorite book, warn him, "I'm going to read you this story, but if the baby wakes up, I'll have to go to him."

Allow your older child to help in small ways, but don't ask him to be too grown up. When a child is solicitous of the baby and wants to help out, if you don't allow him to participate in her care, it's like saying, "Here's a box of candy, but you can't have any." I used to ask my Sara, who liked to do busy jobs, to fill up the nappy box for me. Bear in mind, though, that when a toddler is loving and eager to cooperate, it's easy to forget how young he is. It's not fair to turn a two- or three-year-old into a caretaker.

TIP: A baby can be a sitting (or lying) duck for an older sibling, even one who seems to love and accept her. Never leave your toddler and the baby alone. Even if you're in the room with them, you need eyes in the back of your head.

How Do I Keep My Older Child Quiet When the Baby Sleeps?

Just as you did (hopefully) with your firstborn, you need to respect your baby's need for quiet. Still, it's not always possible to get a robust toddler to use her "quiet voice" even if you request it, or she might not be old enough to comprehend what you mean. If this is the case, be clever. Distract the noisy sibling and play with her as far from the baby's room as your home will allow.

Accept, but don't encourage, regressive behavior. If your child goes through a period of regression, don't overreact. It's quite common. He may want to climb onto the changing table, get into the crib, or try out Baby's toys. That's fine, but the important phrase is "try out." When Sara wanted to go into Sophie's pram, I let her . . . for a moment. But then I said, "Okay. You tried it, but it's not for you. It's for Sophie. She can't walk like you can—she has to go in the pram." The reality is that a keen interest in baby things usually lasts only for the first week or two. When parents allow toddlers to satisfy their curiosity, they happily go back to their own playthings.

Tryouts don't apply to breastfeeding, however. Shana, a mother in Montana who called recently, had weaned fifteen-month-old Anne five or six months before the new baby arrived. A few days after she brought baby Helen home, Anne started asking for Mum's breast, too. Shana was confused. Several of the mothers she'd met through a La Leche League support group told her to offer Anne her breast if she wanted it—and that it would be "psychologically damaging" to deny her. "But that doesn't feel right to me," Shana said. I agreed, adding that I thought it would have been even more damaging to allow Anne to control her mother. My suggestion was that Shana tell her daughter straightaway, "No, Anne, this is the baby's food. We have to save it for her." Since Anne was also starting to eat solid food, at mealtimes Shana could reinforce the difference by pointing out, "Here's our fruit and our chicken. This is the kind of food that Anne and Mummy eat. This [pointing to her breast] is baby Helen's food."

Encourage your child to express how she feels. With all the thought I gave to my second pregnancy, I never expected my Sara to ask, "When is the baby going back, Mummy?" At first, as many parents do, I brushed off her comment as "cute." A few weeks later, though, she told me she "hated" Sophie because "Mummy has only busy time now." She had also taken to emptying the drawers in the nursery whenever I fed Sophie. Child-proofing the cabinets put an end to that mischief. But then Sara starting trying to flush the loo roll down the loo. Obviously, I hadn't taken the time to interpret Sara's behavioral cues or to really listen to how she felt. And it was true: every time she had tried to snare my attention—usually in the middle of a feed or a nappy change—I would say to her, "Mummy's busy right now." Those words obviously stuck with her.

Feelings Alert!

Statements like these aren't "cute." They tell you how your child feels, so pay attention when you hear:

- I don't like it when she cries.

- She's ugly.

- I hate her.

- When is the baby going back?

Realizing how keenly she felt my distraction, I helped Sara put together her "busy bag," a sack of crayons and coloring books with which she could amuse herself whenever I had to feed Sophie or put her down. We made it part of our routine. I'd say, "Let's get your busy bag down from the cupboard, so you have something to do while I tend to your sister."

Whatever you do, *never* try to convince your child that she's being silly or wrong. Don't suggest that she "really" loves her baby brother. And don't take it personally—her sentiments about her new sibling have nothing to do with your parenting skills. Instead, explore her comments through dialogue. Ask, "What is it about the baby you don't like?" Many children say, "His crying." Can you blame them? An infant's crying irritates adults, too, and for your toddler it's an even greater insult considering that the crying immediately captures Mum's attention. Explain that this is the baby's "voice." Remind her, "That's how you talked to me when you were a baby." Or give a more current example: "Remember when you were first learning how to skip and you had to keep practicing? One day our baby will have words like we do, but now all she can do is practice her voice."

Watch what you say. Toddlers imitate whatever they hear and see around them. Your child is always listening, and it's easy to plant ideas in her head. If she hears things like "She's jealous of baby," it can give her ideas.

Also, listen to yourself *from your toddler's perspective.* We parents sometimes forget how traumatic it is for our little ones to feel displaced. When you make statements like, "You have to love your brother," or "You have to protect your sister," your toddler probably says to himself, *Protect her? This piece of flesh that makes noises like a cat and keeps Mummy away from me? I don't think so!* It's also insensitive to say to a young child, "Act your age," which he doesn't understand, or to insist, "You're a big boy now—

Things You Should Never Say to Your Toddler about His Younger Sibling

"You have to take care of him."

"You have to like her."

"Be nice to the new baby."

"You have to protect our baby."

"Don't you love your new baby?"—Then when the toddler says, "No," you say, "Oh, yes you do."

"Play with your sister."

"Look after your little brother."

"Watch your sister while I'm cooking dinner."

"Share with your brother."

"You're a big girl now."

"Act your age."

---

with a big boy bed, big boy toilet." Children don't feel "big," and besides, what two-year-old wants that burden?

> **TIP:** *Never use the baby as an excuse, as in, "We have to leave now because it's Jonathan's nap time."*

Take your older child's complaints seriously. Justine was three when her little brother, Matthew, was born. She seemed fine at first, but by the time the baby was four months old, all hell had broken loose. Although Justine had been potty trained for months, she started wetting her bed and smeared feces in the bathroom. She balked at taking a bath and had tantrums at bedtime. "We don't know this child," Justine's mum, Sandra, said. "Normally, she's really good, but now she's mean. We try to reason with her, but nothing works."

"Do you like baby Matthew?" I asked Justine, who came in with her parents. But before she had a chance to answer, Dad interjected, "She loves her baby brother, don't you?"

Justine glared at her father as if to say, *Do I? Hell, no!*

Reading her face, I continued the dialogue, "What don't you like about him? What things does he do that you don't like?"

"Crying," Justine answered.

"That's his voice," I explained. "Until he learns words, that's how he tells us what he wants. One type of cry means, 'Mummy, I want food.' Another is, 'Mummy, I need my diaper changed.' It would really be good if you could help Mummy figure out what Matthew's cries mean."

I could see the little wheels turning in Justine's head, as she weighed whether or not she even *wanted* to help. "What else don't you like?" I said.

"He goes in Mummy's bed," she offered.

"Don't you take your dolly in bed?"

"No." (Meanwhile, Dad again contradicted her, "Yes, you do, sweetie.")

"Well," I continued, "Mummy takes the baby to bed just to feed him. What else don't you like?"

"I have to take a bath with him."

"Well, maybe we can do something about *that*," I offered, glad that she finally had hit on something that her parents could change.

As Justine lost interest in my conversation and returned to her play, I explained to Sandra and her husband, "If Justine has always viewed her bath as a special time, and now she's not happy and won't go into the bathroom, you've got to look at that. I know it's quicker for you to put the two of them into the tub together, but she doesn't like it. She obviously misses her time with you and is taking her sadness and anger out on her baby brother." I suggested that they give Matthew a bath first, and then let Justine have the tub to herself. "Double baths are a small price to pay for peace," I added.

Granted, there's a difference between listening to a child and letting her run the house. When your child complains, look at her history: is this something she was used to and now feels deprived of? Consider the nature of her request, too. If what she wants is reasonable—and it doesn't hurt or exclude the baby—then accommodate her.

Mary in the Middle

When a new baby arrives, the middle child is often more traumatized than her older sibling was when she was born—she has a double whammy. Still smarting from the resentment heaped upon her by the firstborn, now there's *another* one displacing her. Suddenly Mum is saying, "I've brought home a baby for you to love." Who asked for it? As far as the second child is concerned, there are no benefits to this crying creature. And it's not just Mum whom she misses. She doesn't understand why her baby-sitter doesn't have the time to take her to the playground anymore. To make matters worse, everyone tells her, "You have to take care of your baby brother." What three-year-old wants *that*?

TIP: *Try to "catch" your child being kind and loving to his sibling and praise him: "What a good brother you are," or "That's so sweet of you to hold Gina's hand." (See also pages 57–58 about praise.)*

Let your child know what you expect. If you're busy with the baby, say so. Your child has to get used to hearing it. When she is mean or harms the baby, tell her. In Daniel's case, because his parents felt "sorry" for him, they were reluctant to discipline him. Not surprisingly, he then hit or pinched his brother every chance he could get. When I asked his mother why she wasn't intervening, she said, "He doesn't know any better." I told her, "Well, then *you* had better teach him."

Unfortunately, without realizing the problem they're creating for the whole family, parents often make allowances for or pity the first child: "Poor thing—he feels left out." Or they insist, "He loves the new baby", a few moments after the little darling has taken a ballpoint pen to his little sister's scalp. Rationalizing or denying a child's behavior won't change it. Instead of saying, "You have to love your brother," when Daniel pinched the baby, I told his mother to reiterate the rule: "You may not pinch Crocker. That hurts him." She should acknowledge his feelings ("I can see that you're frustrated"), but

Nip It in the Bud

When your toddler feels neglected, he is not able to say, "By the way, Mummy, I need your attention for the next half hour." He becomes angry and impulsive instead. And he knows that hurting the baby will get your attention. So whenever your little one decides to have a go at the new baby, do what you would in the situations we described earlier. Restrain his hand, and without anger, say, "You may not stay here if you pinch the baby. That hurts her." Remember that discipline is *emotional education* (see page 209). The lesson here is that it's not okay to act out your feelings by bullying another human being or animal.

also help him deal with the current reality: "I have to spend time with him and take care of him, just like I did with you, because he's only a baby."

Anticipate "testing"—but be firm about your boundaries. Though her parents insisted, "Be nice to your baby sister," three-year-old Nanette kept testing them. She would climb into eight-week-old Ethel's crib whenever the coast was clear, unaware that a camera was positioned overhead. Nanette would poke and jostle until the baby cried. The first time her mother saw Nanette's sneak attack on the TV monitor in the kitchen, Elaine ran in, whisked Nanette out of the crib and told her she couldn't have any more juice. Nanette protested. "I was just kissing her." Elaine said nothing, preferring to let the incident slide rather than call her three-year-old a liar.

Elaine walked on eggshells around her toddler. Fearful that Nanette's whining would turn into a full-blown jealous tantrum whenever she picked the baby up, Mum had begun to hand off Ethel to the nanny or Grandma. Elaine also told relatives and friends who bought gifts for the baby that they'd better bring a present for Nanette, too. "I hate to discipline her," Elaine admitted when she related the situation to me a few weeks later, "because she already feels left out."

On the day I visited, Elaine was preparing to take Nanette to the park. "Why don't you take baby, too?" I asked.

"Nanette doesn't want her to come," she answered, not realizing that she was allowing a two-year-old to call the shots. Just then, we glanced at the television monitor. Nanette was in the crib again, except this time she was about to swat Ethel.

"You've got to go in there right now," I urged. "Tell her you've seen her do it and that it's totally unacceptable."

This situation could have easily turned into a time-buster, because Elaine was reinforcing her toddler's most selfish and demanding behavior—and putting baby Ethel at risk. At my urging, she went into Ethel's room immediately and said, "No, Nanette! That hurt Ethel. You may not hit the baby. Now you have to go to

When the Older Child Has a Tantrum

A mother's worst nightmare is being alone with a young baby and a screaming toddler. In fact, your toddler usually *chooses* times when you're involved with the baby to act out. What better time to have a meltdown? They know you're captive—and you are. Someone has to wait, and it can't be the baby.

As I instructed Elaine, "The next time Nanette has a tantrum when you're busy with Ethel, finish what you're doing with the baby, put her into her crib, and then give Nanette a time-out." I also pointed out that aside from wanting to keep the baby safe, the reason you deal with her first is to send a message to the older child that tantrums don't get your attention. (See pages 233–239 and 271–274 for tantrum tactics.)

your room." Elaine went into Nanette's room with her and stood by as she proceeded to have a dramatic meltdown. "I can see you're upset, Nanette, but you still may not hit the baby," Elaine told her. From then on, whenever Nanette went to pinch Ethel, Elaine removed her from the situation. In contrast, when she was the least bit nice to her baby sister, Mum praised her. Eventually, Nanette realized that the kind of attention she got when she was good was a lot better than having a time-out in her room.

Elaine also stopped responding to Nanette's whiney song-and-dance routine. Instead of handing Ethel to the nanny when her older daughter protested, Elaine said, "I won't talk to you when you whine, Nanette. Use your best voice." She also let her child know, in no uncertain terms, that she wasn't going to cave in. "I have to help the baby right now. She needs my attention, too. We are a family."

Try to not overreact. When your toddler pulls an impish stunt to get your attention, it can frustrate the Dickens out of you—and your instinct is to blow your top. However, as I explained in detail in Chapters Seven and Eight, overreacting only reinforces bad behavior. One time when I was getting ready to go to Sunday lunch at my Nan's, I had gotten my girls all spiffed up in their white dresses. Unbeknownst to me, Sara led Sophie right into the coal bin. When I discovered Sophie, covered in black coal dust from head to toe, I took a deep breath, ignored Sara, and calmly said to Sophie, "Oh, it looks like we'll have to change you, and we'll be late for Nana's."

Liana, whose daughters, Karen and Jamie, are two and a half years apart, recalls the first few months after Jamie was born: "I had to watch out for pinching, bent fingers—mostly when I was nursing the baby. To prevent it, I'd suggest that Karen get a book and look at it while I fed her sister. Sometimes it worked, but sometimes it didn't. I just had to accept that Karen would have her moments, no matter what I did. There were lots of instances where she'd get red in the face and frustrated because she didn't have my attention. But by not making a big deal of them, they passed."

TIP: Keep up your routine. As Liana points out, "Having a solid routine helps with discipline, because I can always say, 'We don't do that now.' " True, the baby isn't on the same kind of routine as your firstborn, but to her it's all she knows. In other words, schlepping about with her older sibling is her routine.

Don't try to make your child love or even like the new baby. Margaret was beside herself. After a month of telling Liam to "be nice" and reminding him, "It's your brother," her elder son seemed to be getting worse around the baby. Visiting this family, I saw why. Liam would raise his hand as if to strike Jesse and then look at his mum. In a sweet, almost apologetic voice, Margaret would say, "No, Liam, we don't hit the baby." Later, she'd run an errand with Liam and buy him a new toy.

"You're not being firm enough with him," I told her, "and I suspect it's because you're afraid that if you really put your foot down, Liam will resent Jesse. But he already does. You can't make anyone like anyone else. All you can do is accept Liam's feelings and be clear about your rules." I also suggested that when he accompanied her on an errand, instead of buying him a toy out of guilt, inform him ahead of time, "We're going to the store to get Jesse some diapers. If you want a toy, bring one of yours with you."

Stop the Madness!

You won't be able to prevent sibling squabbles altogether, but you might be able to minimize them.

- Make explicit rules. Instead of a vague admonition, like "Be nice," say, "You may not hit, push, or call each other bad names."

- Don't wait too long before stepping in.

- Don't overprotect the baby. With children under three or four, situations quickly spiral out of control.

- Treat each child as an individual. Be aware of their weaknesses and strengths and their tricks.

- Discuss discipline with your partner when the children aren't around. Never disagree in front of them.

TIP: Helping your toddler manage his emotions is critical during the first few months after the baby's arrival. When you notice him start-

ing to spin out of control, remember the One/Two/Three rule (pages 227–230) and don't let him go too far over the top. A simple, timely intervention, such as, "Are you getting excited?" can show him that you're paying attention and that you're there to help him, too.

Don't allow "the baby" to break the rules either. When you hear crying, your natural reaction will be to see your younger child as the "innocent victim," but this isn't always the case. Often, this is what actually happened: Your older child spent the morning on a LEGO project, carefully constructing a castle, and along comes Mrs. Shufflebottom to ruin everything . . . again. Empathize with your toddler. To be sure, when the baby is old enough to crawl or walk, she's old enough to start learning "no." Studies show that babies as young as eight or ten months begin to connect and develop a rapport with their siblings. By fourteen months, they can even anticipate an older sibling's actions. In other words, your little one is probably more conscious than you think.

> **TIP:** *Don't constantly ask the older child to share or make excuses when the baby invades, or destroys, his playthings. Hearing "Oh, he's just a baby—he doesn't know what he's doing," will frustrate the older child even more. Because your toddler doesn't have the maturity to make allowances for that annoying little creature with grubby hands, his first instinct might be to retaliate physically.*

Set up a special place for your older one. She is constantly told to "be nice" and to share, but then she goes to play with a doll and finds little teeth marks in it. She reaches for a favorite book only to discover that pages are missing. She attempts to play a CD but can't because it's covered in baby gunk. Respect is a two-way street. Protect your older child's space and belongings by helping her create a sacred space out of the baby's reach.

Liana, an exceptionally calm and very pragmatic mum, shared some excellent suggestions: "You can't really baby-proof your house with a three-year-old because they love little things, so I created 'Karen's place'—a card table that was exclusively for her, where she could do puzzles, LEGO, or play with other toys that had small pieces. I'd tell her, 'If you don't want Jamie to get into something, you have to take it up to your special big girl place.' "

Visiting with Liana and the girls in a hotel room, it was easy to see how Jamie, then just beginning to toddle, could get on her sister's nerves. Jamie tried to grab anything that Karen played with. She didn't mean harm; she was just trying to copy. Seeing Karen increasingly annoyed—and from past experience knowing that her fuse, like any child's, got shorter when she was tired—Liana averted a potential blowup. Pointing to an overstuffed armchair in the corner, this wise mum suggested, "Let's make that your big girl chair." Karen understood immediately that climbing into that big chair would protect her from Jamie's onslaught. Sure enough, a few minutes later, Jamie made a beeline for the chair, but Liana distracted her with a spoon and a plastic bowl so that she wouldn't disturb her older sister.

Treat each child as an individual. It's often easier to keep the peace when each child is dealt with fairly and individually. Even though you love both children, you can't possibly feel the same about them—*they* are different. One child wears your patience thin; another amuses you. One is inquisitive, the other laid back. Each one has different talents and vulnerabilities and will approach life in a unique way; each needs his own attention, space, and possessions. Take all this into consideration when your children interact, and acknowledge *your* feelings as well. If one child has a better attention span or follows directions more easily, you might even have to modify rules to be in keeping with his needs. Apply my One/Two/Three technique here, too (pages 227–230). If the baby ends up screaming every time your older son plays with his blocks, stop allowing the same drama to unfold. Give the big boy a special place to build and take the baby elsewhere. Also, avoid comparisons ("Why can't you be as neat as your brother?"). Even subtle hints, such as, "Your sister is sitting at the table," are damaging. Furthermore, if your child doesn't want to cooperate, believe me, mentioning her sister or brother might just have the opposite effect.

Of course, even with the best intentions, conflicts occur; you act quickly and even unfairly, and discipline goes awry. The best any parent can do is be aware and get yourself back on track.

The Benefits of Siblinghood

The next time your toddler pinches the baby, or the baby knocks down the older one's LEGO castle, remind yourself that research reveals good news about siblings, too.

* **Language.** Even when your older child is making goo-goo eyes at the baby, he's teaching him to converse. Often a child's first words are the direct result of these lessons.

* **Intelligence.** Obviously, younger siblings imitate and thereby learn from their elders. But it works the other way as well: children's intellect grows whenever they help another child solve a problem, even one who is younger. Siblings also spur each other on to explore and be creative.

* **Self-esteem.** Helping a brother or sister and having someone who praises you and loves you unconditionally boosts confidence.

* **Social skills.** Siblings watch and model one another. From their elder brother or sister the younger one will learn the rules of social interaction, figure out how to behave in various situations, how to get a parent to say "yes."

* **Emotional sustenance.** Siblings can help one another travel the rocky terrain of life. An older sibling can help a younger one prepare for new experiences and show her the ropes; a younger sibling can cheer an older one on. Having a sister or brother also gives children practice in airing feelings and developing trust.

Have a long-term outlook. When you're tired of being a juggler and referee, remember that your children won't be a baby and a toddler forever. Besides, competition isn't all bad. Having a sibling can bring out different aspects of a child's personality, and differences can also make a child appreciate his uniqueness. Through their sibling relationships children learn how to negotiate, and they build up their tolerance for the kind of give-and-take they'll later experience with friends and classmates. In fact, there are a wealth of benefits to siblinghood, for both the younger and older child (see box).

On many days you'll feel like Liana: "My job was keeping them apart for the first year!" At times, she admits, her daughters' waking hours are still exhausting. "If I have any agenda other than the two of them, it's a disaster." But the rewards are there, too. Now that Jamie is one, mobile and starting to talk, the girls are having more fun together. Just as important, Karen trusts that Liana is still there for *her* and that she's not going to lose her mum to her younger sister. Thanks to her parent's sensitivity and fairness, they've all made it through the first year, and Karen understands a bit more now about what it means to be part of a family.

Couple Conflicts

The bigger a family gets, the more complex its dynamics. As we saw in Chapter Eight, children's problems, acute or chronic, can cause friction between parents. But the reverse is true as well: when parents don't work as a team or when unresolved issues fester, it can also *cause* a child's behavior to spin out of control. Following are thumbnail sketches of several common types of couple conflicts, why they are harmful, and what you can do to keep them from leading to more serious family problems.

Chore wars. Although many men nowadays spend some time with their children and pitch in with household tasks, a still common complaint is that Dad considers himself "a helper." To be sure, chore wars plague many modern relationships. The woman may make excuses for her mate ("He works late"), or try to manipulate him ("I pretend I'm sleeping on Saturday mornings, so *he* has to deal with Christy"), but she still feels resentful. The man may protest ("If I could do more, I would") or get defensive ("What's the big deal? She does a great job with the kid"), but doesn't do much to change.

The fact is, if two adults live in a household, it's better for children to have the input of *both* people. Their different personalities and talents enrich a child's potential, and just as important, when it comes to discipline, two heads are far better than one. The truth is, when both parents are involved in everyday chores, there's less of a chance that the child will save up his misbehavior for just one of them. For instance, when Mallory and Ivan, the couple you met in Chapter Eight, started to take turns putting two-year-old Neil to bed every other night, the benefit was twofold: it gave Mallory a break, and just as important, the hands-on contact helped little Neil connect with his daddy in a new way. Not so incidentally, Neil didn't try to manipulate Ivan as much. This had less to do with Ivan and more to do with the fact that toddlers generally test and reserve their best tricks for the parent with whom they spend the most time.

When a woman asks me, "How can I get my husband to participate more?" I urge her to look at her own attitudes and behavior. Sometimes Mum unconsciously thwarts Dad's involvement (see sidebar, page 86). I also suggest that she sit down with her partner and ask him what jobs he enjoys. Sure, it's unfair for a woman to get stuck with the disagreeable tasks, but she needs to be realistic. With the kind of guy who thinks baby-sitting means plopping the kid in front of the TV while he's watching a Lakers game, getting him to do even his favorite jobs is a start.

Document the Baby, Too

Charles, father of two girls, one four, the other three months old, recently confided, "The first time around, Minnie and I were so excited about her pregnancy. We went to classes, kept a journal, and took pictures every month. When Erin finally arrived, we took a thousand photos in the first few months alone, and we have this beautifully bound, three-inch-thick photo album to prove it, not to mention a shelf full of videos. I'm ashamed to admit that I have maybe six or seven shots of Hari, and they're lying around loose in a top drawer."

Minnie and Charles are typical of many couples. They go wild, documenting every moment of their firstborn's life. By the time the second one comes along, it's business as usual. Or they're afraid to make the older child jealous by focusing too much on the baby. But what happens when Number Two grows up and wants to look at *her* baby pictures? So as not to disappoint her, make sure that you capture and preserve her milestones, too.

As my Nan used to say, "You get more flies with honey than with vinegar." If *you* are fair and generous, it often encourages the other person to be fair and generous, too. Jay takes Madeline to the park every Saturday afternoon, so that Gretel can meet a friend for lunch, take in a movie, or have her nails done. However, if Jay's date with Maddy happens to conflict with a football game he's dying to watch, they either get a sitter or Gretel forgoes her plans.

Don't-Tell-Mom. One day, Frank and Miriam were driving home with Zachary. At the entrance of their long, winding driveway, Frank said to his two-year-old son, "Hey, Zack. Wanna drive home for Daddy?" Frank put the car in park and, despite Miriam's protests, lifted Zack out of his safety seat and plopped him on his lap. "Steer for Daddy," he directed. Zack, naturally, was beaming ear to ear.

Thereafter, whenever father and son were in the car alone Frank allowed Zachary to "drive home" (up the driveway), cautioning his son, "Don't tell Mommy." One day, though, Miriam caught sight of Zack on his father's lap and went ballistic. "I told you not to do that," she lambasted her husband. "It's dangerous." Frank laughed and insisted it was harmless fun—after all, it was "only the driveway."

Whether the issue concerns eating ("Don't tell Mommy I bought you this cupcake"), behavior ("Don't tell Daddy I let you try on my lipstick"), or veering from the normal routine ("Don't tell Mommy we read four books tonight instead of two"), when one parent subverts the other's authority, it teaches children to sneak, lie, and become defiant. And the other parent is

---

Mom's Still *the One*

No matter how close women get to the glass ceiling and even when they crash through it, in the majority of households, mothers continue to be the gatekeepers of the family. Fathers certainly are more hands-on with their children nowadays. One in four spends 75% or more of his free time with the children, for a total of more than 20 hours a week. Still, men aren't necessarily doing the grunt work. When over 1000 parents were asked how chores are divided, the respondents admitted that it is Mum, not Dad, who:

- Takes the child to the pediatrician (70%)

- Stays home when a child is sick, even though both parents work (51%)

- Usually gives children their bath (73%)

- Does most of the housework (74%)

- Feeds the children their meals (76%)

Source: Online survey from Primedia's americanbaby.com, June 2001.

---

eventually forced to deal with the fallout. To wit, after a few weeks of Zack's covert driving experiences, when Miriam tried to get her son to sit in his car seat, he balked. He wanted to sit on her lap and "drive."

My recommendation in these cases is, first, be up front. *Never collude with a child.* Second, negotiate how you might handle your differences. Children can learn that parents have different expectations and standards—one will buy junk food but the other doesn't, one reads two books at bedtime, the other four. But the issue here is not rules, it's deceit and the message that it sends. If Dad can undermine Mom's discipline, why can't the toddler? This type of dynamic teaches toddlers to manipulate and lays the groundwork for the divide-and-conquer behavior you see in older children, especially teens.

(By the way, where safety is at stake, there is no room for negotiation. Frank was not merely disobeying Miriam's rule or standards; children are required to ride in safety seats. By allowing Zack to sit on his lap, Frank was actually breaking the law. The fact that he was "just in the driveway" is immaterial. A two-year-old doesn't know the difference between a back road and a highway.)

Avoiding Chore Wars

- Be fair.

- Make reasonable compromises.

- Whenever possible, allow each partner to do what he or she likes best and/or is best at doing.

- Make time for each other.

- Get a baby-sitter or ask Grandma or a good friend to pitch in.

My Way Is Better. "What do you mean you let Jordy sit on the sidelines during the entire class?" Gordon raged at his wife, Deanna. "That's ridiculous—you're babying our son. Next time, *I'm* taking him." Gordon, a former football player and now director of a health club, had come from a family of athletes. Throughout Deanna's pregnancy, he had eagerly anticipated the arrival of his "little quarterback." When Jordy arrived, several weeks early, Gordon was shocked to see that the image he'd carried for nine months was nothing like the scrawny child who feared noise and bright lights. Even as Jordy got stronger and blossomed into a sturdy toddler, he cried whenever his father threw him in the air or tried to play more roughly than Deanna did. Gordon repeatedly accused her of "making him into a sissy." Now, hearing that eighteen-month-old Jordy was reluctant to participate in a "baby class" like Gymboree, Gordon was sure that it was Deanna's "fault."

Deanna and Gordon's situation is not unique; parents often lock horns over what's "right." They typically disagree about *manners* ("Why do you let her smash her food like that?"); *discipline* ("Why are your letting him put his shoes on the couch like that? *I* never do"); or *sleep* ("Let him cry it out" versus "I can't bear to hear him crying like that").

Instead of ironing out their difficulties with each other, they argue over their toddler's head, accusing each other either of "protecting" the child or of being too strict or too lenient. In fact, when one parent veers to an extreme, the other does tend toward the opposite pole. Their antagonism is extremely harmful to their child. Even if he doesn't understand their words, he feels the tension.

I urge these parents to start talking to each other. It's not a matter of *who* is right, but what will work best for *their child*. Interestingly, each argument usually has some merit, but each parent is too busy being "right" to hear the other person. If, instead, the two of them stopped and actually listened, they might learn from one another and could perhaps come up with a plan that incorporated *both* sets of ideas.

I tried to get Gordon and Deanna to look at Jordy through unbiased eyes, and at the same time, to assess their own agendas. "Pushing Jordy is not going to change his personality," I told Gordon. "Also, listening to you and his mum argue could upset him and make him even more fearful and reluctant to leave Mum's side." Deanna had to honestly evaluate her behavior, too. Was she perhaps *over*compensating for her husband's macho approach? It's important to know your child and allow him to proceed at a comfortable pace, but perhaps Gordon had a point, too: she needed to encourage Jordy a bit more, even as he sat on the sidelines. To their credit, Deanna and Gordon were able to listen. They stopped arguing in front of their son. They strategized together. And as a team, they decided it probably would be a good idea for Gordon to take Jordy to Gymboree—but to cheer him on, not to "fix" him. It took another six weeks, but Jordy finally joined in. We'll never know whether it was the parents' strategy or the fact that their son was finally ready. However, if the adults hadn't started working together, I suspect that Gymboree would have been the least of their problems.

Martyr Mom/Devil Dad. Charmane, a former television executive, has been a stay-at-home mother since Tamika's birth fourteen months ago. Her husband, Eddie, a record company executive, works long hours, and Tamika is usually in bed by the time he gets home. Charmane feels resentful bearing the sole burden of parenting, but she also covets her exclusive territory. On the weekends, she insists that she wants Eddie "to become more involved," but she criticizes everything he does: "No, Eddie, Tamika doesn't like it when you do that. . . . She likes to play with her fire truck after breakfast. . . . Why did you put her in *that* outfit? . . . Make sure you take her teddy bear if you're going to the park . . . bring a snack . . . no, not Goldfish; bring carrots—they're better for her." On and on she prattles. It's enough to make the most loving Dad say, "So long—she's all yours today."

Instead of telling Eddie how angry and isolated she feels during the week, Charmane secretly wants him to make it up to her. And yet, she is ambivalent about giving up the control. She wants Eddie to participate, but she also wants to tell him what to do and how to do it. Additionally, playing the martyr is exhausting, so that even when Eddie spends time with Tamika, Charmane never relaxes or replenishes her energy.

The person suffering the most, of course, is little Tamika, who cries or pushes Eddie away when he tries to play with her—her nonverbal way of saying, "I want to play with Mum, not you." Granted, she's at an age when many toddlers prefer their mums. It's not just Daddy—Tamika won't go to anyone else if Charmane's in the room. However, when Charmane exits, Tamika fusses for only a few minutes and then she's fine, which tells me that this problem is less about a toddler's separation anxiety than the fact that her mother is reluctant to let go. What's more, Tamika *hears* her mother monitoring and reprimanding her dad. She may not understand the words or precisely what Charmane means, but the feeling behind the barrage of criticism is all too clear. If this continues, Tamika will become even more skittish when Eddie approaches. Mum the martyr will have succeeded in painting Dad as the devil.

Both parents' feelings have to be aired and respected. Charmane has to admit her resentment and be willing to give up the control. Eddie has to talk about how Tamika's criticism makes him feel. He also has to take responsibility for not being more available. When a parent says, "I have to be at work," he is making a choice. If Eddie truly wants to be involved in his daughter's life, he might have to make different choices that give him more free time, and Charmane has to make a place for him at home.

"Instead of merely insisting, 'Tamika won't play with Eddie,' " I told Charmane, "you could problem solve. Figure out ways to make her more comfortable with her father. Compliment him more and criticize less. Encourage her and help him gradually build up their time together."

Eddie had to change his approach to Tamika, too. One of Charmane's complaints was that he was sometimes "too rough" with their daughter. Men do tend to play with children in a more rough-and-tumble manner. Tamika wasn't used to such frisky play and her tears told me she clearly didn't like it. "Maybe she'll change when she gets a little older or maybe not," I explained to Eddie. "In any case, for the time being you have to respect what she's telling you. When you toss her in the air, if she cries for her mum, that tells you she's unhappy. Change whatever you're doing."

I suggested that it's not necessarily a matter of Tamika preferring her mother. Rather, she likes the way her mum plays with her. "Maybe she'd rather be jiggling the dials and levers on her busy box, and she associates that kind of activity with Charmane, not you. Start making her comfortable and doing things she enjoys— and then perhaps you can stretch her limits."

Unresolved business. Problems from the past can pollute a relationship and even choke the life out of it. Ted, a carpenter who designs and builds one-of-a-kind furniture, had an affair before his daughter Sasha was born. His wife, Norma, a vice president in a large corporation, uncovered the affair just as she found out that she was pregnant. They reconciled for the sake of their unborn child, and from the outside, they looked like a very happy family once the baby was born. Sasha was healthy, Norma a great mom, and Ted a devoted dad. After a year had passed, the parents started talking about having another baby. But when Norma weaned Sasha, she was suddenly flooded with loss. Her obstetrician assured her that many women had an intense emotional reaction when they stopped breastfeeding, but Norma knew that her feelings went deeper. She was still angry about the affair. Meanwhile, Ted was in a whole other place. He never imagined how much he would love being a parent, and now he wanted another child.

Ted could put the past behind him, but Norma couldn't. She insisted on couples therapy, where they revisited the trauma. Norma, now less focused on Sasha, got angrier and angrier in the weeks that followed. "When are you going to let this go?" Ted kept asking. "We have a beautiful daughter now. Our lives are back on track."

Sadly, instead of dealing with the pain of Ted's affair *before* they had children, Norma had immersed herself in her pregnancy and in coping with Sasha's first year. Now, the two of them were on different sides of the fence, getting increasingly disconnected from each other. She wanted to clear away the wreckage; he wanted a new baby to save their marriage.

Norma and Ted split up by the time Sasha was three. She couldn't get past her anger, and he got tired of waiting and feeling guilty. Norma was right about one thing: having another baby wouldn't have solved anything. She learned too late that one has to go *through* problems instead of around them.

In my first book, I mentioned Chloe, who had been in labor for twenty hours because her firstborn, Isabella, had gotten stuck in the birth canal. It was a terrible delivery—and Chloe was still talking about it *five months later*. I had suggested then that she express her feelings, even consult a professional, rather than let the emotions fester. Now Isabella is nearly three. As it turns out, Chloe blamed Seth but never really talked it out with him at the time. She held on, not to only the horror of her delivery, but to the belief that Seth hadn't helped her through it. She felt abandoned by him. They talked about the situation over and over—how the doctor had disappeared, how the epidural wore off, how helpless he felt, how angry she was. Chloe still couldn't let it go. For months, Seth tried to be understanding, but Chloe was becoming more strident, frequently criticizing his fathering skills.

Seth became increasingly frustrated. At one point, when he suggested that they "move on" by having another child, she blew up at him. "After all I've told you," she screamed accusingly, "you still have no idea of what I've been through." Eventually, Seth left.

The moral of this and Norma and Ted's story is the same: when you see yourself holding on to bad feelings, you need to express them and, in all likelihood, seek professional help.

Problem Prevention

- Air resentments instead of letting them fester—but don't argue about them in front of your toddler.

- Attempt to solve problems *together*; make a plan for dealing with sleep, meals, outings. At times you may have to agree to disagree.

- Toddlers do best with consistent standards, but they can handle differences, as long as you're up-front about them: *You can have three books with Dad, but when Mommy puts you to bed she reads two books.*

- Try not to polarize your positions by going to one extreme because you think your partner is at the other.

- Listen to what you say to your child. When Dad says, "Mommy doesn't like it when you put your feet on the couch," it tells your child you disagree and subtly undermines Mom's standards.

- Don't take your child's reactions personally—children behave differently with each parent.

- If fighting becomes chronic, seek professional help.

Could Chloe and Seth's marriage have been saved if Chloe had gone into therapy early on, or if a good couples counselor had helped them tease out the real reasons for their discontent? Maybe, maybe not. I do know they'd have had a better chance if they had not let their resentment fester.*

Many variations on the above themes exist, but the details aren't as important as the fact that couple conflicts, in any shape or form, are dangerous to children's well-being. If you see yourself in any of these situations, take heed. Every dispute calls for creative problem solving; in the sidebar on page 316 are some important points to keep in mind.

Time for You/Time for Your Relationships

One of the best ways to guard against couple conflicts, of course, is to replenish your own energy and to protect your adult relationships—not just your marriage but your friendships as well. Though you're nurturing a child or children, you also need to care for yourself and maintain your status as an adult—a grown-up with connections to the adult world. The following suggestions are a matter of common sense, but in the hustle and bustle of family life, we often forget them.

Make specific plans for adult time. It's not enough to say "I need some time to myself," or "We need time together." You'll have to schedule it. Ideally, you have a structured routine to begin with (how could you not, after reading this book?). Pencil in time for yourself, as well as for your relationships. Have a regular date-night rendezvous with your mate; plan luncheons and dinners with

---

*Sadly, almost one in two marriages ends in divorce, and the majority of couples who separate have children under age five. Even if you live in a different house from your partner, it's vital that you stay in your child(ren)'s life and commit to some form of coparenting. It's not easy, but it is possible to cooperate with an ex-spouse for the sake of the children. Seek the help of a counselor and tap into good resources, one of which is the book *Families Apart: Ten Keys to Successful Coparenting*, by my coauthor, Melinda Blau (Perigee Books).

friends—and don't let childless buddies drop by the wayside. If you have trouble making plans with other adults, ask yourself, *What's stopping me?* Some parents feel that they're "bad" if they leave their children; others enjoy the role of martyr. Remember that *not* taking time to replenish your energy can have disastrous results. In contrast, a well-rested, satisfied, and self-preserving person is less likely to scream at the children or dump his or her frustrations on a partner.

E-mail: Carving Out Couple Time

My husband and I find it very hard to find time for each other since I am a full-time mother with a bedtime schedule close to our son's—around 9:30 P.M.—and Mike (my husband) works 5 days a week from 4 P.M. until 2 A.M. So we have developed a "love journal." We write little notes to each other whenever we think of it or whenever we have time. It's fun to find the love journal on each other's side of the bed when there's a note in it. It could be a love note; it could be telling about something that made a difference in our day at home or at work; it could be anything we want. It's a little reminder that we *are* married and that we love each other and care about each other.

When you take a break, really take a break. When you're out for the evening with your partner, *don't* talk about the children. When you have lunch with friends, discuss what's going on in the world, the latest fashions, or how sexy the yoga instructor is, but don't swap parenting stories. Don't get me wrong, luv. I'm all for parents discussing new developments in their children's lives and solving problems together, and I think it's great to share strategies with other parents, but you have to give it a rest at times.

Find ways to take brief respites. You don't have to wait for that "big escape" to steal a bit of downtime. Take a walk around the block, alone or with your partner. Put your toddler in the playpen so that you can climb the StairMaster or read a magazine. Take a catnap to refresh yourself. If your partner's at home, and you feel so inclined, have an extra cuddle and a smooch. Get up fifteen minutes earlier to meditate, write in a journal, or review the day with your honey.

Exercise. Do it on your own, do it with your mate or a friend. Find a walking buddy in the neighborhood. Go to a gym. Take your child with you if you can't find a sitter. The important thing is to get your blood flowing and feel the oxygen coursing through your lungs—ideally, for at least thirty minutes a day.

Pamper yourself. I don't mean a day at the spa, luv, although if you can pull *that* off, more power to you. Just make sure that, once a day, you take time to breathe a bit more deeply, rub some delightful scented body lotion all over yourself, stretch, or luxuriate in a hot tub. Even five minutes of catering to yourself is better than nothing.

Keep the sparks glowing. In your relationship, keep the courtship going. Make time for romance as well as for sex. Do nice things and surprise one another (see the sidebar, page 318, for one couple's innovative suggestion). Nurture your own passions, too, and embrace new interests. As your children grow, don't let yourself stop growing. Take classes. Find a new hobby. Go to museums and galleries and college campuses, places where you're bound to meet fascinating people.

Create a parent support system. Parenting can be a very isolating experience. Hence, it's important for parents to become part of the larger community. Visit the local *Y* or community center to see what these facilities offer families in the area. Enroll in a parenting class with your toddler, or start a play group. Network; find other families that have similar-aged children.

Enlarge your definition of "family." Make sure that your social life is not restricted to two-foot-tall dynamos with eternally sticky hands. In addition to getting out occasionally, it's also important to invite people *in*. Encourage grandparents and other relatives to be part of your life. Have regular family dinners and holiday fetes. Include friends in your family gatherings as well. It's wonderful for children to grow up relating to a variety of adults.

TIP: All parents, not just single parents, ought to seek out other adults to spend time with their child. The more adult connections a young child makes, the better equipped she will be to face the many different personalities she'll encounter in the world at large.

Don't forget to ask for help. Serious physical and emotional problems can develop in a family when one or both of the adults is on overload. Tell your mate if you're more exhausted than you can bear. Hire help if you can afford it, even part of the time. If you are in play group and are comfortable with one of the other mum's parenting styles, suggest that the two of you trade babysitting time.

Self-care is the key to juggling. Otherwise, we start to feel like it's all too much. We fight with our partners, yell at our children. Resentment builds and frustration mounts. Parenting is hard and ever changing. "You have to wear a lot of hats," as my Nan says, and for most of us, meeting our own needs is usually last on the list. Only a resentful martyr keeps going and going till she drops or explodes. It's not an admission of failure to ask for help—it's the sign of a wise parent.

Some Final Thoughts

One looks back with appreciation to
the brilliant teachers, but with
gratitude to those who touched our
human feelings. The curriculum is so
much necessary raw material, but
warmth is a vital element for the
growing plant and for the soul of the
child.

—Carl Jung

Being a good parent is both gratifying and self-affirming, but it's also a hard job, harder still with a toddler underfoot. Every day ushers in breathtaking change, and the stakes seem higher than in the good old days when a feed or a diaper change was often all that was needed to make your child happy. Now the issues are more complex. Is he walking okay? Talking enough? Will he have friends? Will people like him? Will he be scared on his first day of preschool? And how can I make it all happen. . . *now?*

A Last Reminder

As your child grows, keep in mind the themes of this book—the essence of baby whispering. They are no less applicable to teenagers than to toddlers.

- Your child is an individual—know him for who he is.

- Take the time to observe, listen, and talk *with* your child, not at her.

- Giving your child the respect he deserves will inspire him to respect others as well.

- Your child needs a structured routine to give her life predictability and safety.

- Be a balanced parent, one who limits as well as loves.

This book has been about all that you can do to help your toddler negotiate this daunting life passage. But I end it by stressing as well what you *cannot* do. You can encourage and nurture, but you can't push. You can step in to avert or solve problems, but you cannot rescue. You can, and should, be in charge, but you cannot control who your child is. No matter how eager you are to have him reach the next developmental plateau or get past a difficult phase, he will walk, talk, make friends, and develop in ways that even you can't imagine . . . on his time, not yours.

My granddad, whom I admired for his tolerance and understanding, once told me that a family was like a beautiful garden and children its flowers. A garden needs tender, loving care and patience. Strong roots, rich soil, good planning, and proper placement are also essential. After you plant the seeds, you must stand back and watch as the buds take shape on their own. You can't tug at them to make them sprout faster.

Still, the garden needs your constant attention. You must continue to feed the soil, water the plants, and nourish it all with love.

Only by ministering to the flowers every day will you help them bloom to their fullest potential. If you notice weeds threatening to choke the plants or insects eating the leaves, you must take immediate action. Surely, families need to be safeguarded in much the same way as a garden, and children cared for with at least as much watchfulness as rare roses or prizewinning peonies.

Granddad's analogy rings as true today as it did over a decade ago when my children were toddlers. He was trying to tell me then that I had to be observant but that I also had to have patience—and so must you. Cheer your child on, love her unconditionally, help her prepare for life, and give her all the tools she'll need to carry on without you. And when she's ready, the world and everything in it will be waiting for her.

Index

About the Authors

TRACY HOGG is a nurse, lactation educator, and newborn consultant with more than twenty years' experience. Her uncanny ability to understand and calm babies led to her nickname the "baby whisperer." In 1995, she founded Baby Technique, through which she consults with parents individually and organizes and teaches group classes. Originally from England, she lives in Los Angeles and is the mother of two daughters. You can visit her Web site at www.babywhisperer.com.

MELINDA BLAU is an award-winning journalist specializing in family and health topics. She is the author of ten other books and countless magazine articles. The mother of two grown children, she lives in Northampton, Massachusetts.